Emily Dickinson from a daguerreotype about 1848

Emily Dickinson

Richard Chase

The American Men of Letters Series

GREENWOOD PRESS, PUBLISHERS
WESTPORT, CONNECTICUT

The Library of Congress cataloged this book as follows:

Chase, Richard Volney, 1914–1962.
    Emily Dickinson. Westport, Conn., Greenwood Press
₍1971, c1951₎

    xii, 328 p. 23 cm.

    Includes bibliographical references.

    1. Dickinson, Emily, 1830–1886.

PS1541.Z5C5 1971   811'.4 [B]   70–136058
ISBN 0–8371–5208–9   MARC

Library of Congress   71 ₍4₎

Originally published in 1951 by William Sloane Associates,
New York

Reprinted with the permission of William Morrow & Company, Inc.

Reprinted from an original copy in the collections of the Brooklyn
Public Library

Reprinted by Greenwood Press, Inc.

First Greenwood reprinting 1971
Second Greenwood reprinting 1973
Third Greenwood reprinting 1977

Library of Congress catalog card number 70-136058
ISBN 0-8371-5208-9

Printed in the United States of America

For my Mother and Father

Contents

Acknowledgments

IN WRITING such a book as this, one's indebtedness accrues in so complicated a manner that one cannot possibly acknowledge it systematically. Yet one is conscious of the pleasure and, one hopes, the justice of recording certain specific debts. Every student of Emily Dickinson must be grateful to George F. Whicher, whose *This Was a Poet* (1938) was the first dependable biography. Mr. Whicher's biographic account will doubtless remain somewhere near definitive as an establishment of fact, and although I have sometimes departed from it in my interpretations of the poet's life, my debt to his book is extensive. In contemplating Emily Dickinson against the Puritan background, I have relied rather heavily on the work of Perry Miller, on his *Jonathan Edwards* (an earlier book in the American Men of Letters Series) and on his *The New England Mind: The Seventeenth Century*. Among critics who have written about the poetry of Emily Dickinson I am particularly grateful to Allen Tate, R. P. Blackmur, and Yvor Winters.

I should like to express my debt to Mr. Thomas H. Johnson for his encouragement at several stages of my work and for his helpful criticisms of the manuscript. We early decided that it would not be appropriate for me to make use of any of the unpublished Dickinson papers of which he is the prospective editor. His welcome suggestions for the improvement of my book have been entirely *ex officio*. One may salute in advance Mr. Johnson's future editions of the poems and letters, for these may be counted on to bring what textual accuracy can finally be brought to the published writings of the poet and to establish as far as can be done a dependable chronology of these writings.

Thanks are due to the editors of the American Men of Letters Series and to Miss Helen Stewart of Sloane Associates for their critical assistance. I am especially grateful to Lionel Trilling and Mark Van Doren for encouragement and suggestions for improvement. Mr. F. W. Dupee, Mr. Quentin Anderson, and Mr. R. W. Flint have rescued me from a variety of mistakes of judgment and style. I hope this is the appropriate occasion to express a long-standing debt of gratitude to Mr. Dupee for various forms of assistance and advice, during the last ten or twelve years, which I find it easy to sense in their magnitude but difficult to express in particular.

I want, finally, to thank Mrs. Carol Trosch for her conscientious secretarial assistance.

Emily Dickinson

Origins

FORTUNATELY there is no need to reconstitute the fame of Emily Dickinson. Most critics seem agreed that she stands, perhaps with Whitman, at the top of the American achievement in poetry, and that she is the greatest of women poets. Anyone who reads poetry at all is likely to cherish the utterance, original yet already classic, exact yet magnificent, which we hear in the well-known lines.

> After great pain a formal feeling comes—
> The nerves sit ceremonious like tombs,

or

> Because I could not stop for Death,
> He kindly stopped for me,

or

> The manner of the children
> Who weary of the day,
> Themselves the noisy plaything
> They cannot put away.

Relieved of the task of promoting his poet to a higher position in public favor, the critic-biographer may occupy his mind with understanding the poems, commenting on them if he can, and trying to distinguish the failures, which he may think were many, from the successes. And with his sense that the reputation of the poet is secure, he can the more easily confront such problems as whether she is praised for the right reasons or for the wrong.

Our high estimation of Emily Dickinson's poetry goes back to the 1890s and the response of such capable readers as Alice James and Howells. We readily give assent to what was implied in the words of the witty and intelligent sister of William and Henry James, who wrote in 1892: "It is reassuring to hear the English pronouncement [probably that of Andrew Lang] that Emily Dickinson is fifth-rate—they have such a capacity for missing quality; the robust evades them equally with the subtle. Her being sicklied o'er with T. W. Higginson makes one quake lest there be some latent flaw which escapes one's vision." We agree with Howells that the poems of Emily Dickinson are a "distinct addition to the literature of the world." If she has not become quite world-famous, to the extent that Whitman has, she has nevertheless "got out of New England," as an early critic said, and is known and admired in many parts of the world. So nearly unique is her work that it is hard to trace in particular her influence on later writers. Yet many modern poets, including Hart Crane, W. H. Auden, Mark Van Doren, and Marianne Moore have admired and profited by her work. In the 1920s—that generous and vigorous age of American letters upon which, these days, we can hardly look back without nostalgia—she was regarded as one of the great visionary or "mystic" poets and as an impressive example for writers in revolt against standard taste and in search of a more complex and brilliant poetry. In the 1930s her great reputation remained intact among those who regarded her at all, although there was clearly a tendency to praise her less as a poet than as a brave and emancipated woman who had outwitted the provinces and escaped their stagnation.

She is newly relevant to our contemporary experience. Her sense of the anguish of personal existence and of the precariousness of human life recommends her to a time in which new philosophies of existence have come forcefully to our attention. Her vigor, her curious and reconnoitering mind appeal to a period which has been given too much to apathy and suspicion of the spirited imagination. Her rigorous psychology and her sense of the virtue of definition, of intellectual severity, of the exclusions which the mind must make if it is to preserve its precarious "economy," of the powerful consequentiality of fact and circumstance, of the hostility or indifference of the universe to man—all these attitudes recommend Emily Dickinson to an age which is seeking secular modes of thought more severe, more realistic, and more durable than the easier optimisms which have sometimes characterized American intellectual life.

In his function as biographer the writer who addresses himself to the life of Emily Dickinson must deal with two difficult circumstances. The first is the dearth of material. The biographer must share the regret of Henry James who in writing his study of Hawthorne was as much struck by what was missing from the personal and social life of his subject as by what it included. Hawthorne was a shyer and more renunciatory man than most of his fellow New Englanders. Yet compared with Emily Dickinson he led a remarkably overt and active life. James might even more aptly have been commenting on Emily Dickinson than on Hawthorne when he wrote that Hawthorne's life was "almost strikingly deficient in incident, in what may be called the dramatic quality." More and more after 1862 and almost absolutely after 1870, the poet was in good earnest a recluse. As everyone knows, she became an almost complete stranger to the world outside her father's house in Amherst.

Her gradual seclusion decreased the number of incidents and dispelled the drama her life might otherwise have had. But this seclusion produced, one might say, a vacuum which legend-makers rushed to fill up. This circumstance is the second major difficulty confronting the biographer. Playwrights, novelists, biographers, and even dancers have interpreted Emily Dickinson's "letter to the world." The shy, small, nervously intense young woman passing among her father's guests at his annual Commencement tea, the timorous but gallant girl quaking before her father's rapacious tyranny, the broken-hearted priestess of love dressed in vestal white in honor of this army engineer or that clergyman, the aging spinster fleeing in panic from the knock on the door or lowering gingerbread by means of basket and string from her second-story window to the children waiting below, the sibylline visionary writing her inspired verses on the backs of old envelopes and recipes—these are items, more or less faithful to fact, in the Dickinson myth.

The idea of seclusion will always fascinate those who live in a culture which, like our own, professes a public, or at least a non-private, ideal of existence. Sanctioned as it is in America, public opinion will always be suspicious of private opinion. It will regard the recluse with an excessive and sometimes with a morbid interest, and it will eagerly invest his seclusion with a wealth of fantasy. (Some of the details of Emily Dickinson's seclusion, such as her reluctance to address letters in her own hand and her habit of conversing with guests from the hall while they sat uneasily in the parlor, clearly took on the coloring of the extraordinary and actively invited the kind of interest of which I speak.) It is therefore proper to refer to our American *myth* of seclusion, and to observe that most of our best writers have discerned its meaningfulness and importance in American life and have given it a wide variety of fictional representations—from Ishmael in his private world at the masthead of the *Pequod* to Hepzibah Pyncheon in the ancestral House of the Seven Gables.

Besides our own native readiness to make a legendary figure out of Emily Dickinson, one must note in the poet herself a certain self-conscious, deeply felt necessity to contribute to her own myth—a readiness to assume her part with appropriate flourishes and fitting décor, a tendency to play the coquette with her friends, with the culture in which she lived, and with posterity.

No wonder, then, that biographical treatments of Emily Dickinson, before George F. Whicher's work, should not only have taken note of the Dickinson myth but should also have lost their way in its labyrinth. The poet herself wrote, one needs continually to recall, that her life had been "too simple and stern to embarrass any." This does not mean that her life is of no interest, but we ought not to forget the emphasis of her disclaimer. Having only the first volume of poems to go by, Howells wrote in 1891 that "there is no hint of what turned her life in upon itself, and probably this was its natural evolution, or involution, from tendencies inherent in the New England, or the Puritan, spirit." The problem in writing about Emily Dickinson is how to modify the myth of her life in the light of her own assessment of its sternness and simplicity and in the light of the persuasive idea that the course of her life was "natural." The biographer may ideally lament the dearth of exciting events in the life of his subject. Yet his duty is to refrain from inventing what is not there and, as did the poet herself, make a virtue out of frugality.

Emily Dickinson's retirement from the world had, of course, a tradition behind it. For it has always been a possible way of life for New England spinsters and widows, among them Hawthorne's mother and Alice James herself. Yet this is not the only sense in which she belonged to New England. For however much of the particularity of her New England circumstances Emily Dickinson transcended to make her great impression upon us, she remains profoundly a poet of her milieu. No one was more conscious than she herself that the consequences of having lived at a certain time in a certain place and in a certain way may be all but absolutely decisive. We must begin, at least, with New England if we hope to gain a true perspective of the myth, the poet, and the poems.

Emily Elizabeth Dickinson was born on December 10, 1830, in the solid and capacious brick house which her grandfather had built in his days as a leading citizen of Amherst. In the manner of New England towns, the plainly but gracefully designed white and yellow buildings of Amherst asserted themselves sharply against the rolling hills and the mountains of the surrounding country, making a kind of aggressive virtue out of the very newness of the civilization they represented. Seen against the impressive natural surroundings, the Congregational meetinghouse and the three or four buildings which in 1830 constituted Amherst College gave the onlooker (if one may trust the paintings and drawings which have been preserved) a sense that the life of the inhabitants consisted a good deal in the strong assertion of independence and righteousness in the midst of an expansive universe. Riding in a stage across the plain which leads in an easterly direction from the Connecticut River and North-ampton to Amherst, a new student at the college beheld the prospect in the autumn of 1846 and then wrote in his diary: "This village, which is probably to be my home for the next three years, stands upon a hill, almost at the center of a huge amphitheater formed by the hills or mountains which bound the horizon. The prospect is splendid, and the village itself a neat and pretty place."

Although in her poems and letters Emily Dickinson appears to be entirely uninterested in her ancestors, she could have boasted, if she had wished, of an eminently respectable line of descent. Hers was the eighth generation of the family on American soil, counting down from Nathaniel Dickinson, who removed from England to Massachusetts in 1630. In passing we may note an important fact—that her generation was the last in direct descent from the pilgrim patriarch; her brother's two sons died without issue, one as a child, the other at thirty-five. The poet's generation was the fifth to live at Amherst. The Dickinson ascendancy among the citizens of the town, who gave the title of "Squire" to the men of the family, began with Emily's grandfather, Samuel Fowler Dickinson. He was the last of the Dickinsons who genuinely lived with his Calvinist Maker. He is said to have been a "flaming zealot for education and religion" and to have "believed like fury." Like his son and grandson he was a lawyer and a leader in providing for the welfare of Amherst College. We may suppose that in Samuel, the last of the family to bear an Old Testament name, the shackles which bound the ways of God to the affairs of this world were not yet seriously strained and we may consequently suppose him to be the last of the line for whom the legal profession and the task of educating the young were still instinct with the legalistic spirit of the Covenant Theology and the intense emphasis of the primitive New England pedagogy. Emily's father found in the profession of law and the duties of citizen and father an almost, if not quite, complete religion. He seems to have had no more than a conventional belief in the divine Lawmaker. And he was certainly more interested in the material progress of Amherst College than in whether the course of studies was bringing the young to Christ.

Samuel Fowler Dickinson made a reputation as the best lawyer of the district; he served a term in the Massachusetts Senate; and was a deacon of the church for forty years, a position which he gravely assumed at the age of twenty-one. His missionary zeal was extraordinary, and indeed his great effort to assist in "the bringing in of the Kingdom" exceeded his ability to bring in the family income. His selfless devotion of time and money to the building of the college is said to have reduced him nearly to ruin before he died at sixty-two, discouraged in this world but with hopes of a place in heaven.

The difficult question of Emily Dickinson's father and

of his effect upon her, I shall not touch on here, beyond saying that although he was obviously of great importance in the formation of his daughter's personality and of her imagination, he was not, certainly, the tyrant and lover-in-disguise that he is sometimes assumed to be. Nor does Higginson's characterization of him as "thin, dry, and speechless" quite do him justice. If as his daughter said "he never played," it was perhaps because he never learned how, rather than because he was suffering from any actually inhuman and destructive rigidity or coldness. He was, of course, a man of rectitude in his own eyes and in those of his neighbors, a man of integrity, boldness, and outspokenness to those with whom he did business, a firm and protective, but, it would seem, in many ways a timid father to his family—firm, that is, and even legislative in matters of family policy but timid and largely embarrassed by the emotional events of family life. The divine mission of Samuel Fowler Dickinson was transformed in his son into a prudential public career. Edward Dickinson could be counted on not to bankrupt himself in order to bring in the Kingdom. The sense of mission he still had, but it took the form of "public spirit." Besides his flourishing law practice, he served as the treasurer of Amherst College for thirty-eight years before turning the task over to Emily's brother Austin. He was a figure in the Whig politics of the state and he spent two years in Washington as a Congressman. He was active, conscientious, energetic, and high-minded, and we may suppose that in Edward Dickinson we discern also that anxious gravity and that disposition to melancholy solitude which Tocqueville saw in the successful Americans of the time. We find a hint of what Edward Dickinson was like in the portrait of Waymarsh in Henry James's *The Ambassadors*—Waymarsh the grave and anxious American who seemed to sit stiffly on the edge of his seat as he traveled through Europe, more intent upon some illusive disquiet which he beheld in the distance than upon the monuments of art and culture he had come to survey. For though Edward Dickinson scarcely imagined the possibility of going to Europe, he is described as having sat similarly in a state of disquiet throughout a memorable family excursion to Northampton to hear Jenny Lind, whose singing he did not enjoy. Nor is there any doubt (if the reader will allow me to carry out the figure) that Edward Dickinson passed through life on the edge of his seat.

Emily Dickinson's mother was born Emily Norcross. About her there seems to have been almost nothing to say. She was endlessly and exclusively domestic, even "oppressively tidy," as an observer thought. She sometimes embarrassed her daughter by the insistence with which she hovered around guests to inquire if there was not one more cake or cup of tea which would complete their felicity. She figures hardly at all in the meager store of what we know about the Dickinson family, and one gathers from this that she was unusually passive and retiring and possessed no ostensible power of being or of mind. By her very passivity, the mother must have been more influential upon her daughter than we would gather from the scraps of evidence. If she was not Emily's kind of recluse, she was yet a recluse in her own style, the style of thousands of self-effacing Victorian wives. Emily Dickinson's striking remark to Higginson—"I never had a mother. I suppose a mother is one to whom you hurry when you are troubled"—is not the end of our conjectures about the relation of daughter to mother but only the beginning. But it is an inward drama which demands a good deal of caution in the biographer. The "world" must have judged that Emily Norcross Dickinson was an eminently successful mother and that her married life had turned out pretty much as Edward Dickinson had desired when he wrote characteristically to her just before the wedding: "Let us prepare for a life of rational happiness. I do not expect or wish for a life of pleasure. May we be happy and useful and successful and each be an ornament in society and gain the respect and confidence of all with whom we may be connected."

It is difficult to gain a clear sense of what life was like in the Amherst of Emily Dickinson's girlhood. From our viewpoint, so much the viewpoint of national and global totality, the Amherst of one hundred and twenty years ago is remarkable first for its spirit of independence and then for its paradoxical social condition, which without being either aristocratic or equalitarian nevertheless preserved a feeling of rank and at the same time a feeling of candid democracy. Doubtless the same paradox appears in modern America. The difference is that early in the nineteenth century—when in provincial New England our modern money capitalism and equalitarian ethos had only just begun to be operative—the farmer was more sharply conscious of the difference between his manners and morals and those of the few local "squires" and that the local squire, when he hoed his own garden or hauled his potatoes to town, as Edward Dickinson did, was genuinely aware of his kinship with the farmer. The peculiar envy which a belief in equality inspires was well enough known in early nineteenth-century Amherst, but one is perhaps not inventing archaic utopias by conjecturing that the desire for equality took at that time a rather more generous and manly and, as was sometimes said, "Roman" manner than it has in later times.

However stark and unrelated to its environment early American architecture may have seemed to the cosmopolitan eye of Henry James, the buildings of Amherst were undeniably emblems of a sturdy independence. There was a personal independence, based, of course, upon American political beliefs and deriving from the Puritan heritage. This personal independence sometimes grew neurotic and exaggerated and produced the New England crank. But somewhere this side of crankiness there was the realm of the "characters." Like other New England towns Amherst had its complement of characters—Lavinia Dickinson, Emily's sister, became one in later years —and the willingness or desire to be known as a character shows, at least, a commendable impulse to lend drama and color to an otherwise monotonous existence. The personal independence of the individual citizen was mirrored in the economic and cultural independence of Amherst itself. Its citizens subsisted largely off the rich Connecticut Valley land and depended on local artisans for goods and services. And not until Amherst College began bringing in students and speakers from the outside and sending its graduates to remote parts of the globe as missionaries did the town begin to be curious about the rest of the world.

When William Gardiner Hammond, the new student whom I quoted above, came to Amherst from Newport, he remarked that "it is not considered anything out of the way for even pious men to take a walk on Sunday, and it is the universal practice here. This is a little country place, and such a thing does not tend to countenance dissipation as it would in Newport." Hammond's observation testifies to a pragmatic and common-sense democracy of conduct which provincial Amherst allowed itself exactly because of its isolation. We may be sure that it does not testify to any laxity of religious principles in Amherst as compared with Newport. On occasion at least, Amherst still felt the intense afterglow of its Calvinist orthodoxy. By heritage it was among the Connecticut River townships which had constituted in the time of Jonathan Edwards's grandfather Stoddard an almost separate confederacy, divorced by principle as well as by geography from Boston and the whole northern New England seaboard. And not six miles from Amherst, at Northampton, Edwards himself had steered his perilous course through the Great Awakening of the late 1730s and '40s. In his altogether brilliant manner he had reaffirmed, on new grounds, the main tenets of orthodox Calvinism. His influence was snuffed out by the enemy he had bitterly fought during his life: the liberalizing tendencies of deism and Unitarianism which were cultivated in the cities, especially Boston. But in the first decades of the nineteenth century Amherst still retained a strong feeling that it was a citadel of orthodox godliness and that its business was to fend off influxes of liberalism. When Amherst College was founded in 1820-21, Noah Webster, one of the founders, wrote that the purpose of the college was to "check the progress of errors which are propagated from Cambridge." And indeed, from Webster's point of view, they needed checking, for Harvard had as early as 1805 appointed a Unitarian to its chair of divinity. The town of Amherst in 1826 (the population was about 2600) had five churches, all Congregationalist. But the wall of orthodoxy was to be slowly battered down. A small Baptist group appeared in Amherst in 1832; an Episcopal church was established in 1864, and a Methodist mission in 1868. And Samuel Fowler Dickinson would surely have despaired of the coming in of the Kingdom had he known that his son's tolerance would finally extend so far as to allow him to favor the building of a Roman Catholic church in Amherst.

But in 1820 the Puritan zeal still ran high, and where that was wanting, community zeal took its place. The brief picture of the construction of the first college building left us by Professor Tyler, the historian of Amherst College, is a striking glimpse of the confidence and generosity with which the citizens spontaneously joined together, to construct, as they said, a Charity Institution "for the Classical Education of indigent young men of piety and talents, for the Christian Ministry." It amounted to a sort of miniature religious revival, a long series of which extended back into the history of New England Puritanism:

> The stone for the foundation was brought chiefly from Pelham by gratuitous labor, and provisions for the workmen were furnished by voluntary contributions. Donations of lime, sand, lumber, materials of all kinds, flowed in from every quarter. Teams for hauling and men for handling and tending, and unskilled labor of every sort, were provided in abundance. Whatever could be contributed gratuitously was furnished without money and without price. The people not only contributed in kind but turned out in person, and sometimes camped on the ground and labored day and night, for they had a mind to work like the Jews in building their temple, and they felt that they too were building the Lord's house.

Here was an example of the astonishing "tumult" that Tocqueville heard when he stepped on the American shore. Here too was an example of the "public spirit" of independent men working in concert which Tocqueville came to value more highly than any other phenomenon of American society. For it was the township which impressed this observer as the moral center of our democracy and as its best guarantee of endurance. "The township of New England," he wrote, "is so constituted as to excite the warmest of human affections, without arousing the ambitious passions of the heart of man." In the ordinary events of small-town life he discerned an unconscious "ritual observance" of institutional freedom. He regarded the township as the highest political form evolved by the Americans and took it to be their best safeguard against tyranny.

The poetry of Emily Dickinson has its obvious relations to the American environment out of which, in spite of her seclusion, it grew. In its bluntness, its factuality, its candid roughness of form, its wit, its terseness, its peculiar combination of pragmatic practicality and supernaturalism, its lyric intimacy with power, melancholy, love, death, and infinite futurity—in all these we discern the lineaments of the culture from which it stemmed. We may suppose the ravages that provinciality and loneliness made on the mind of Emily Dickinson to be extensive and entirely regrettable, however hard it may be to conceive of her mind as being anything far different from what it was. But we should be undeniably right in saying that, along with the romances of Hawthorne, her poems are the subtlest and most profoundly rooted flower of provincial American life in its most coherent and successful form. Beside Emily Dickinson, Emerson is a cosmopolitan, and Thoreau reflects not so much a political and religious culture as an idea of nature and the quirks of his own mind, whereas Melville and Whitman speak of America at large. "It takes a great deal of history to produce a little literature," Henry James observed in considering the work of Hawthorne. In the long line, and the arduous struggles, of the Dickinsons from Nathaniel to Emily we have evidence of the rightness of James's remark. In considering the history of the Dickinsons we sense also the extraordinary difficulty of establishing a provincial culture in a new land as well as the difficulty of achieving excellence in literature in such a culture once it is established.

Yet whatever one may find to say, with Tocqueville, in admiration of the township society Emily Dickinson grew up in, one must admit its emotional tenuousness, its cultural isolation, and its heavy uniformity of manner, sensibility, and opinion. Emily Dickinson must surely have been speaking out of the chagrin of provincial genius when she wrote in a poem called "Much madness is divinest sense" that the "majority" comes near to having the power of life and death over the spirit of man. Dissent from majority opinion is, by the prevailing standard, insanity. But it is also necessary. The soul, as she wrote in another poem, must "seek its own society."

If in its own society the adventurous soul must seek intellectual and emotional freedom, it must also seek richness and drama. The culture of Amherst did, to be sure, make attempts at relieving the monotony and furnishing out the bleakness of existence. As Tocqueville might have pointed out, its political ritualism and its centering of emotional life upon the community could be construed as attempts to adorn the gray fabric of day-to-day life. Doubtless many of the citizens could still, during the early years of Emily Dickinson's life, invest the universe with the terrific persons and principles of the Puritan theology. During the long sessions in church on Sunday, morning, afternoon, and perhaps evening, the believer could still find himself reassured that the universe was a richly eventful place wherein one might daily experience the emotions of terror or joy. At twenty-one Emily Dickinson was an unbeliever; yet, as the following excerpt from a letter to her brother shows, she was able to catch the excitement of the old theology:

> Oh, Austin, you don't know how we all wished for you yesterday. We had such a splendid sermon from that Professor Park—I never heard anything like it, and don't expect to again, till we stand at the great white throne. . . . The students and the chapel people all came to our church, and it was very full, and still, so still the buzzing of a fly would have boomed like a cannon. And when it was all over, and that wonderful man sat down, people stared at each other, and looked as wan and wild as if they had seen a spirit, and wondered they had not died.

The town offered a certain meager variety in its architecture and its material embellishments. From the austere church, of whose pews and galleries Mr. Whicher says that they were "as square and orthodox as the preaching" and whose pulpit looked like "a pine coffin on end," Emily Dickinson would return to the relatively rich variousness and grace of the family house—a house which still remains as a monument, among its charming elm trees, lilacs, and gardens, to eighteenth-century American architecture. Inside the house the eye that was tired of the austere geometry of the church might rest gratefully upon the heavy and coolly elegant marble of fireplace and table-top, upon the white woodwork and the contrasting mahogany furniture or the whale-oil lamps or the solidly built square piano which Emily's father bought for her in 1845. In later years, one might observe a rich Brussels carpet, whose generous pattern of flowers was the delight of visitors. Or one might study upon the walls engravings of "The Forester's Family," "The Stag at Bay," or "Arctic Night."

Besides the political, religious, and domestic life of Amherst, there was the public festivity known as the Cattle Fair, a rural institution which is today one of the very few surviving remnants of genuine American folk culture. William Gardiner Hammond has left a somewhat youthfully supercilious account of the Cattle Fair (or Show as it was also called) with its attending social activities:

> A great cattle show and fair in the village today. A rich display of human as well as animal nature. . . . The evening, however, was *the* occasion. All the big turnips, etc., were cleared away, and nothing left but the tables of the ladies' society. Went up into the parlor after tea, and escorted Sabra Howe to the hall. It was crowded: the beauty and the fashion of Amherst were there in full array, going about seeking whom they might sell something to; many of the students there and every inch of room filled with a dense mass of rowdies and nobodies. It was full to suffocation. Everybody was present, even the faculty, *en masse*. One could neither walk, stand, nor sit in peace, nor hardly preserve his *individuality*. Crowded about, made an unsuccessful speculation in the ring-cake, and walked home with Mrs. Warner. Then up to Academia [a college literary society] and helped them adjourn. Back to the fair: crowded about and talked to various ladies. . . . Went home with Sabra, of

course, and stayed a little while. Then to the fair again; had my fortune told with great success; saw the end of all things, and finally went home with Miss Shepard. Thus endeth the cattle show, brute and human.

At the Cattle Show of 1856, so we are told, Emily Dickinson gained a second prize with a loaf of her "rye and Indian bread."

The college Commencement exercises also assumed the proportions of a general community ritual, attracting spectators not only from the town but from the surrounding countryside. The ceremonies lasted throughout the day and as many as fifteen or twenty orations, some in Latin, were likely to be heard. Perhaps Commencements at Amherst were not far different from the one at Williams which caught the attention of Hawthorne while he was vacationing in 1838. In his *American Notebooks* he has left a striking picture of the occasion: the handsome young graduates, the wrestlers who provided relief from the academic proceedings, the salty talk of the neighborhood farmers, "the queer, humorous recitative" of a peddler who sold a "heterogeny of articles" to the crowd, a pathetic Negro lost in the throng.

Well-to-do people like the Dickinsons could afford a rare and exciting trip to Boston. In the summer of 1846 Emily Dickinson visited Bunker Hill and the Horticultural Exhibit, and attended two concerts. She went to the Chinese Museum, where she saw two reformed opium-eaters, one of whom played and sang, while the other wrote her name in Chinese for twelve and a half cents.

Life for the citizens of Amherst, as we see, did have its small measure of variety. But one's final sense is rather of the meagerness of the variety and of a consequent heavy and imprisoning mediocrity and uniformity. After being amazed by the "tumult" of American life, Tocqueville quickly came to perceive the spiritual inertia and emotional monotony which hung upon the hearts of Americans. Contrasting aristocracy with democracy, he wrote that in the latter

> the good things and the evils of life are more equally distributed in the world: great wealth tends to disappear, the number of small fortunes to increase; desires and gratifications are multiplied, but extraordinary prosperity and irremediable penury are alike unknown. The sentiment of ambition is universal, but the scope of ambition is seldom vast. Each individual stands apart in solitary weakness; but society at large is active, provident, and powerful. . . . If there be few instances of exalted heroism or of virtues of the highest, brightest, and purest temper, men's habits are regular, violence is rare, and cruelty is almost unknown. Human existence becomes longer, and property more secure: life is not adorned with brilliant trophies, but it is extremely easy and tranquil. Few pleasures are either very refined or very coarse; and highly polished manners are as uncommon as great brutality of tastes. Neither men of great learning nor extremely ignorant communities are to be met with; genius becomes more rare, information more diffused. . . . Almost all extremes are softened or blunted: all that was once prominent is superseded by some mean term, at once less lofty and less low, less brilliant and less obscure, than what before existed in the world.

And Tocqueville ends his admirable summation by professing himself "saddened and chilled" by "the sight of such universal uniformity."

When we are tempted to think too honorifically of Emily Dickinson's poetry as the last fine utterance of New England Puritanism or the New England Renaissance or as the subtle poetic expression of a grandly energetic civilization-building America, we shall do well to remember the negative, the disintegrative side of the culture she lived in —the leveling-out, the slackness, the mediocrity, the softness and bluntness of moral and intellectual experience, the anxious isolation, and the monotony of both private and public life. When we think of her poems in relation to her culture, we must think of them as a privately constructed emendation, even a repudiation, of the township life she knew. Her best poetic tendency is everywhere away from the slackness and mediocrity of her society, and to speculate that in some sense this may be true of every poet is only to reaffirm in one's mind the striking divergence of Emily Dickinson's poetry from the emotional tone of her society. If her society was broad, expansive, and vague, her verse, at its best, was rigorously limited in its scope of experience, was concentrated and precise. If the mind of her society moved slowly and loosely to commonplace conclusions, her mind grasped truth in moments of sudden intuition. If her society was lacking in institutional or sacramental variety, she evolved in her verse a private system of hierarchal existence. If her society was exaggeratedly public in its emotional life, her poetry celebrated the drama of the private soul. If the impetus of her society was to level emotion and intelligence out into a uniformity neither limited nor deep, the intention of her poetry was to affirm a universe in depth, a universe in which dramatic distinctions must be made between society, man, nature, and God.

To rival Hawthorne as the finest product of the New England township culture, Emily Dickinson had to adopt a point of view which gave both assent and dissent to the society it surveyed. For despite her strong dissent, the mark of mid-nineteenth-century American life—with its blunt factuality, its healthy roughness of manner, its wit, its undercurrent of lyricism—is deeply impressed upon her poetry. One regrets that some of the less admirable American characteristics are also impressed upon it; for—however much we may regard it as an imaginative emendation of her society—we can hardly help also seeing that it helplessly reflects some of the failings it seeks to repudiate. Even her most ardent admirer must surely admit to the powerful feeling of monotony that one gets from her poems if they are read more than two or three dozen at a time. The monotony of the culture remains in the less successful of her poems, as do the spasmodic and unstable emotional texture, the vague verbal abstraction, and the sense of pervasive incompleteness.

The sources, then, of our poet's "articulate inarticulateness" (as Samuel G. Ward called it) are to be found in her culture and her relation to it. Loneliness, as Ward said in a letter of 1891 to T. W. Higginson, was the most striking characteristic of the New England existence, both in Puritan and in later times. He might have noted, as did Howells, that Emily Dickinson's poetry bespoke a mind which the New England scene had made better acquainted with death than with life. Perhaps no highly developed culture has provided so few modes of sympathy as our own. Emily Dickinson's life and poetry are certainly strikingly native in the strong imprint of isolation which they bear. No one knew better than she what she called "the lone effort to live, and its bleak reward." And of course this lone effort was not confined to recluses and poets. We have Emily's word for it that her father, whose typicality as the successful New England lawyer was almost painfully apparent, suffered from the inner disquiet of loneliness. Edward Dickinson, his daughter wrote, led a "lonely life" and met a "lonelier death." Much in the experience of her father, whom she loved, remained in her own experience.

Early Years

WHEN, in 1862, T. W. Higginson began to receive epigrammatic and sometimes obscure letters from "E. Dickinson" of Amherst, he wrote to inquire into the background of his odd correspondent. What did she read? How did she live? How old was she? Was she religious? Where had she gone to school? Who were her companions? His correspondent replied that she read Keats, the Brownings, Ruskin, Sir Thomas Browne, and Revelation, that her companions were the hills and a dog as large as herself, that she lived with her father, mother, brother, and sister, that they were all religious but she was not. And she reported to the man she hoped would consent to be her new "tutor" that she "went to school, but in your manner of the phrase had no education."

This latter was a little more self-effacing than necessary. Emily Dickinson had an education, though it was somewhat amorphous and discontinuous. Of course there entered into her education several forces which were not confined to the schoolroom, so that if we are to sketch out the cultural influences upon her during the decade of 1840-50, we must take account of several different kinds of education. Besides the course of studies at Amherst Academy, which the young Dickinsons attended in the 1840s, there was, for one thing, the "American humor" of the time. There was the serious religious and ethical idealism of the advanced young men at the college. There was the cult of sentiment which Emily and her friends shared. And there was the missionary Puritanism of Mt. Holyoke Female Seminary, which she attended in 1847-48.

The first words we hear from Emily Dickinson show us that she wrote well even at the age of eleven. In 1842 she wrote complainingly to her young friend, Jane Humphrey, who, it would seem, had lived in the Dickinson house while she and Emily studied at Amherst Academy:

> I have been looking for a letter from you this long time but not receiving any I plucked up all the remaining courage that I had left and determined to make one more effort to write you a few lines. I want to see you very much for I have got a great deal to tell you about school matters—and besides you are one of my dear friends. . . . I miss you more and more every day, in my study in play at home indeed every where I miss my beloved Jane. I wish you would write to me. I shall think more of it than of a mine of gold.

There can be little doubt of the romantic ardor of her temperament in these early years. Even in later years one finds that as in this letter to Jane Humphrey she repeatedly, though always gently, chides her friends for not writing soon enough or for not declaring themselves her friends with sufficient warmth. Her letter continues on the subject of "school matters":

> this afternoon is Wednesday and so of course there was Speaking and Composition. There was one young

man who read a Composition the Subject was think twice before you speak. . . . he is the sillyest creature that ever lived I think. I told him that he had better think twice before he spoke. What good times we used to have jumping into bed when you slept with me. I do wish you would come to Amherst and make me a great long visit. how do you get along in Latin. I am in the class that you used to be in in latin. besides latin I study History and Botany. I like the school very much indeed. . . . I can think of nothing more to say.

One hears in this the overtones of a particular kind of satire successfully managed only by precocious girls—that sharp and somewhat giddy critical comment on human foibles which is tinctured by the exaggeration or emotionalism it satirizes. Emily Dickinson might well have produced something like Jane Austen's charming mock history of England or her *Love and Friendship* had not American humor been so devoted to the satirical effect of oratorical overwriting and had it not remained untouched by Restoration and Augustan wit.

Amherst Academy, the "mother of Amherst College," was opened in 1814. Emily and her younger sister Lavinia were enrolled as early as 1840 and both attended off and on until 1847. There were four terms each year, and for most students attendance was somewhat irregular. There were likely to be a hundred or more students at the Academy at any given time. Neither at the Academy nor later at Mount Holyoke Seminary did Emily Dickinson receive the rigorous education then current at Amherst College. At the Academy she studied English, Classics, French, Latin, History, Botany, Geology, Mental Philosophy, and German. She practiced at the piano, but never achieved real competence. Like many of the girls at the Academy, Emily made and fondly tended an herbarium.

In her teens Emily Dickinson had gained among her contemporaries the reputation of a humorist. It was also clear to them that she had less of conventional piety than most of them had. She regarded herself as a "free spirit," a distinction she cherished in company with her friend Abiah Root, to whom she faithfully wrote for five years after Abiah Root left Amherst in 1845. Emily's letters show that she and Abiah partly based their friendship on their sense of being different from "the prim, starched up young ladies" who "are perfect models of propriety and good behavior": "don't let your free spirit be chained by them," Emily beseeches her friend. The letters make clear, however, Emily's feeling that she was a freer spirit than her friend could ever be—a fate which she contemplates with signs of dismay. Yet in contrast to her wit and her impiety, she continues in these and other letters the often gravely poetic extravagance of friendship which she displayed in her early letter to Jane Humphrey. On a Sunday morning in 1848 she writes to Sue Gilbert, her brother's intended:

> Thank the little snowflakes because they fall today rather than on some fair weekday when the world and the cares of the world would try so hard to keep me from my departed friend. And thank you too, dear Susie, that when the world is cold I am sure of one sweet letter, one covert from the storm.
> The bells are ringing, Susie, North, East and South and your own village bell and the people who love God are expecting to go to meeting; don't you go, Susie, not to their meeting, but come to me this morning to the church within our hearts, where the bells are always ringing and the preacher whose name is Love shall intercede for us.

. . . thank you for my dear letter which came on Saturday night when all the world was still, thank you for the love it bore me and for its golden thoughts and feelings so like gems that I was sure I gathered them in whole baskets of pearls.

The verbal and emotional excesses of this letter assume a rather different meaning for us when we discern that Emily is writing a literary composition, experimenting with words, and that Susie, though undeniably beloved, is being made a literary occasion for an already practicing artist. The concluding words of the following excerpt from the same letter may convince the reader that the young writer's experiments were not in vain:

I think of you, dear Susie—now I don't know how or why, but more dearly as every day goes by and that sweet month of promise draws nearer and nearer, and I miss July so differently from what I used to—once it seemed parched and dry and I hardly loved it any on account of its heat and dust, but now, Susie, month of all the year the best. I skip through violets and the dew, and the early roses and the robins—I will exchange them all for the angry and hot noon day when I can count the hours and the minutes before you come.

The image of "angry and hot noon day" was to find its way into more than one of Emily Dickinson's poems to indicate a final clarity or revelation of the mysterious paradox of time and eternity. And although in this early letter it hardly signifies anything so complicated, one senses in the letter an implied background of melancholy and death and what one can only vaguely describe as "otherness." A poem which Emily sent to Sue Gilbert in the same year concerns a robin whose annual flight to the South is obviously a visit to an eternal world, where, before returning to her, he basks

> In a serener Bright
> In a more golden light.

But such thoughts cannot have been, in these early years, the sustenance of life. At eighteen Emily Dickinson could doubtless still feel some of the glamorous (though slightly self-satirizing) expectation which she expressed two or three years earlier. "I have grown tall a good deal, and wear my golden tresses done up in a net-cap." And again, "I am growing handsome very fast indeed. I expect I shall be the belle of Amherst by my 17th year. I don't doubt that I shall have crowds of admirers at that age." Actually the belle of Amherst in Emily's generation was Jane Gridley, if we may trust William Gardiner Hammond. When he was not busy with Demosthenes and Xenophon, Hammond had an eye for the girls of Amherst, an eye which Emily Dickinson seems never to have caught.

The "golden tresses" are mythical. Emily had Titian hair, and everyone remarks upon its fineness and richness —largely, one gathers, because there was little else to remark about her appearance. Even the Dickinson cultists have never maintained that the poet was anything but plain. Large, intelligent brown eyes she surely had, but they do not seem to have turned many hearts. As a girl she cherished flirtations. So we gather from a letter she wrote Abiah Root in 1850 in which she naughtily hints at dark goings on: "If you were here I would tell you something— several somethings—which have happened since you went away." And the letter is signed: "Your very sincere and *wicked* friend." But we do not know of any man with whom, in her teens, Emily Dickinson may incontestably be said to have fallen in love. That she formed a number of idealistically amorous attitudes towards a number of young men seems certain. Still, it must be noted that those of her biographers who see in the ardent language of her letters the proof of a love affair with this or that young man forget too easily that she wrote with the verbal excess of girlish feeling, of the sentimental fiction of the day, of copious but unformed literary energy, and of "American humor."

The ardent and rather heavy romanticism of Emily's inner adolescence found its adequate relief in the wit and impious gaiety which her contemporaries noted in her. At sixteen she was not above the popular humor of the time. "I have just seen a funeral procession go by of a negro baby, so if my thoughts are rather dark you need not marvel"—so she writes in a letter to Abiah Root. On the same occasion she displays a freedom with hallowed names which was more remarkable in 1846 than now: "I have lately come to the conclusion that I am Eve, alias Mrs. Adam. You know there is no account of her death in the Bible, and why am I not Eve? If you find any statements which you think likely to prove the truth of the case, I wish you to send them to me without delay." A related fantasy occurs in a Valentine poem composed in 1852 and sent, with humorous intentions, to a friend:

> Put down the apple, Adam,
> And come away with me;
> So shall thou have a pippin
> From off my father's tree.

Another stanza in the same poem is more closely in the style of genteel Victorian light verse:

> Unto the Legislature
> My country bids me go.
> I'll take my india-rubbers,
> In case the wind should blow.

But the most interesting example of Emily's early humorous writing is purely American. One of Melville's earliest compositions was a humorous treatment of the advertising methods of Phineas T. Barnum, and it appears to be true of Emily Dickinson that her first published work was a piece of satirically grandiose humor in which the writer, like Melville, took as much pleasure in the outrageous tall talk she was satirizing as she did in satirizing it. In later years, a schoolmate recalled that at the Academy Emily was a contributor to the school magazine known as *Forest Leaves*. "Emily Dickinson and Mary Humphrey," she reports, "were the wits of the school, and the humorists of the 'comic column.' " We hear that Emily often wrote "in the style of funny little sermons," an established mode of humorous writing in her time. Another form which the humor of the time took was, as we have noticed, the comic Valentine, and one of these written by Emily in 1850 is the fullest extant example of her humor. It was addressed to George Gould, an Amherst student and friend of her brother Austin. Gould roguishly printed the Valentine in the college paper of which he was an editor and which was called (presumably after Leigh Hunt's journal) the *Indicator*. Emily had written as follows:

> Sir, I desire an interview; meet me at sunrise, or
> sunset, or the new moon—the place is immaterial. In
> gold, or in purple, or sackcloth—I look not upon *rai-*

ment. In coach, or in wagon or walking, the *equi-page*, far from the *man*. With soul, or spirit, or body, they are all alike to me. With host or alone, in sunshine or storm, in heaven or earth, *some* how or no how—I propose sir, to see you.

And not to *see* merely, but a chat sir, or tete-a-tete, or confab a mingling of opposite minds is what I propose to have. I feel sir that we shall agree. We will be David and Jonathan, or Damon and Pythias, or what is better than either, the United States of America. We will talk over what we have learned in our geographies, and listened to from the pulpit, the press, and the Sabbath School.

This is strong language, sir, but none the less true. So hurrah for North Carolina, since we are on this point.

Our friendship sir, shall endure till sun and moon shall wane no more, till stars shall set, and victims rise to grace the final sacrifice. We'll be instant, in season, out of season, minister, take care of, cherish, soothe, watch, wait, doubt, refrain, reform, elevate, instruct. All choice spirits however distant are ours, ours theirs; there is a thrill of sympathy—a circulation of mutuality—cognationem inter nos! I am Judith the heroine of Apocrypha, and you the orator of Ephesus.

That's what they call a metaphor in our country. Don't be afraid of it sir, it won't bite! If it was my *Carlo* now! The Dog is the noblest work of Art, sir. I may safely say the noblest—his mistress' rights he doth defend—although it bring him to his end—although to death it doth him send!

But the world is sleeping in ignorance and error, sir, and we must be crowing-cocks, and singing larks, and a rising sun to awake her; or else we'll pull society up by the roots, and plant it in a different place. We'll build alms houses and transcendental State prisons, and scaffolds—we will blow out the sun and the moon, and encourage invention. Alpha shall kiss Omega—we will ride up the hill of glory—Hallelujah, all hail!

Yours, truly, etc.

Anyone who has read the mock orations of early nineteenth-century humor, those of Davy Crockett for example, will take Emily's Valentine to be a genuine part of the tradition, with its pleasure in high-flown verbosity, its grandiose progressivism, its invocation to the power and the unlimited future of America, its restless fantasy of societies built and abandoned overnight.

But Emily Dickinson's Valentine oration is different from run-of-the-mill American "screaming" because the ideal it poses is intellectual and moral. A really heartfelt mission of moral and cultural improvement underlies the calculated fraudulence of the language. An apotheosis of exalted minds is to occur through the exchange of ideas, the final meeting of minds is to be a felt revelation of spiritual community. It is time, as she seems to say, that our lonely American minds should join with all choice spirits. Then shall we achieve "a thrill of sympathy—a circulation of mutuality—cognationem inter nos!" In the same year of 1850 and but a few miles to the northwest of Amherst, in Pittsfield, another American writer was posing a similar goal for American spirits. By proudly confessing to the world the genius of Hawthorne, this author wrote, "you confess others; you brace the whole brotherhood. For genius, all over the world, stands hand in hand, and one shock of recognition runs the whole circle round." So wrote Melville in "Hawthorne and his Mosses."

As a critic has suggested, the shock of recognition within American culture has been largely the privilege of mod-

ern readers who cast an eye back over our strangely discontinuous heritage, whereas the great writers, whom we
are now able to see in some sort of historical relation, were
vouchsafed only the burdensome "shock of *un*recognition."
This small, and in itself unimportant, coincidence between the thoughts of Emily Dickinson and Melville reminds us again of our American cultural disjunctions. Had
there ever been, until nineteenth-century America, a
highly developed civilization in which an Emily Dickinson and a Herman Melville could have lived and died
without ever having heard of each other? Or, for that matter, a Henry James and a Herman Melville? The point
bears emphasis because some, at least, of the anxiety and
sadness of Emily Dickinson's life issued from her strong
need for intellectual companionship and her failure to
find it.

There can be no doubt, however, that the desire she expressed in her Valentine found a measure of satisfaction in
her early years while she was still youthfully enthusiastic
and even awestruck by the academic life of her college
town. Her teachers at the Academy, of whom she speaks
with the greatest enthusiasm ("I am always in love with
my teachers"), were influenced by the intellectual climate
of the college and some of them were young graduates of
the college. When Emily was in her late teens and just beginning to gain the competence to respond to reading and
to new ideas, the college had already changed—fallen
away, as the orthodox might think—from the Calvinist zeal
of its first days. Well-to-do students, such as William Gardiner Hammond, had begun to attend the college and the
severe atmosphere of an institution originally devoted to
"indigent and pious young men" was somewhat molli-

fied. When Emily Dickinson was fifteen, a new intellectual tone was established by the new president of the
college, Edward Hitchcock. Though a minister of the gos-
pel who insisted, as an historian reports, that his teachers
be "heartily Christian," "in lively sympathy with reviv-
als," and "consecrated to the cause of charity, humanity,
and God," Hitchcock was a notable scientist. And far from
taking such thinkers as Darwin, Huxley, and Lyell to be
instruments of the devil, he insisted that the Christian
could meet the scientist on his own ground and demonstrate the harmony of Scripture with the discoveries of
geology and evolution. Ostensibly, in the Amherst of the
'40s and '50s no spiritual retreat was being made before
the new sciences; but among the advanced young people
of Emily's generation the Calvinist foundations were falling into disrepair.

Nevertheless the very adventurousness of the new spirit
introduced by Hitchcock provided a temporary stimulus
to intellectual activity, and the earnest love of ideas which
is discernible in the young men of the time whom Emily
admired, such as Leonard Humphrey and George Gould,
must bring a good deal of nostalgia to serious minds at
Amherst today. There can be no doubt that provincial
American intellectual life in the early nineteenth century,
where it existed at all, was a good deal superior in its seriousness and its general literacy to that of our century. In
spite of his priggishness and his moralism William Gardiner Hammond struggling manfully with his headaches
in order to conquer Livy, Cicero, Tacitus, Locke, and Edwards presents a spectacle which may well appeal to the
modern academic, beset as he is with the slide-rule and
test-tube culture of his students.

Despite this general truth, the fact remains that Emily Dickinson never, throughout her life, knew anyone of really great or original intelligence. The Reverend Charles Wadsworth, whom she later admired and with whom she seems actually to have fallen in love, possessed fervor and eloquence but no striking intelligence. George Gould, the student to whom Emily addressed her Valentine, was thoughtful and serious and gained a reputation at Amherst for the eloquence of his orations and essays. Obviously an advanced spirit, he is said to have spent his senior year in an "attempt to combine the philosophy of Dugald Stewart with that of Ralph Waldo Emerson." Emily thought very highly of Gould's abilities and his college expected great things of him. But his career of pastorates in Springfield, Hartford, and Worcester was undistinguished, and the speciousness of one of his sermons (recorded by Miss Taggard) does not inspire respect for the final development of his mind: "The Bible is a practical book; it, therefore, never arrays God's sovereignty and man's freedom in an attitude of antagonism to each other, but always in rational coincidence and in perfect practical harmony." Emily Dickinson came to know better than that. (We may note at this point that Miss Taggard's extensive attempt to show that Gould was the object of Emily Dickinson's love now appears mistaken. Mr. Whicher is probably correct in saying that "Gould passed completely out of her life soon after his graduation from Amherst in 1850.")

The most admired member of the group of advanced spirits which included Emily, George Gould, and Emily's brother was Leonard Humphrey, whose early death, as Mr. Whicher has well suggested, had meanings for Emily Dickinson and her friends very much of the same kind that the death of Edward King had for the Cambridge contemporaries of Milton. Humphrey was graduated from Amherst in 1846, and gave a valedictory address on "The Morality of States." To Emily's great joy, he became principal of Amherst Academy, holding this position during her last year there. He later attended Andover Theological Seminary, returned to Amherst briefly as a tutor at the college, and died unexpectedly in 1850. Both Gould and Humphrey had intellectual interests in advance of the academic courses of their time. If Gould concerned himself with Emerson, Humphrey was learning to speak in the prophetic moral strain of Carlyle and was further modifying his theological training with the ideas of Wordsworth. In the short time when Emily Dickinson was able to call Humphrey "my tutor," he seems to have been trying to shape a philosophy of life which stressed the "imagination," as described and illustrated in *Lyrical Ballads*, and which included a cult of romantic solitude. Miss Pollitt quotes from Humphrey's notebook a passage which makes us feel that Emily's youthful teacher had developed a kind of ethical romanticism of the mind but that he showed no signs of extraordinary intelligence: "To those who have suffered from the inexorable rule of Common Society,—who know the compulsory effort to talk, or the grievous burden of listening,—how delicious is that freedom of intercourse in which the soul is suffered to pause in the abundance of its thoughts, and need speak only when the thoughts overflow. It is said that if a silken thread be tied around a perfectly molded bell at the moment of sounding, the bell will burst asunder, and shiver into a thousand pieces. So is it when a heart of perfect and delicate harmony in itself seeks to manifest its life among other hearts;

the slightest revulsion is enough to destroy the expression forever." However serious the intellectual life of these young people may have been, one nevertheless suspects that among Emily Dickinson's friends this ethical romanticism of the mind often passed for genuine intelligence. It belonged to the high-minded young men of the day and it made a smaller impression on Emily Dickinson than she herself may have thought. When she ventures upon intellectual matters in her early letters, she tends to be either downright and factual or else elaborately facetious—two tendencies which sharpen and combine into the epigrammatic manner of the later letters. And her poetry was to show qualities of mind undoubtedly beyond the reach of those whom she had idolized at eighteen or twenty.

The clichés of Humphrey's obituary in a local paper do not tell us much about Humphrey. But they have the historical value of clichés: they tell us what the public opinion of the time held the ideal young man to be:

> Thus suddenly has passed away one in the midst of life and in the fullness of hope. Mr. Humphrey was a man of great promise, highly cultivated and of fair attainments. As a Scholar, few of his age stand higher in the number and value of their acquirements.
> He was patient, accurate, and thorough in his investigations. Possessing a mind exact and logical, yet tasteful and elegant, his productions were always rich in thought and beautiful in form. Few possessed the power of more deeply interesting by their exhibition of truth than the deceased. . . . Religion had shed also over all his natural endowments her chastening influence.

There is no reason to suppose that Emily Dickinson loved Humphrey in any way beyond what she meant when she said that she was always in love with her teachers. There is very good reason to accept the story that Humphrey's intention of marrying another Amherst girl was well known among his young friends. Humphrey may well have particularly impressed and delighted Emily. Yet though obviously heartfelt, her letter concerning his death (written in January 1851) is rather more literary, in the post-Miltonic, romantic style of melancholy, than her letters usually are.

> I write Abiah to-night, because it is cool and quiet, and I can forget the toil and care of the feverish day, and then I am *selfish* too, because I am feeling lonely; some of my friends are gone, and some of my friends are sleeping—sleeping the churchyard sleep—the hour of evening is sad—it was once my study hour—my master has gone to rest, and the open leaf of the book, and the scholar at school *alone*, make the tears come, and I cannot brush them away; I would not if I could, for they are the only tribute I can pay to the departed Humphrey.
>
> *You* have stood by the grave before; I have walked there sweet summer evenings and read the names on the stones, and wondered who would come and give me the same memorial; but I never have laid my friends there, and forgot that they too must die; this is my first affliction, and indeed 'tis hard to bear. . . . I don't think there will be any sunshine or any singing-birds in the spring that's coming. I shall look for an early grave then, when the grass is growing green; I shall love to call the bird there if it has gentle music, and the meekest-eyed wild flowers, and the low, plaintive insect.

These are not the words of someone personally overwhelmed with grief and loss after the death of a beloved one. They are the words of a sensitive and intelligent young woman trying to master the *idea* of grief and loss, seeking for attitudes and modes of expression out of immediate emotional necessity. Yet there can be no doubt that this "first affliction" was a momentous event in Emily Dickinson's life. It was the first time she felt the immediate impact of death—the impact, that is, of what was to be the main theme of her poetry. At twenty-one she knew only the language of sentimental romanticism, though later she was to discover a sharper, more severe language. The theme of immortality, we may note here, begins to appear in her letters after the death of Leonard Humphrey.

Besides their humor, their religion, their scholastic studies and their ethical romanticism, the young people of Emily's acquaintance had in common a cult of sentiment. The generally amorphous quality of their intellectual life left them more exposed than they might otherwise have been to the sub-intellectual and partly unconscious assumptions of popular belief—that undeclared and unobserved body of attitudes and emotional habits which helps to characterize the culture in which it exists. In a highly developed culture this body of assumptions is fully taken account of—transmuted and used or simply rejected—by the life of intelligence. In a less developed culture the life of intelligence tends to be permeated by popular assumption and is more or less at its mercy. The intellectual life of Emily Dickinson and her young friends was indeed highminded and serious on the one hand and humorous and even satirical on the other. But it was also susceptible to a thoroughly vulgarized sentimentality.

We sense an established communion of sentiment between Emily Dickinson and her correspondents. The holiness of home, the pathos of graveyards, the transport of joy at the thought of immortality, the cult of scenery—these were shared assumptions. Writing in 1851 to her brother Austin, who was teaching school in Boston, Emily expresses her loneliness in a manner which strikes one as actually ghoulish: "I wish you were here, dear Austin; the dust falls on the bureau in your deserted room, and gay, frivolous spiders spin away in the corners. I don't go there after dark whenever I can help it, for the twilight seems to pause there, and I am half afraid; and if I ever have to go, I hurry with all my might, and never look behind me, for I know who I should see." She tells Austin that when she sets the table she often forgets that "we are not all here" and sets a place for him; she then "brushes a tear away in memory of my brother." Apparently Austin, an adherent of the cult, found nothing uneasy in his sister's somewhat self-indulgent flirtations with ideas of death.

The popular sentiment of the time was a watered-down version of two cultural phenomena: New England Puritanism and Romanticism. It is not surprising that Emily Dickinson should have found sustenance in this popular sentiment, since she herself was a product, even in her best poetic moments, of the same cultural influences. It is only a little surprising that a mind which would soon be capable of great poetic acts should have been so fully absorbed in an inferior image of itself.

For Emily and her friends the cult of sentiment achieved the fine flower of its expression in a book called *Reveries of a Bachelor* (1850) by Donald Grant Mitchell, otherwise known as "Ik Marvel." Emily thought Mitchell capable of "the very sweetest fancies" and of "exquisite language." Such an author could have been born only on a glorious, golden day when the clouds are sailing through a beautiful blue sky. So she writes to Austin in 1851, deliciously sharing with him a spiritual world which their father disapproved, as could be gathered by his remarks about wasting time with these "modern literati" who write "rev-e-ries."

Mitchell's book, subtitled "A Book of the Heart," became a handbook of sentiment for its time. The author assumes a pose of gaiety and freedom. Insouciantly he roams at will through the airy realms of imagination. He is young, though his twenty-six years give him just enough seniority to impress his even more youthful readers at Amherst. He loves nothing better than to sit by the fire and discern interesting phantasms and moralistic symbols in fire, smoke, and ashes. His youthful humor and his sense of delight in fanciful ruminations are tinged with melancholy, with thoughts of death and eternity. Accompanying him through the regions of dream is his noble dog Carlo, after whom Emily Dickinson would seem to have named her own dog, if she did not take the name from St. John Rivers's dog in *Jane Eyre*.

Mitchell was reassuring to young people who cultivated the arts but who seldom reflected on aesthetics. It is only by accident, Mitchell says, that his "floating visions" have found their way into book form. He might of course have made a novel out of his fancies. But, as he says, "I have chosen the honester way of setting them down as they came seething from my thought, with all their crudities and contrasts, uncovered." This was a credo which Emily Dickinson herself never entirely abandoned. It is only "cold critics," Mitchell remarks, who speak of something as "art-

fully done." Nature, not mere art, produces the most beautiful flowers of thought. It is much better to write without
"art," to set down for oneself one's own honest ideas. Having proclaimed that his book had been written without
thought of publication, Mitchell went on to say that fame,
with its "plumes waving in zephyrs of applause," might be
attractive, but more important is the personal necessity of
releasing the tumults of affection from the depths of one's
soul, as the lava flows from the "seething heat of a volcano."
And with this too Emily Dickinson always agreed.

Mitchell loved the transports of Infinitude. Ideally, he
exclaimed, "this heart would be at length itself; striving
with everything gross, even now as it clings to grossness.
Earth's cares would fly. Joys would double. Susceptibilities
be quickened; Love master self; and having made the mastery, stretch onward, and upward toward Infinitude." He
had a cult of the physical manifestations of death, and his
reader might be sure that when Mitchell described a
maiden's hand as white (as he repeatedly did) he was
never praising its vital beauty; he was noting the first signs
of the encroaching specter. What is the use in getting
married? he asks, in a mood of desolation symbolized by
the ashes in the fireplace.

> How anxiously you watch that step, if it lose not its
> buoyancy; how you study the color on that cheek, if it
> grow not fainter; how you tremble at the lustre of
> those eyes, if it be not the lustre of Death; how you
> totter under the weight of that muslin sleeve—a phan-
> tom weight!

Death has its rewards, of course. There is the "nice coffin,
a very nice coffin. Pass your hand over it; how smooth!"
And death may be ultimately defeated, just as life may be

transfigured, by love. "Love . . . unlocks the door upon
that Futurity where the isles of the blessed lie like stars.
Affection is the stepping stone to God. The heart is our
only measure of infinitude." Mitchell's "reveries," we cannot doubt, stirred the imagination of a poet who was to
speak of the superiority of the heart over the head, of the
transport of religious joy, of the anatomy of death, of
achieving immortality through love, of the "volcano" of
passion in the human breast, of the fire and ash of human
feeling.

Though it is not a matter of great importance, Mitchell
helps us to understand at least one of Emily Dickinson's
poems better than we otherwise might. It is not a good
poem, with or without Mitchell.

> More life went out, when He went,
> Than ordinary breath,
> Lit with a fine phosphor
> Requiring in the quench
>
> A power of renowned cold—
> The climate of the grave
> A temperature just adequate
> So anthracite to live.
>
> For some an ampler zero,
> A frost more needle keen
> Is necessary to reduce
> The Ethiop within.
>
> Others extinguish easier—
> A gnat's minutest fan
> Sufficient to obliterate
> A tract of citizen.

In his valuable essay on Emily Dickinson's poetry, Mr.
R. P. Blackmur correctly judges that this is a mere "exer-

cise," that the argument is incoherent, and the language vague. Mr. Blackmur has a good deal of understandable trouble with the word "anthracite" and guesses that Emily Dickinson wished to indicate by that word "the effect of something hard and cold and perhaps black." Initiates into the mysteries of Mitchell, however, will understand what she meant. Mitchell's second "revery" is entitled "By a City Grate" and makes a distinction, of psychology or humors, between two types of human being. One is the "sea-coal" or "bituminous type, characterized by a mercurial, shallow, unsteady, brilliant sensibility. The other is the "anthracite" type, characterized by stable, devoted, dependable, and profound ardor. Thus in Emily Dickinson's poem he who has died was the anthracite type, and it is her way of praising him to say that it took a great deal of cold to extinguish his heat. "So anthracite to live" is nonsense grammatically, but we must paraphrase: "The temperature of the grave was just adequate to quench the fire of one who when he lived was so much the anthracite type." The "others" who "extinguish easier" are presumably like sea-coal. The argument is a little more meaningful than Mr. Blackmur senses, though the poem is scarcely better.

Mitchell imparted to his receptive young readers an ambiguous cult of woman. It begins with the little girl and the faithful dog. The cult requires that one or the other die, and if it is the dog (Emily reported to Higginson in 1865 that her Carlo had died) the girl grows up in the cult. Her emotional life is presumed to be chaste and not far out of touch with God. Without God a man "is the football of Destiny." How much more, then, does the woman need God. Underneath the surface of Mitchell's prose there is a kind of unventilated morbidity and a diffused eroticism.

If the young woman is the "sea-coal" type—that is, openly sexual and flirtatious—she is beneath contempt. If she is "anthracite," she will take one of two courses. She will marry and be a sisterly and domestic helper and an inspiration to her husband. Or—what appears to be even nobler —she will renounce the world and remain a spinster, making a cult of the "lares" of her childhood home, angelically tending, it may be, her sick father, and leaving at her death a packet of beautiful and inspiring letters describing her ordeal.

One can imagine Emily Dickinson, who at twenty-one already knew her fear of leaving home and had ventured the opinion that she would never do so, looking into the mirror of Mitchell's prose. The ideal woman, he said, the woman who is "anthracite," has "an angel face; no matter for curious lines of beauty; no matter for popular talk of prettiness; no matter for its angles or its proportions; no matter for its color or its form,—the soul is there. . . . It tells of honesty, sincerity, and worth; it tells of truth and virtue;—and you clasp the image to your heart, as the received ideal of your fondest dreams." We cannot doubt that Emily clasped.

She must have been particularly interested in the image of Bella, who in Mitchell's final revery is the spinster-recluse who stays home though her young friends and relatives have gone out into the world. After her death, Bella's letters tell her story.

I have come back now to father's house; I could not leave him alone, for they told me he was ill. I found him not well; he was very glad to see me, and kissed me so tenderly that I am sure, Cousin Paul, you would not have said, as you used to say, that he was a cold man. I sometimes read to him sitting in the deep library-window, (you remember it,) where we used to nestle out of his sight at dusk.

And so the letters continue until finally Bella gives herself up to the better world beyond this one. So Emily Dickinson cared for, and even read to, her father in his latter days.

Certain images used by Mitchell have a distinctly Dickinsonian ring:

Then the iron enters the soul.

But courage, and patience, and faith, and hope have their limit. Blessed be the man who escapes such trial as will determine limit.

Our souls indeed wander. . . . to a home-land . . . until like blind flies, they are lost in the blaze of immensity.

But I do not wish to claim for Mitchell's book too strong an influence upon the developing mind of Emily Dickinson. I should judge that it had its specific influence, but it served also in a more general manner to confirm in her mind the popular assumptions about life which she felt her culture to make. Mitchell was a heady dose, more so than the pious unction of his manner would indicate. For beneath the gaiety and idealism and melancholy sentiment there lay powerful forces. An erotic pleasure in the idea of death, a hatred of sexuality, a resentment toward children, a contempt for order and intellect, a boundless and foolish optimism, and a simple-minded idea of the relation of man to God.

Emily Dickinson's year at Mount Holyoke Female Seminary, in 1847-48, was a crucial period in her intellectual development. She continued with the same general kind of courses she had studied at Amherst Academy. But, more important, the year at Mount Holyoke was the occasion of her single religious crisis.

A full year before she entered the Seminary, Emily was characteristically full of intense anticipation: "I fear I am anticipating too much, and that some freak of fortune may overturn all my airy schemes for future happiness." When Emily Dickinson arrived at the Seminary in South Hadley, Massachusetts, there were (she said) nearly 300 students there, though another estimate places them at 235. Writing to Abiah Root six weeks after her arrival, she proclaims herself to have survived the first attacks of homesickness and to be "contented and quite happy." She is pleased to find "ease and grace" among the students, "a desire to make one another happy," and only occasional exhibitions of those "rough and uncultivated manners" which, with a sudden access of gentility, she had feared to find. Her account of the schedule of a day at Mt. Holyoke befits a school which prided itself on the number of Christian missionaries it was able to send to the heathen:

At 6 o'clock we all rise. We breakfast at 7. Our study hours begin at 8. At 9 we all meet in Seminary Hall for devotions. At 10¼ I recite a review of Ancient History, in connection with which we read Goldsmith and Grimshaw. At 11, I recite a lesson in Pope's *Essay on Man*, which is merely transposition. At 12 I practice calisthenics, and at 12¼ read until dinner, which is at 12½, and after dinner from 1½ until 2, I sing in Seminary Hall. From 2¾ until 3¾ I practise upon the piano. At 3¾ I go to Sections, where we give in all accounts for the day, including absence, tardiness, communications, breaking silent study hours, receiving company in our rooms, and ten thousand other things which I will not take time or place to mention. At 4½ we go into Seminary Hall and receive advice from Miss Lyon in the form of a lecture. We have supper at 6, and silent study hours from then until the retiring bell, which rings at 8¾, but the tardy bell does not ring until 9¾.

By the standards of modern women's colleges, Emily Dickinson's schedule was severe. But Mt. Holyoke was no place of horrors. It was not Lowood School, and no Jane Eyre cowered before the inhumanity of teachers or suffered the rigors of institutionalized poverty. Nevertheless Miss Mary Lyon, the founder and headmistress, set a rigorous standard of Christian living, which entailed not only the learning of precepts and praying for redemption but also the active service of the girls in maintaining the domestic economy of the school. Emily Dickinson's task was to lay out the knives in the dining hall in the morning and at noon and to wash and wipe them at night.

More freedom than one might suppose was granted to the students. The first time William Gardiner Hammond made the nine-mile trip from Amherst to South Hadley, he rang the bell at the Seminary in great terror of Miss Lyon "and the assistant dragonesses" and was amazed to be led into the parlor "without any inquisition preparatory." A friend of his succeeded in spiriting a student across the Connecticut River to a hotel for tea and in bringing her back as late as 9 P.M. without incurring the displeasure of the authorities. And Hammond testifies that it was possible to see the students at calisthenics: "Saw some of the young ladies exercise at calisthenics, a species of orthodox *dancing* in which they perambulate a smooth floor in various figures, with a sort of sliding stage step. . . . The whole movement is accompanied by singing, in which noise rather than tune or harmony seems to be the main object. . . . Had a capital chance to look at the girls during the evolutions, and especially when they defiled before us out of the room hand in hand. . . . Saw one or two pretty girls there; but the majority of *transcendent* ugliness." Young Hammond had apparently surveyed on this occasion no rout of dryads, no company of nymphs, no Thesmophoriazusae, no Atalanta, no Diana.

If there was any real hardship at Mt. Holyoke in Emily Dickinson's time, it was the spiritual hardship of the nonbeliever. In her schedule of daily events, Emily writes "at 4½ we go into Seminary Hall and receive advice from Miss Lyon in the form of a lecture." She neglected to say that "we" referred only to the relatively small body of "impenitents" who did not stand up when Miss Lyon asked the assembled students which ones were saved. From the journal of Miss Susan L. Tolman, one of the teachers, we learn that the inquisition of 1847-48 (as it may be called) began very shortly after the arrival of the students in the fall. On October 2, the names of "those who have a hope, and those who have not were taken. . . . I saw more than one weep as her name was put down 'no hope'." On October 11, Miss Tolman notes that the religious meetings have commenced, the praying circles meeting at 7:30 in the evening and the impenitents at 4:30 in the afternoon. Miss Lyon's meetings with the impenitents continued through the fall, and by December 20 Miss Tolman could write that "there is attention and some awakening but little *deep* feeling yet." Miss Lyon continued to address the impenitents "in regard to the salvation of their souls, of seeking it in earnest and now." On the eve of Christmas, Miss Tolman noted a new immediacy in the Spirit's presence but sadly observed that "we are not yet where we should be, low at the foot of the cross." After an austere and Puritan Christmas, which involved neither the pagan festivities of weaker sects nor a vacation from school, Miss Lyon continued her crusade, upbraiding unsaved souls "for not *now* seeking salvation, and submitting to Jesus."

> She showed how vain they were, how vain they would seem in the light of Eternity. The closing remark was, "How vain to resist God. Did you ever see the little insect fall into the flame, see it struggle and strive to escape? how vain— Just so you are in the hands of *angry* God! What if you do resist? Which are *you*, a feeble worm of the dust? Oh! how vain! how much better to submit."

We have at least some hints of the quality of Emily Dickinson's life during these winter months while the persuasive and accomplished Miss Lyon grappled for the souls of the impenitent. The logic of the Puritan theology and the Jonathan-Edwards-like rhetoric of Puritan evangelism were always capable of engaging Emily Dickinson's mind and of stirring her imagination. We may easily deduce this from many of her poems and from her idolization, after 1854, of the Reverend Charles Wadsworth. One of the few remaining specific references to her during these months shows that she was drawn very nearly to the final step of confessing her salvation. Later in January, after one of her "lectures," Miss Lyon announced an evening meeting for "all those who had today felt an uncommon anxiety to decide." Of this occasion, the assistant head-mistress wrote to a friend: "Seventeen attended a meeting in the evening for those who felt unusually anxious to choose the service of God that night, and it was a very solemn meeting. Emily Dickinson was among the number." The evidence indicates that this was the crisis of the poet's religious life. The clear and momentous fact is that she definitely drew back from the final commitment. She does not seem to have attended any further meetings of the impenitents.

Her letters give us some insight into the state of her mind in relation to religious matters during these early years. Even at sixteen she knew that her assent to Christianity, if she ever gave it, would not be easy—not nearly so easy as it was to her friend Abiah Root, to whom she wrote: "I have perfect confidence in God and His promises, and yet I know not why I feel that the world holds a predominant place in my affections." And again she writes: "I do not feel that I could give up all for Christ, were I called to die. Pray for me, dear Abiah, that I may yet enter into the Kingdom, that there may be room left for me in the shining courts above." Emily envied and admired the happy repose conversion was bringing to girls of her acquaintance: "I presume you have heard from Abby," she writes to Abiah Root, "and know what she now believes—she makes a sweet girl Christian, religion makes her face quite different, calmer, but full of radiance, holy, yet very joyful. She talks of herself quite freely, seems to love Lord Christ most dearly, and to wonder and be bewildered at the life she has always led. It all looks black and distant, and God and heaven are near. She is certainly very much changed." Very characteristically feminine are these thoughts of the post-adolescent Emily Dickinson, combining as they do the Augustinian-Puritan emphasis on conversion and rebirth with the tender feeling of girl for girl, with the interest in the changes of a girl growing up, the successful passage from the bewildering time of adolescence to the radiance and hope of new life. Emily must have found very painful her inability to receive the grace which had come to so many of her friends.

Of her painful anxieties during the year at Mt. Holyoke we gain some immediate sense from a letter she wrote to Abiah Root after the long contest between herself and Miss Lyon had ended in failure.

> I tremble when I think how soon the weeks and days of this term will all have been spent, and my fate will be sealed, perhaps. I have neglected the *one thing needful* when all were obtaining it, and I may never, never again pass through such a season as was granted to us last winter. Abiah, you may be surprised to hear me speak as I do, knowing that I express no interest in the all-important subject, but I am not happy, and I regret that last term, when the golden opportunity was mine, that I did not give up and become a Christian. It is not now too late, so my friends tell me, so my offended conscience whispers, but it is hard for me to give up the world.

She apparently felt a good deal of guilt over her spiritual intransigence, so that when she refers to herself as "one of the lingering *bad* ones" who "slink away and are sorrowful" and turn their backs on the sacredness, solemnity, and radiance of the Christian life, she is only partly ironic. There can be no doubt that missing her "golden opportunity" to become a Christian gave her something like the full poignancy of that sense of loss for which in later years her inner life was so notable.

What was going on in Emily Dickinson's mind that kept her finally from taking the step to the Christian life? She surely had more potential capacity for religious experience than any of her young friends, and, as we have seen, she was very strongly drawn by Miss Lyon's evangelizing.

One influence that held her back may have been that of the advanced young men she knew at Amherst, with their talk of Emerson and Carlyle and their interest in science. More important, one may suppose, was the fact that Emily was a Dickinson. No matter how publicly respectable her father may always have been, he was also always a sternly independent man. He himself did not join the church until 1850 when he was forty-seven, though his father, as we have noted, had been a deacon at twenty-one. It is said that when he came to his pastor to announce his decision, the pastor complained that "You want to come to Christ as a *lawyer*—but you must come to him as a *poor sinner*—get down on your knees and let me pray for you." The unbending individualism of Edward Dickinson, his feeling that to join with others in public expressions of emotion is vulgar, intolerable, and unworthy of a self-sufficient New Englander, was strongly ingrained in Emily Dickinson's temperament. When Edward Dickinson died, a calling card was found in his wallet which read: "I hereby give myself to God." The legal language betrays the enormous reservation. We may imagine the troubled self-questionings of Emily's father as he tried to understand why a successful lawyer, a Whig, and an American should need God and how, without compromising himself in the eyes of his fellows and in his own soul, he could ever bring himself to fall upon his knees as "a poor sinner." We may suppose that his daughter, who facetiously refers to her Whig politics in an early letter, had the same or analogous troubles. The individualism displayed by Emily Dickinson when she remained seated while the other students stood up to signify that they were Christians was an abiding characteristic.

But we are dealing with an emergent artist. Emily Dickinson seldom thought at length or explicitly about art and the artist, and there are few overt signs that in these early years she thought of herself as a dedicated poet. She wrote poems at seventeen or eighteen, but most of her friends did too, her sister Vinnie for one. And four or five years later she humorously warns her brother Austin not to presume to write any more poems, because in doing so he is trespassing on her private preserve. But we hear no clearly enunciated dedication to poetry from Emily Dickinson; it would be astonishing if we did. In the seventeenth-century England a Milton might elaborately declare himself a poet. But nineteenth-century Amherst offered no tradition or cultural context within which such declarations might be made.

Nevertheless Emily Dickinson's mind when she was eighteen or twenty cannot be adequately conceived without remembering that at thirty-two she was capable of writing great poetry. She was not an Abiah Root. This she realized, as we gather from a letter to Abiah written in 1851.

> You are growing wiser than I am, and nipping in the bud fancies which I let blossom—perchance to bear no fruit, or if plucked, I may find it bitter.

The shore is safer, Abiah, but I love to buffet the sea
—I can count the bitter wrecks here in these pleasant
waters, and hear the murmuring winds, but oh, I
love the danger! You are learning control and firm-
ness. <u>Christ Jesus will love you more. I'm afraid he
don't love me *any*</u>.

Like Melville, Emily Dickinson was finding Christian
belief impossible to accept in the nineteenth century. Almost in the very language Melville used to describe intellectual and imaginative dauntlessness, she voices her conviction that Christianity has come to represent passivity,
spiritual surrender, and mediocrity. Surely this is the implication of her words. It is rather a stretch of the imagination to compare her to Melville's heroic Bulkington, who
in *Moby-Dick* sets sail so daringly upon the sea, having
found but meager sustenance for the spirit ashore. But in
leaving the safe shore, seeking the dangers, and risking the
wrecks, they are undeniably fellow voyagers—fellow voyagers in respect at least to their need to transcend the
mediocrity of spirit which they found in mid-nineteenth-
century America. We may say of Emily Dickinson that in
her early years she joins those American geniuses who
have radically revolted against the spiritual slackness and
flaccidity of intelligence which they discover about them.
Emily Dickinson hardly possessed the intellectual powers
of Jonathan Edwards or Melville, but in her radical response to her culture she is of their company.

The passage I have just quoted belongs to the letter in
which Emily speaks of "the departed Humphrey." It is a
stock-taking letter, in which, as she does on one or two
other occasions in the early letters, she imagines herself
as an old woman: "I dream of being a grandame, and

banding my silver hairs, and I seem to be quite submissive to the thought of growing old." She looks backward also, imagining Abiah and herself as playing at being children again. She is seriously surveying her life, though in a half-whimsical way. It is a time of crisis for her, and we must not fail to note what she conceives to be the difference between herself and Abiah Root. The difference was that beyond the boundaries of the conventional Christian belief (which Emily had rejected three years earlier at Mt. Holyoke) there lies a realm of "fancies" which, she says, "I let blossom." Abiah, being "wiser," nips them in the bud. It is characteristic of Emily Dickinson that even when she speaks of "fancies" it would not occur to her to speak specifically of poetry. But whether she refers actually to her plans to write poems or merely confesses to a burgeoning and unruly but exciting life of the imagination which she knows cannot belong to the Abiah Roots of the world, we have a strong sense, as one might say, of a mind behaving poetically.

To the possibility that Emily was kept from committing herself to Christianity by such influences as the enlightened young Emersonians and Carlyleans of Amherst or the inherited Yankee individualism of the Dickinson family we must add the fact that she was a poet. We must add also, of course, that she was a poet who found that the poetic content of Christianity was, for her, incompatible with a formal commitment to Christian dogma and the Christian church. One of the most extraordinary qualities of Emily Dickinson's character was her power of making final choices. She exercised over herself a kind of power politics of the soul. At eighteen or twenty she had made one of her arduous choices. She had chosen poetry.

We do not have to accept the entire import of Mr. Allen Tate's fine essay on Emily Dickinson to agree with him generally on the historical view he there takes up. Very briefly rendered, his argument is that Emily Dickinson appeared at the poetically propitious moment when to minds such as hers the New England theology was finally proving unacceptable as dogma, as a mode of habit and automatic belief, and when consequently this theology became exclusively the property of the imagination. According to this view a powerful imaginative release and efflorescence occurs at the moment in history when a religion finally relaxes the bonds of dogma. The imagination rises vigorously to the task of keeping alive in the personal experience of the individual what had hitherto been kept alive by habit and belief. This is not, of course, the only historical crisis which is productive of poetry, but it belongs to a type of crisis which may perhaps be discerned in other cultures at other times. Mr. Tate speaks of the situation of the poet who finds himself balanced upon the moment when a homogeneous culture and world view are "about to fall," when they "threaten to run out into looser and less self-sufficient impulses." And he goes on to say that the world order of the Puritan theocracy "is assimilated, in Miss Dickinson, as medievalism was in Shakespeare, to the poetic vision; it was brought down from abstraction to personal sensibility." Mr. Tate believes that this kind of historical situation provides the poet with particularly fruitful modes of tension between abstraction and sensation, and that when it is possible for a poet to exploit this historical crisis with "the greatest imaginative comprehension . . . we have the perfect literary situation." "Only a few times in the history of English poetry," he says, "has this situation come about, notably, the period between about 1580 and the Restoration. There was a similar age in New England from which emerged two talents of the first order —Hawthorne and Emily Dickinson."

Mr. Tate's remark about the poet balanced at a moment between epochs when the older one is running out into loose impulses will surely remind the reader of Emily Dickinson's poem "I felt a cleavage in my mind," which concludes as follows:

> The thought behind I strove to join
> Unto the thought before,
> But sequence ravelled out of reach
> Like balls upon the floor.

This is not demonstrably a direct comment on the historical plight of the poet or of nineteenth-century New England, but it is certainly striking proof that the kind of intellectual experience involved in this historical plight was well known to our poet. Some of her other poems, however, leave no doubt that she had reflected very consciously on what was involved for her personally in the decline of the religious life and the rise of secularism, commerce, and science. She does not, of course, philosophize at length on these matters. She contents herself with brief expressions of nostalgia for the time when it was still possible to believe. The reasons for her nostalgia are specific: with the decline of religious belief, life has become petty, common, drab, and dull. She yearns as a poet, and not as a would-be theologian. She regrets that life is bereft of the pomp and drama which the Puritan belief once gave it. What a blank day, what a day of denial it was when "the Heaven died." We are "dying in Drama," as she wrote in a memorable phrase, and it is the business of the poet to preserve the dramatic quality of existence which religious belief no longer guarantees. In the poem beginning "Those, dying then, knew where they went," she says that now God cannot be found. The "abdication" of belief has made behavior "small." Drama and the significant existence must somehow be preserved. And she comes to her conclusion:

> Better an *ignis fatuus*
> Than no illume at all.

As we have here suggested, our poet's theme of renunciation finds one of its sources in the historical situation which forces her to give up the dramatically significant life she believes she would have had as a birthright in more Christian times and forces her, furthermore, to take up the arduous task of constructing a privately dramatic life through imagination and poetry. Her idea that the "ablative estate" is "sweetest"—that whatever is slipping away into desuetude and dissolution provides the most poignant of spectacles—also finds its analogue in her historical situation. And the same may be said of the small series of poems, like "I bring an unaccustomed wine," which speak of bringing vital liquors to a dying man or animal just too late to restore life. "A dying tiger moaned for drink" is the most striking of these, and the most overtly religious in its symbolism. The poet says that she searches in the desert for water, finds the dripping of a rock, bears the water in her hand to the dying tiger, which dies, however, just as she reaches it. Nothing is left but the entranced "vision" on the retina of the tiger's eye, a vision of water and the poet.

Plainly Emily Dickinson was conscious of being in the

historical situation Mr. Tate has propounded for her. She would have felt it in her own family history. We have had occasion in the preceding pages to document the historical crisis of New England Puritanism as it impinged on the Dickinsons. In the transition from her grandfather's Calvinism to her father's conventional and reluctant Congregationalism, as well as in the decline of orthodoxy at Amherst College, she could hardly have avoided the sense of momentous change in the New England spiritual life. One would not, of course, wish to assert that the crisis of history under discussion happened all at once or in any specific year between 1830 and 1850. It might be argued, indeed, as Perry Miller sometimes seems inclined to do, that history had forced Jonathan Edwards, one hundred years before, to be more of an artist than a theologian.

The amalgam which Emily Dickinson made out of romanticism, popular sentimentality, and Calvinist Christianity becomes more plausible to us when we reflect that Calvinism, in the form still available to her, was an inner, personal drama. It was thus the substance of sensibility as much as were romanticism and sentiment. Even in her mature poetry, her religious ideas, as Mr. Tate remarks, are "no longer the impersonal symbols" we find in Herbert or Vaughan. They have become, as with Donne, "the terms of personality; they are mingled with the miscellany of sensation." And Mr. Tate discovers in both Donne and Emily Dickinson a "singularly morbid concern, not for religious truth, but for personal revelation." If we keep these observations in mind, we shall be less surprised at the cult of sentiment which so impressed our poet, and we shall find it less difficult to reconcile her commitment to this kind of sensibility with her commitment to Calvinism.

Finally, we may note again that Emily Dickinson's resistance to the evangelism of Miss Lyon was an episode in the emergence of a poet. She sensed that, for her, Christianity could be honestly understood and accepted only as privately reconstituted by the poetic imagination and that consequently it must be abandoned as dogma and convention. To give in to Miss Lyon would have meant "nipping in the bud" the "fancies" which she knew she must "let blossom."

Two Tutors

IN A letter to Colonel Higginson written in 1862, Emily Dickinson said: "I had no monarch in my life, and cannot rule myself; and when I try to organize, my little force explodes and leaves me bare and charred." Though she spoke, at the age of thirty-two, as if her life were already over, it remained true throughout her life that she found no monarch, no writer or teacher who could exercise the kind of definitive influence upon her which she felt she needed. She had, however, a series of "tutors," as she chose to call them. With a severe seriousness somewhat mollified by a half-kittenish femininity, she proclaimed herself the "scholar" of those men of her acquaintance whom she considered her intellectual superiors. Emily Dickinson's image of herself as a "scholar" was attractive to her on several counts. She genuinely felt the desire for instruction. She never, even at fifty-five, entirely gave up the "little girl" part of her character. It may be, also, that the term "scholar" had been made resonant for her by the essays of Emerson.

In the years after her formal schooling, she had three

tutors: Benjamin Franklin Newton, the Reverend Charles Wadsworth, and Colonel Higginson. The tuitional influence of Newton may be dated 1848-53, that of Wadsworth 1854-62 (though they seem to have corresponded until Wadsworth's death in 1882), and that of Higginson from 1862 on. This chapter will have to do with Newton and Wadsworth.

In another letter of 1862, also to Higginson, our poet wrote these biographically crucial words:

> When a little girl, I had a friend who taught me Immortality; but venturing too near, himself, he never returned. Soon after, my tutor died, and for several years my lexicon was my only companion. Then I found one more, but he was not contented I be his scholar, so he left the land.

Dickinson biography has been largely, and I should think a good deal too largely, an attempt to deduce from this passage the actualities of Emily Dickinson's life. Miss Pollitt's candidate for the tutor (and lover) who "left the land" is Major Edward B. Hunt, the first husband of Helen Hunt Jackson, who wrote popular fiction under the name of "H. H." and who was a friend of the Dickinsons. Miss Taggard thought that Leonard Humphrey was the tutor who died and George Gould the tutor (and lover) who left the land. Mr. Whicher believes that the first tutor was Newton and the second Wadsworth. We may note one minor difficulty with Whicher's interpretation before accepting it as manifestly correct. The friend who "taught me Immortality" could refer to Humphrey. The phrase "Soon after" makes it all but necessary to conclude that the "friend" and the "tutor" are not the same person (as Whicher assumes) but two different people, and that con-

sequently Leonard Humphrey may have been more important to Emily as friend and preceptor than Whicher admits. The "tutor" was undoubtedly Newton, who died in
1853, three years after Humphrey. One more difficulty is
her remark that she had no tutor but her lexicon "for several years" after the death of her tutor. Yet she first met
Wadsworth in 1854. In order to get around this difficulty,
we must assume that although she met Wadsworth in 1854
and was undoubtedly strongly impressed by his preaching
and his personal character, she did not consider him a tutor
until later when the relationship was more firmly established, either by the correspondence that had sprung up
between them or by the visit of Wadsworth to Amherst in
1860.

Newton was one of the several young men who from
time to time served as apprentice-lawyers in the law office
of Emily's father. He was nine years older than his
"scholar" and seems to have possessed a strongly independent mind which may have set him apart, for Emily, from
the other young men—lawyers and students or instructors
from the college—who visited the home of Edward Dickinson. A native of Worcester, Newton came to Amherst during the winter of Emily's year at Mt. Holyoke Seminary, a
conjunction of events which helps to explain her strong
attachment to Newton and her strong dependence upon
his mind. For Newton was a Unitarian and a radical, and
Emily Dickinson had just discovered that the belief and
practice of orthodox Calvinism were not for her. She had
suffered a good deal, as we may suppose, during the ordeal
of her discovery. And in her inevitable disappointment
and her inevitable reaction, she found in Newton's ideas
a justification of her decision and a release for her emo-

tions. During Newton's two years in Amherst, she came to cherish her father's law student in a manner she herself eloquently expressed in a letter to Newton's pastor:

> Mr. Newton was with my Father two years, before going to Worcester, in pursuing his studies, and was much in our family. I was then but a child, yet I was old enough to admire the strength, and grace, of an intellect far surpassing my own, and it taught me many lessons, for which I thank it humbly now it is gone. Mr. Newton became to me a gentle, yet grave Preceptor, teaching me what to read, what authors to admire, what was most grand or beautiful in nature, and that sublime lesson, a faith in things unseen, and in a life again, nobler and much more blessed.
>
> Of all these things he spoke—he taught me of them all, earnestly, tenderly; and when he went from us, it was as an elder brother, loved indeed very much, and mourned and remembered. During his life in Worcester he often wrote to me, and I replied to his letters. I always asked for his health, and he answered so cheerfully that, while I knew he was ill, his death indeed surprised me. He often talked of God, but I do not know certainly if he was his Father in Heaven. Please, sir, to tell me if he was willing to die, and if you think him at Home.

We know very little of what, specifically, Newton taught his eager scholar. The words she uses in describing the pedagogy of her "grave Preceptor" as well as her implications about what ought to engage a "scholar's" attention— books, nature, things unseen—have a strongly Emersonian ring. And one gathers that Emerson was the great influence upon Newton. One of the letters from Worcester, to which Emily Dickinson refers in her letter to Newton's pastor, was accompanied by a "beautiful copy" of Emerson's poems. And we know from other sources that she was well read in Emerson's essays.

We shall have occasion later to remark upon the relation of Emily Dickinson's poetry to Emerson and Transcendentalism. The presence of the Emersonian spirit—its delight in spiritual aggrandizement, its celebration of the sufficient self and the majesty of the individual—can easily be detected in several of her minor poems. In the years of her attachment to Benjamin Newton, Emerson probably represented intellectual adventure, the stimulation of new and radical ideas, the excitement of prophetic utterance calling the soul to regeneration, to freedom and openness of experience without the threat of dogmatic closure. Could Emily Dickinson, with her youthful desire that the "thrill of sympathy" and the urge to accomplishment should be felt by all great minds, fail to be impressed by an essayist who urged all men to observe and emulate the "action of man upon nature with his entire force"? And did not the inspired essayist in his "Nature" grandly offer examples of such action: the miracles of early antiquity; the history of Jesus Christ; the achievements of principle, as in religious and political revolutions and the abolition of the slave trade; the miracles of enthusiasm as seen in Swedenborg and the Shakers; and the phenomena of Animal Magnetism—not to mention prayer, eloquence, self-healing, and the wisdom of children?

Another author much discussed by Emily Dickinson and Newton was Mrs. Lydia Maria Child. Her book called *Letters from New York* was one of those which Emily and her young friends were accustomed to hide in the bush by the front door or under the piano top so that her father would not spy them and launch one of his tirades against "modern literati." Mrs. Child was heady liquor to the young radicals of the day. A prodigious pundit and general reformer, she wrote novels, miscellanies, "souvenirs," histories, and tracts. She wrote a three-volume work called *The Progress of Religious Ideas through Successive Ages*, which pointed out the similarities among the world's religions and was radically heterodox. As early as 1833 she published an abolitionist tract. She publicly offered to share John Brown's imprisonment in order to nurse his wounds. She crusaded for civil rights, women's rights, prison reform, and education. She cultivated the irreligious literature of the Enlightenment, but, as Whittier pointed out in an introduction to one of her books, she also "loved the old mystics"—Böhme, Swedenborg, and Woolman. *Letters from New York*, though less openly humanitarian than many of Mrs. Child's other works, would have given Emily Dickinson some sense of the socialist and utopian political thought of the time and would have shown her how the revolutionist might conceive of the spiritual beauties of literature as conducing to a new order of things. "I am greatly delighted with Mrs. Browning's 'Aurora Leigh,'" wrote Mrs. Child elsewhere. "It is full of strong things, and brilliant things, and beautiful things. And how glad I am to see modern literature tending so much toward the breaking down of social distinctions!"

It is difficult to suppose that Emily Dickinson ever very seriously entertained any radical political ideas. Had she stepped into the imaginary world of Henry James's *Bostonians* she would have been as ill at ease with Olive Chancellor, the woman's rights crusader, as was the conservative southerner, Basil Ransom. But she was no more conservative than she was radical. She was not directly political at all; she esteemed no institution and no political movement. The kind of strong and massive decision which is involved, or ought to be involved, in political thought she directed inward, making her great personal choices. She was thus entirely proof against the fate of projecting her personal neurotic difficulties into political form, as do the Olive Chancellors of the world. The radicalism of Mrs. Child was exciting to her rather as an experience of novelty than as a commitment to ideas. If Mrs. Child left any mark on Emily Dickinson's mind, it was a tendency, in weaker moments, to rather vague forms of spiritual aspiration and ethical abstraction—the tendency, in short, which she learned more intricately from Emerson. One might add, however, that she may have felt for the first time in the writings of Mrs. Child that it was possible for a woman to exercise, either in practical life or in the life of the imagination, an executive force over people, events, and ideas. This she would not have felt in the politely sentimental fiction by lady novelists which she often read in her late teens and early twenties—such works as Lady Fullerton's *Ellen Middleton* and Miss Annesley's *The Light in the Valley*. Even more effective in impressing Emily Dickinson with the executive force a woman's mind might exert was her reading of *Jane Eyre*, which also occurred during her friendship with Newton.

Perhaps the strongest effect of Newton upon his scholar was not in the realm of specific ideas so much as in a general opening out of the possibilities of the imaginative life. She cherished very dearly the praise he gave her earliest poems. He found in her poetry a genuine talent and encouraged her to go on writing. That this early encouragement was of definitive importance we see from a note to

Higginson in which she says: "Your letter gave no drunkenness, because I tasted rum before—" sibylline words which mean: "Your praise is welcome, but subsequent praise can never be quite like the first." The first praise was without doubt Newton's.

But the Reverend Charles Wadsworth was the "tutor" who made the most lasting impression upon Emily Dickinson. She undoubtedly fell in love with Wadsworth. In the early spring of 1854, the Dickinson family assembled in Washington, where Edward Dickinson was serving as a Member of Congress. During a trip to Philadelphia to visit Lyman Coleman, whom the Dickinsons had known in Amherst, Emily was introduced to Wadsworth, then the pastor of the Arch Street Presbyterian Church. Like all her "tutors," Wadsworth was considerably older than she—seventeen years, in fact. Thus began what Emily Dickinson called in 1882, when Wadsworth died, "an intimacy of many years with the beloved clergyman."

However much Emily may have been in love with Wadsworth, the intimacy was unquestionably a meeting of minds and a sharing of profound sympathy beyond time and space. Wadsworth was respectably and, one gathers, happily married. His behavior was always impeccable, and—so far as is known—he and Emily saw each other face to face no more than four times, perhaps only three. They exchanged letters, she read Wadsworth's published sermons, their meetings were deeply charged with emotion, and beyond this we can say no more about their intimacy. We may specify, however, the occasions of their later meetings. These took place when Wadsworth visited Northampton and Amherst in the spring of 1860, the late summer of 1861 (this is conjectural), and the summer of 1880. It was, as Emily must have thought, a "frugal" relationship.

But there is no question of the enormous emotional commitment she made to Wadsworth. In 1882 she writes to a mutual friend, James D. Clark, that Wadsworth "was my shepherd from little girlhood and I cannot conjecture a world without him, so noble was he always—so fathomless—so gentle." She cherished in him his tendency to "seem almost overpowered" by "spasms of gloom." Once she had remarked to him, "You are troubled." And he had answered, "shivering as he spoke, 'My life is full of dark secrets.'" She had known him as a "Man of Sorrow." He was "a dusk gem, born of troubled waters, astray in any crest below. Heaven might give him peace; it could not give him grandeur, for that he carried with himself to whatever scene." Against the monotony and flatness of Emily Dickinson's provincial life, Wadsworth stood forth with a brilliant and dramatic force. In contrast to the provincial business men, lawyers, students, and professors, in contrast to the undistinguished and colorlessly spiritual wives and daughters among whom she lived, Wadsworth had for her a quality of greatness which made it possible to think of him as an almost mythical being. In his pastorship to the "little girl," in the "Man of Sorrow," she felt the image of Christ. In the dark secrets of his life there was the romantic suggestion of a demonic inner mystery, such as Emily and Charlotte Brontë attributed to Heathcliff and Rochester. In his fathomlessness, in the spasms of gloom that almost overpowered him, there was the awful heritage of the Calvinist theology. He was even a divine hero from another world whose mission, like that of Moses, was announced by his having been born a "dusk gem," in a casket, as we may suppose, which floated on "troubled waters."

Taking Wadsworth to be such a man and feeling the presence of his sympathy and his support, Emily Dickinson had some assurance of an outward correspondence to the inward events of the imagination. As Jane Eyre sees the world as a newly dramatic and consequential place after meeting Rochester, so Emily newly felt in the world the dramatic reality of the emotions and ideas which bestirred her poetic mind. The forcefulness of Wadsworth's pulpit manner, the stern exclusions of Calvinist dogma, the profundity and the aspiring joy of the spiritual life to which he summoned the wayward were cherished warrants for those inner decisions and finalities of the feminine mind. The determined confrontation of the demonic, the mythical, and the divine which Wadsworth made in his sermons was the justification and his the guiding light of Emily Dickinson's impulse to regard life under the rubric of its most sacred and dramatic occasions—the occasions of marriage, of loss and renunciation, of sacramental insight into nature, of the receiving of grace, and of the ultimate revelation, death.

In actuality Wadsworth was a rather shy man who maintained as few personal relationships with his parishioners as possible. Like Jonathan Edwards he used no physical gestures while preaching and his eyes betrayed no recognition of the existence of his audience. Like Edwards he relied upon the sheer eloquence of his utterances from the pulpit, which he entered from below through a trap door. His preaching, it must be confessed, was not on the level of Edwards's. In those late days of the faith, the rhetoric tended to grow hollow and the references to God's providential selection of America as the world's guide to salvation had more than a little of the ring of nineteenth-century American self-aggrandizement. Still, such a sermon as that which Wadsworth preached on Thanksgiving Day of 1855 contained genuinely moving passages. The sermon took its text from Esther: "And who knoweth whether thou art come to the Kingdom for such a time as this?" The message of the sermon was that just as Esther had been chosen as the instrument of the world's redemption through her people, so America from all Providential indications is "a great spring, or lever, or wheel, in that vast and complicate machinery whereby Omnipotence is outworking" the redemption of the modern world through Christian truth, freedom, liberty of conscience, and civil rights. (Emily Dickinson, who so often speaks of her elevation to royal estate, would have cherished Wadsworth's description of how God had raised Esther "from poverty to a throne," and had "brought her to the queenship of that great oriental kingdom.") America, he went on to say, showed wondrous signs of proving itself the worthy instrument of God. The genius of American institutions seemed assured and their success in delivering the world from European intolerance, inequality, and corruption as well as from African and Asian squalor could probably be counted on. Nevertheless, a "foreboding of disaster" darkens our joy. Intemperance reels through the streets, and there is an unholy lust of conquest in our political life. We must fear the "poor lunatic" who preaches disunion in the misguided attempt to free the southern bondman, whom God will free in His own good time. Anti-Catholic bigotry is dangerous to the body politic, and we must give up the foolish fear that "this Anglo-American people are to go back in any considerable masses to the drivelling mummeries of the Tiber's haggard superstition." There is danger that through disunion and disbelief and falling away from the word of God the "light and loveliness of our political and evangelical beatitudes" will finally go out in the shadow of death. Let not America, he concludes, be an "effete engine" of God's will. For if we do, that engine will as surely be destroyed by the flash of God's thunderbolts as is every engine which is chosen but fails to fulfill its divine instrumentality.

There cannot be the slightest doubt that Wadsworth touched the depths of Emily Dickinson's mind a good deal more intimately and fruitfully than anyone else of her acquaintance was able to do. The appeal of the Calvinist ideology was stronger for her than the appeal of Emerson's ethical spiritualism. It had the quality of exclusion and finality and rigorous limitation which characterized the profounder motions of Emily Dickinson's mind. On this score such a passage from Wadsworth as the following must have moved her a good deal more than the epigrammatic prophecies of Emerson, with all their fuzziness and lack of outline and inner structure:

> This fair world was not rounded into beauty and hung amid the stars, to remain forever a stronghold of the apostate. In the first hour of its disloyalty to Jehovah, it was, *a priori*, to be expected that God would either sweep it out of being, or redeem and restore it.

Surely, whatever one's beliefs, this is both more beautiful and more intelligible than such a passage as the following, fine though its first sentence is:

From the earth as a shore, I look out into that silent sea. I seem to partake its rapid transformations: the active enchantment reaches my dust, and I dilate and conspire with the morning wind. How does nature deify us with a few and cheap elements?

Emerson's words convey to the mind an idea of immediate, if muted and tenuous, experience; they give one the feeling of aspiration; and they imply an openness of vision in an open universe. For such a mind as Emily Dickinson's, the universe could not be so open as it was for Emerson. In Wadsworth's view of things, she might think, one could at least distinguish among man, God, and universe, and one could not miss the idea, either, that acts may have irreversible and absolute consequences.

I perhaps ought to remark that here as elsewhere I am using Wadsworth and Emerson typically as well as specifically in speaking of their influence on Emily Dickinson. They are representative of the two streams of thought which find their way into her poems: Calvinist Christianity and nineteenth-century Romanticism and Transcendentalism.

. There is no doubt that Wadsworth supplied Emily Dickinson with certain verbal usages and with certain poetic images. There was, for example, his habit of using words like "complicate" as if they were past participles. There was his fondness for ending words with "-less," as in "strengthless" and "resistless." There was his vocabulary of jewelry, involving gems, carbon, and diamonds, and his vocabulary of royalty, involving thrones, robes, and, particularly, diadems.

Yet Wadsworth's influence on Emily Dickinson was not so much that he gave her words and images, or even ideas that she had never known before. For most of these she must already have discovered in Protestant hymns, in Congregational sermons, and especially in the course of indoctrination administered by Mary Lyon at Mt. Holyoke Seminary. His influence was personal and emblematic. His letters and sermons sustained the deepest and most creative qualities of her mind, at the same time that his almost miraculous presence in the world was a warrant for the reality of her strongest inner emotions. It does not seem to me illiberal to suppose that Emily Dickinson's mind, being so fully and finely feminine, deeply sensed its need of possessing an ideal image such as Wadsworth as its warrant of externality, of the mind's grasp upon outer circumstance, of the reality of an ordered and consequential universe. Such an establishment of ego she could not find in a Mary Lyon or a Benjamin Newton or in the Transcendental literature of her century. And the influence of Wadsworth was all the stronger because he did not ask her to believe in the mechanics of his dogma, but only to imagine and to delimit and define.

One does not think of Emily Dickinson as oscillating between intellectual positions—the respectable belief of her father, the orthodox Congregationalism of Mary Lyon, the radicalism of Newton, the Presbyterianism of Wadsworth. All of these attitudes she finely contained from her earliest years to her latest, so much a product was she of her time and place. She was superior to those who influenced her, and they could effect in her mind no radical innovations. But they could and did affect the disposition of those original qualities which were bequeathed to her. Wadsworth figured largely in the most profound and creative disposition of the intellectual and imaginative properties of her mind. She would never entirely give up her Emersonism, her romanticism, or even her cult of sentiment and "reveries." But Wadsworth's Calvinism assured her that she would never be at the mercy of these influences, as sometimes she seemed to be in her youth.

"Emilie"

DURING the period from 1848 to 1862 Emily Dickinson often signed her letters "Emilie." The "Emilie" period divides itself into the years 1848-53, when she was Newton's scholar, and 1854-62, when, very generally speaking, she was Wadsworth's scholar. Unimportant in itself, the false spelling of her name yet signifies certain facts about her life during these years. The change from "y" to "ie" gave her name a kind of romantic quality, perhaps calling to mind a certain aura of the French or the medieval. A certain fairy-tale queenliness may be implied. The new spelling indicates a new self-consciousness, and a consciousness of the attitude of others toward the developing young woman who presented to them a questionable and elusive symbol, an alias, a pen name. The name "Emilie" indicated that its bearer was different from most of her friends and from her family. It hinted at intellectual emancipation and exciting adventures of the spirit. It suggested an enigmatic complexity of character which expressed itself with insouciance and "harum-scarum" humor but which was equally ready to confess to a sense of loss and renunciation, a growing reluctance to think of leaving home, a new dependence on the affection of friends, a steady contemplation of death, and a longing for immortality. All these implications are to be discerned in the self-projected person called "Emilie." But the most general and the most important implication of the name is that it asserts the poet's sense of her difference from most other people. In 1854 she wrote to her brother Austin, with whom she shared the spiritual adventures of "Emilie," to ask what it was that made him and a few other emancipated spirits of their acquaintance so different from the generality of mankind. And she added that it was a question she often asked herself.

Emily's early humor (we have already noticed her cultivation of American "screaming") was a part of her intellectual rebelliousness. Father, it was true, "never played." But Emily and her brother were playful, by temperament and almost on principle. They allowed themselves a license of mind quite unknown in their elders. The poet who could later write a poem beginning "It is easy to work when the soul is at play" was remembering, it may be, the gaiety of her late teens and early twenties.

Sometimes she indulged in mere facetious whimsy, as in her long letter of 1850 to Abiah Root in which she related how she caught a cold. A "little creature pounced upon a thin shawl I wore." He had a red nose and a huge handkerchief. He kissed her immoderately and refused to loose his tight embraces. "I sneezed so loud one night," she writes, "that the family thought the last trump was sounding and climbed into the currant bushes to get out of the way." But of course, she concludes, mocking the language of such preceptors as Miss Lyon, these are more fictions, "vain imaginations to lead astray foolish young women."

While still at Mt. Holyoke Seminary she begins to cultivate the facetiousness which in her late teens and early twenties she shared with Austin. "Your welcome letter," she writes on one occasion, "found me all engrossed in the study of Sulphuric Acid." And with the sly satire on age and authority which both brother and sister enjoyed, she remarks that she has thought of showing the letter to Miss Whitman to ease her mind in case she suspects that it may possibly "savor of rebellion or an unsubdued will." In another letter to Austin the following rather giddy badinage appears: "Has the Mexican War terminated yet, and how? Do you know of any nation about to besiege South Hadley? . . . I suppose Miss Lyon would furnish us all with daggers and order us to fight for our lives in case such perils should befall us." This has the tone of the grandiose humor of the screamer, though not so plainly enunciated as it is in a letter of 1850 to her uncle Joel Norcross in which, by way of chiding him for not writing her as he had promised, she calls him a villain, a doer of crimes, a scoundrel, a disturber of the public peace, and a state's prison filler, and invokes upon his head the destructive force of fire, water, light, tempest, hungry wolves, lightning, and thunder.

Though it is hardly one of her main themes, social satire of considerable skill is to be found in some of Emily Dickinson's poems. Her letters demonstrate her early competence in this style. Most of this satirical observation of manners is directed at her family, usually her father. For example, she writes to Austin in 1851 to complain of the pall of sobriety which father, Nature, and the Sabbath have conspired to throw over the Dickinson home now that the gay and talkative brother for whom she yearns has gone off to Boston to teach school.

> . . . we are a rather crestfallen company, to make the best of us, and what with the sighing wind, the sobbing rain, and the whining of Nature generally, we can hardly contain ourselves. . . . Father thinks it's "amazin' raw". . . . Mother is warming her feet, which she assures me are "just as cold as ice." I tell her I fear there is danger of icification, or ossification, I don't know certainly which.
>
> Vinnie is at the instrument, humming a pensive air concerning a young lady who thought she was "almost there." Vinnie seems much grieved, and I really suppose *I* shall betake myself to weeping; I'm pretty sure that I *shall* if she don't abate her singing.

Of a friend of her father's who had visited the Dickinson home she sends to Austin the probably very penetrating observation that so far as she can judge he's for "law and order." Her brief picture in another letter of their parents' Sabbath behavior has the air of satiric authenticity: "Father and mother sit in state in the sitting-room perusing such papers, only, as they are well assured, have nothing carnal in them." A similarly brilliant brief portrait shows us Edward Dickinson at the Jenny Lind concert. "Father sat all evening looking *mad* and *silly*, and yet so much amused you would have *died* a-laughing. When the performers bowed, he said 'Good evening, sir,' and when they retired, 'very well, that will do.' It wasn't sarcasm exactly, nor it wasn't disdain, it was infinitely funnier than either of those virtues, as if old Abraham had come to see the show. . . ." In a letter of 1853 she describes for Austin the visit of some relatives: "They all agree beauti-

fully with father on 'the present generation.' They decided that they hope every young man who smoked would
take fire, I respectfully intimated that I thought the result
would be a vast conflagration, but was instantly put down.
. . ." And as for conflagrations, there was the spectacular
fire at Mr. Kimberly's barn. "Father and Mr. Frink took
charge of the fire . . . the men all worked like heroes, and
after the fire was out, father gave them commands to march
to Howe's where an entertainment was provided for them.
After the whole was over they gave 'three cheers for Edward Dickinson,' and three more for the insurance company."

Emily and her older brother had formed, as we see, a
league of mutual support in their rebellion from the
more conventional and colorless part of life in the Dickinson home. Austin very clearly displayed that sort of semi-
cultivated waywardness which characterized him through
his career; for though he ostensibly followed in his father's
footsteps as private and public citizen, he was, as we shall
have occasion to notice later, a very different sort of man.
Their younger sister Lavinia shared only distantly the
spiritual and intellectual adventures of Emily and Austin.
She had no intelligence of the kind that would lead her
either seriously or humorously to the realm of ideas. Emily
always loved her sister and respected her faithful and un-
questioning pursuit of her domestic duties, even though
most of her references to Vinnie do not fail to betray her
constant amusement at Vinnie's rather awkward comportment, her well-intentioned gaucherie, and, in later years,
her small-town cantankerousness.

The dependence of Emily upon her brother was very
great during the years between 1848 and 1854, when

Austin returned from his Harvard law studies to Amherst. There may be a measure of romantic or "literary" exaggeration in the brother-sister relationship which developed between them. Yet it was undoubtedly a close spiritual connection. Their letters exhibit the kind of romantic idealism which they may both have imbibed from Emily's "tutor" of these years, B. F. Newton. It is this Emersonian impulse toward ideality which Emily has in mind when, in a letter of 1851, she addresses Austin as "my romantic brother" who, unlike conventional people, is capable of "delight" and a "very high style of rapture." We have already had occasion to notice how this romantic unconventionalism could sometimes take the form of a cult of sentiment, such as was set forth by "Ik Marvel." There is certainly no doubt that Emily's mind was both more stable and more profound than that of her brother. Her dependence upon Austin stemmed from her need for intellectual companionship rather than guidance, which in these years she was finding in Newton. Any event which particularly interested her immediately roused the desire that Austin should share her experience of it. If Professor Park delivered an especially moving sermon, she would be sure to conclude her report of it by saying, "How I wish you had heard him. I thought of it all the time." If a particularly magnificent electrical storm swept over Amherst, moving one's mind to contemplate the awful powers of nature, Emily would write to her brother: "Then came the wind and rain. . . . I wish you had seen it come, so cool and refreshing—and everything glistening as if with a golden dew—I thought of you all the time."

It was perhaps inevitable that in the literary flights of their aspiring minds they should sometimes have succeeded only in baffling each other. In 1851 Emily writes: "You say you don't comprehend me, you want a simpler style—gratitude indeed for all my fine philosophy!" There is, in fact, very little of mysterious philosophy in her letters. One would conjecture, however, that the peregrinations of Austin's muse were rather more wayward. And they may have verged on the tactless. In 1853 Emily writes: "I have had some things from you to which I perceive no meaning. They either were very vast or they didn't mean anything, I don't know certainly which. What did you mean by a note you sent me day before yesterday?" The language is unusually downright and severe. Had Austin clumsily verged upon impropriety as well as obscurity? The cult of sentiment which they shared certainly offered no protection against either impropriety or obscurity. It actively fostered the strange license of the perfectly innocent. Had she lived in our less innocent age, it is scarcely conceivable that Emily would write to her brother ". . . never mind faded forests, Austin, never mind silent fields—*here* is a little forest, whose leaf is ever green; here is a brighter garden, where not a frost has been; in its unfading flowers I hear the bright bee hum; prithee, my brother, into *my* garden come!"

Emily and Austin were agreeing as early as 1847, while Emily was at Mt. Holyoke, that the domestic scene presided over by "Mr. E. Dickinson" was very stiff and dull—"like a funeral," as Austin complained. We learn from Emily's letters that they had both clashed openly with their father on a number of occasions, though no serious breach is recorded. Without Austin, Emily says in 1852, there are no jokes at home and no poetry, "father having made up his mind" that there is nothing much in the world of any value except "real life." And she adds that "Father's real life and mine sometimes come into collision but as yet escape unhurt." After the famous denunciation of these "modern literati" delivered by Edward Dickinson, and apparently inspired by his feeling that the letters passing between Emily and Austin were frivolous, Emily felt that she had had "quite a trimming" and in fact that she had received an "insult" which she bore only by imagining the probably noble and unshaken mien Austin himself would have presented in the face of such an insult. That Austin and his father had clashed we learn from a letter of 1853 in which Emily expresses her amusement at the way in which father and son do nothing but "fisticuff" when Austin is at home and then become devoted friends as soon as Austin goes away.

Emily records two dreams about her father, of which we may observe that one describes the destruction of Edward Dickinson and the other expresses Emily's hostility at his coming between herself and Austin. "Lo!" she exclaims gaily, "Father had failed, and mother said that 'our rye-field, which she and I had planted, was mortgaged to Seth Nims.' I hope it is not true; but do write soon and tell me. For you know [she continues with curiously Joycean redundancy] I should expire of mortification to have our rye-field mortgaged." She both fears and desires, it may be, to find that something precious and belonging privately to her mother and herself has fallen into the hands of someone other than her father—someone whom she is unable to admire, for Seth Nims is a "loco," as she notes with derisive humor. The second dream expresses, at least, Emily's uneasiness at the thought of her father's probable disapproval of the literarily frivolous letters brother and sister have been exchanging. "I waked up this morning," she tells Austin, "thinking for all the world I had had a letter from you—just as the seal was breaking, father rapped at the door. I was sadly disappointed not to go on and read. . . ." It was father's custom to awaken Emily by a rap at her door.

In her twenties Emily Dickinson easily saw through the conventional pretensions of her father, and her reverence for him in his publicly respectable guise, as we have noticed, was a good deal modified by her perceptive understanding of the man under the guise. It nevertheless seems certain that she actively resented and was embarrassed by every relaxation of his imposing mien which Edward Dickinson might choose to indulge. "Father in a palm leaf hat, pantaloons tucked in boots: I don't think negligé quite becoming to so mighty a man. I had rather a jacket of green and your barn door apparel," she confides to Austin, "than all the mock simplicity of a lawyer and a man." She did not wish her father to be relaxed, simple, witty, negligé, affectionate, or demonstrative. She felt that he had no talent for any mode of behavior outside of his severe and imperial comportment. A little like the daughters of Howells's Silas Lapham, she was always afraid, because she loved and wished to admire her father, that he would make himself ridiculous, that he would lose caste. Her difficulty stemmed from the society in which she lived, a society which granted the status of pre-eminence to men such as Edward Dickinson but provided no real structure of values by which that pre-eminence might be reinforced and sustained. "Squire" Dickinson lived in a society lacking in the institutional stability which in a genuine aristocracy makes squires unquestionable squires. The society which could give in the same voice three cheers for Edward Dickinson and three cheers for the insurance company was certainly full of social ambiguities and contradictions. It raised Edward Dickinson to the status of an aristocrat but threatened at every minute to pull the purple carpet out from under him. There are thus external, cultural reasons as well as personal, emotional reasons why Emily Dickinson should have been so sensitively conscious of her father's behavior.

In Emily's letters the typical anecdote about her father is ambiguous; it displays her pride in his public preeminence but also her resentment that he has been made to appear somewhat ridiculous, that he has not behaved with the manners appropriate to the occasion, or that there have been no such manners. And typically, of course, she tells the anecdote humorously. The railroad from New London has finally been completed, for example; and father "was, as usual, chief marshal of the day, and went marching around with New London at his heels like some old Roman general upon a triumph day." A Roman general, doubtless, should not go marching "around," or suffer New London to trail at his heels. When Edward Dickinson was about to assume his newly won seat in Congress in 1853, Emily whimsically writes to Austin that they ought to send Vinnie instead, since she might loosen the national purse strings in favor of the Dickinsons. There will be no graft, however, in their father's transactions because "Caesar" is such "an honorable man." It was not much more than a joke to think of father as Caesar, but less whimsical because more real was the spectacle of father as chief church-bell ringer in case of a beautiful sunset. Emily informs Austin that on a certain Monday evening (in 1851) "we were all startled by a violent church bell ringing, and thinking of nothing but fire, rushed out in the street to see." A lovely evening sky colored gorgeously with pink and gold displayed itself to the "wondering and admiring" people who issued from their houses at the squire's authoritative summons. For father had "happened to see it among the first, and rang the bell himself to call attention to it." This generous public act was one of Edward Dickinson's few contributions to the aesthetic life. Both the sunset and his official summons had the sanction of public opinion. Yet as in all such anecdotes about her father, Emily clearly betrays her sense of the social uneasiness of his position. Keeping these anecdotes in mind, we shall find it easier to account for the pervasive imaginative use of the idea of status, of how one achieves one's "estate," in the poetry of Emily Dickinson.

But what of Emily herself in her early twenties? What direction is the inner life of the emerging poet who calls herself "Emilie" taking? For one thing she still asserts, as she had done in her teens, that she resents having to grow up. "I wish we were children now," she complains to Austin in 1853. "I wish we were always children, how to grow up I don't know." This is not surprising in a poet, for we may suppose without undue romanticism that all poets, certainly all nineteenth-century poets, remain children, and desire to do so, in a way which is not true of non-poets. Nor is it surprising when we remember the Victorian cult of "little women," in which Emily Dickinson to some extent lived and thought. For all her great personal integrity, for all her fine and mature femininity, she always paid some obeisance to little womanhood. Her coy and oddly childish poems of nature and female friendship are products of a time when one of the careers open to women was perpetual childhood. So too are such letters as those she exchanged with her cousins the Norcross sisters, wherein, even in later life, she signs herself with names like "Poor Plover" and addresses her correspondents as "little cousins," "little sisters," and "little creatures."

More strikingly personal is the new assertion that part of being "Emilie" is to be, in the eyes of the world, "quaint" and "old-fashioned." "Emilie" seems to have felt by 1853 that the contemporaries with whom she had been abreast in school were now advancing along paths she could not take. She had felt the divergence at least five years before when, at Mt. Holyoke Seminary, she perceived her inability to share her classmates' commitment to Christianity. By 1853 she feels the failure of communication which has finally overtaken the correspondence between herself and Abiah Root. Abiah has asked her to pay her a visit at her home. But "Emilie" replies: "I don't go from home, unless emergency leads me by the hand, and then I do it obstinately, and draw back if I can. Should I ever leave home, which is improbable, I will, with much delight, accept your invitation. . . . I'm so old-fashioned, darling, that all your friends would stare." "Emilie," as we see, was in the anomalous position of being advanced in her thinking but backward in her manners, backward in the sense that she retained her unconventionality in a conventional world. She had decided early in life that she could not, that she did not wish to, keep up with the conventional world. In an early poem she expresses with characteristic decisiveness her acceptance of herself as she is and her hope, almost her assumption, that God will also accept her as she is:

> I hope the father in the skies
> Will lift his little girl,—
> Old-fashioned, naughty, everything,—
> Over the stile of pearl.

Edward Dickinson had done so. Could God do less?

Her cult of sentiment is plainly present in her idealizations of "home," but a passage in a letter of 1851 to Austin has the ring of deep commitment. "Home is a holy thing— nothing of doubt nor distrust can enter its blessed portals . . . here seems indeed to be a bit of Eden which not the sin of any can utterly destroy,—smaller indeed it is, and it may be less fair, but fairer it is and brighter than all the world outside." Once, in a letter of 1850 to Abiah Root, and again, in a letter of 1851 to Austin, Emily records experiences which strikingly illustrate, as in reality they may decisively have confirmed, her growing inability to leave home. On the first occasion her mother is sick and she has had more than her usual share of the domestic duties which, beyond a certain minimum, she always disliked. She begins her letter portentously by saying that "the circumstances under which I write to you this morning are at once glorious, afflicting, and beneficial." And then, after some facetious remarks about her household drudgery, she communicates a great event and an ensuing crisis:

> At noon . . . I heard a well-known rap, and a friend I love *so* dearly came and asked me to ride in the woods, the sweet, still woods,—and I wanted to exceedingly. I told him I could not go, and he said he was disappointed, he wanted me very much. Then the

tears came into my eyes, though I tried to choke them back, and he said I *could* and *should* go, and it seemed to me unjust. Oh, I struggled with great temptation, and it cost me much of denial; but I think in the end I conquered,—not a glorious victory where you hear the rolling drum, but a kind of a helpless victory, where triumph would come of itself, faintest music, weary soldiers, not a waving flag, nor a long, loud shot. I had read of Christ's temptations, and how they were like our own, only he didn't sin; I wondered if *one* was like mine, and whether it made him angry. I couldn't make up my mind; do you think he ever did?

I went cheerfully round my work, humming a little air till mother had gone to sleep, then cried with all my might—seemed to think I was much abused—that this wicked world was unworthy such devoted and terrible suffering- -and came to my various senses in great dudgeon at life, and time, and love for affliction and anguish.

What shall we do, my darling, when trial grows more and more, when the dim, lone light expires, and it's dark, so very dark, and we wander, and know not where, and cannot get out of the forest. . . .

I tell you I have been dreaming, dreaming a *golden* dream, with eyes all the while wide open, and I guess it's almost morning; and besides, I have been at work, providing the "food that perisheth," scaring the timorous dust, and being obedient and kind. I am yet the Queen of the Court, if regalia be dust and dirt. . . . *My* kitchen, I think I called it—God forbid that it was, or shall be, my own—God keep me from what they call *households*, except that bright one of "faith". . . .

Remember and care for me sometimes, and scatter a fragrant flower in this wilderness life of mine by writing me. . . .

We do not know who knocked so dramatically at the door. If it was Newton, we must assume that he was revisiting Amherst at the time, for he had returned to his native Worcester some time in the winter of 1849-50. But, what is more important, we sense in Emily's words an epitome, or an archetype, of her whole emotional and imaginative life. We should certainly gather from her poems that she was a woman whose frugally dramatic experience had consisted of waiting for someone or something, some longed-for visitor, to knock at the door; that she had made great renunciations; that the experience had been a victory because, though it had acquainted her with anguish and affliction, it had conferred upon her a kind of royal status —a kinship with Cinderella, the Queen whose regalia was dust and dirt, a kinship, even, with Christ; that she would henceforth regard this life as a dark forest whose terrors tried the spirit; and that she thought the final benison of her renunciation might be the bestowal of immortality— a place, that is, in that bright household in which we have "faith." It was not, perhaps, until 1862 that Emily Dickinson began to write good poems on these themes. The story of her poetic development between the ages of twenty and thirty-two, if it could be told with any exactitude, would be concerned, as we see, with her technical and stylistic development and her generally advancing maturity rather than with the discovery of her basic themes. For these she already had as early as 1850.

A less elaborate crisis in her encroaching seclusion occurred in the next year. On that intolerably dull and gloomy Sabbath evening when father complained that it was "amazin' raw," when mother confided that her feet were "just as cold as ice," and Vinnie crooned about the poor young lady who was "almost there," Emily suddenly left the house. "I put on my bonnet tonight, opened the gate very desperately, and for a little while the suspense was terrible—I think I was held in check by some invisible agent, for I returned to the house without having done any harm!" The specific intention of this impulsive act is not very clear; presumably she was not very clear about it herself. She speaks of missing Austin "very much" on that evening. Was she going to run away? to flee to Austin? to Newton? to commit suicide? The very vagueness of her specific intent suggests that the real weight and meaning of what she did was symbolic. Her emotions were grievously pent up by her narrow domestic life, and a dramatic gesture such as she made was just enough of a translation of feeling into act to release and quiet her. Her act is surely symbolic of the strong ambivalence she felt, at twenty-one, towards home. She ardently wanted to be free of its limits, yet even more ardently she wanted to seclude herself once and for all within those limits. The act of leaving the house with a blind madness upon one's soul and then of discovering that after all the powerful impulse was countermanded by an opposite force even more powerful was plainly representative of the most profound instinctive dispositions of Emily Dickinson's character. Her act was archetypal (did she not habitually refer to her home as Eden?); and it must have had for her a great moral utility. She could always think that once she had put to the test the possibility of leaving home, had put at the service of this test very powerful emotions, and that a contrary force had countermanded her. Emily Dickinson was not a person who needed several experiences of this kind to convince her of their significance. Despite the

sentimental strain of her early thought and the spiritualism of her later years, her mind at its deeper levels was
always characterized by a severe realism and a conviction of the fateful consequentiality of events. Her brother
Austin might be moved by the romantic idealism and melancholy of his sister's thoughts about leaving home. But
he probably missed the full significance of the stern decision she was making.

We may observe—to conclude our discussion of "Emilie"
between the ages of eighteen and twenty-four—that the
spiritualism of the later years has its origin in the early cult
of sentiment. Emily Dickinson's spiritualism was a religion of friendship and immortality. The first strong
suggestion of this spiritualism occurs as early as 1851 in
her letter concerning the "departed Humphrey," whose
death, as we have noticed, first turned her thoughts to the
serious scrutiny of immortality. In this letter she records
her discovery that the "brief, imperfect meetings" of
friends "have a tale to tell." They remind us, that is, of
"brevity and change," without which reminder we "should
build the dwelling earthward whose site is in the skies."
Indeed, there is a sense in which we must be grateful to
the moth that corrupts and the thief that breaks through
and steals, for without them life would appear so dear a
treasure that we should forget that other world wherein,
we have reason to hope, our departed friends gloriously
sing. And she concludes:

> Earth is short, but Paradise is long—there must be
> many months in an eternal day; then sometime we
> shall tarry while time and tide roll on, and till then
> *vale.*
>
> Your own dear
EMILIE

If there was one indubitably efficient function of the provincial sentimental idealism of Emily Dickinson's time, it was to vulgarize the ideas and the style of earlier times and to reduce the scope of mind, of conscious awareness, which they once possessed. One may find it no less difficult to believe in the heaven of eternal friendship which Emily Dickinson and her correspondents aspired towards than it is to believe in Saint Augustine's City of God or in the Puritan heaven. Yet if one had to choose one would not choose the poet's heaven of friendship. An analogous decline of mind and style is observable in the letter I have quoted above in which Emily declares her sisterly affection for Austin in the language of the Elizabethan erotic lyric. There was, in short, a kind of historically produced, and therefore unavoidable, innocence and mindlessness in the cultural surroundings of our poet. The deepest motions of her imaginative intelligence moved under a preponderant weight of the mediocre, the vulgarized detritus of Western thought. If, as Mr. Tate correctly points out, Emily Dickinson's historical position was in one sense extraordinarily propitious, we must nevertheless remark that in another sense it was the reverse of propitious. For though it allowed her to write some very great poetry, it also imposed upon her the used and shopworn furniture of the bygone cultural traditions of Puritanism on the one hand and Elizabethan and seventeenth-century poetry on the other. Her response to her historical situation issues not only in her best poetry but also, as we may conclude from reading her poems, in a curious personal, poetic convention which can only be called "rococo." Great cultural traditions do not run out without pathos, tension, tragic awareness, and excitement of mind and imagination. But neither do they run out without leaving a good deal of old junk, of foolishness and sentimentality, of frivolousness and vulgarity.

The second phase of the "Emilie" period extends roughly from the death of Newton in 1853 to the departure of Wadsworth for San Francisco in 1862. It is the period in which Emily Dickinson changes from minor versifier to major poet. In the winter of 1861-62 she was writing at her best; in the ensuing spring she was able to send to Higginson such a first-rate poem as "Safe in their alabaster chambers." It is all the more regrettable, therefore, that lacking the letters she exchanged with Wadsworth as well as other materials, we should be able to say so little with certainty about this presumably crucial period.

One can easily see that in these years a new severity, a new gravity of mind settled upon Emily Dickinson. As early as 1852, she was writing to Austin that "our years have made us soberer. . . . I used now and then to cut a timid caper." Though she was probably not in love with Newton, whom, as she said, she mourned as an elder brother, there can be no doubt that his death was an event of considerable importance in her life. The tone of her earnest letter to Newton's pastor, inquiring if her "gentle, yet grave Preceptor" had been "willing to die," leaves no doubt that she was considerably shaken. She had lost a man whom she regarded with an ardent affection; she had lost her guide through the realms of intellectual aspiration—the support of her unconventionality and her idealism; and she had lost the "tutor" who, as she later wrote to Higginson, had encouraged her to write poems. The "lexicon" to which she turned after Newton's death may have helped—

it certainly influenced her style—but we must suppose that it hardly filled the gap left by "my dying tutor."

Always capable of the most poignant, the most profound sense of loss, an experience confirmed and typified for her by the death of Leonard Humphrey in 1850, she must surely have felt that she had sustained another great loss in the death of Newton. In one of her poems she tells us that

> I held a jewel in my fingers
> And went to sleep.
> The day was warm, and winds were prosy;
> I said, " 'Twill keep."
> I woke and chid my honest fingers,—
> The gem was gone;
> And now an amethyst remembrance
> Is all I own.

If, as Mr. Whicher plausibly supposes, this poem refers specifically to Newton, "I never lost as much but twice" refers to three tutors:

> I never lost as much but twice,
> And that was in the sod;
> Twice have I stood a beggar
> Before the door of God!
>
> Angels, twice descending,
> Reimbursed my store,
> Burglar, banker, father,
> I am poor once more.

This poem tells us, if we read it aright, that having robbed her of Humphrey, God reimbursed her with Newton; that having robbed her of Newton, He reimbursed her with Wadsworth; that now (1862) Wadsworth has been taken from her. The loss is hardly less heavy even though

Wadsworth is not, like the others, lost "in the sod," but has been called, merely, to the Calvary Church in San Francisco.

After the death of Newton, she is a "beggar"; she is confused and unhappy at having been left alone with her emerging poetic capabilities; she begins more acutely than before to feel the measure of her "difference from the others"; she is chafing against the repressive influences of her home and, though the issue has perhaps already been decided, she suffers the conflicts which are involved in her approaching seclusion; she knows with fresh awareness and with increasing profundity the "anguish and affliction" of which, she has told Abiah Root, she had first been made strongly aware in 1850. Edward Dickinson's invitation to his family to visit Washington in the spring of 1854 may have been partly motivated by the general family concern over Emily's health and state of mind and a family agreement that a change of scene might do her good. The fateful visit to Philadelphia introduced her to Wadsworth at a time when, if ever, she despairingly sensed the emptiness of her life and the directionless drift of her intellectual and poetic attempts.

She was deeply in love. Her love gave her joy. Yet the connection with Wadsworth was not destined to be Emily Dickinson's liberation from the pattern of life which had been imposed upon her and which she had made her own. Marriage with Wadsworth was out of the question from the beginning, so that like every other great and definitive experience in her life, her devoted commitment to him involved its own renunciation. It is barely conceivable that if he had been single and a marriage had taken place, Emily Dickinson might have changed, might have developed more widely than she did, might have grasped life more variously. Some such efflorescence might have ensued upon her liberation from the fateful pattern of events that pointed toward her complete seclusion. One may doubt, however, that this would have taken place. More even than most women, Emily Dickinson displayed the enormous conservatism of temperament which after the first two or three decades discourages any radical liberation or mutation of personality. Wadsworth was, in any case, respectably married. To love him, as Emily knew, was to lose him. It seemed to be her destiny.

Though lack of concrete evidence makes it difficult to estimate with much particularity Wadsworth's influence on the life of our poet, it was surely extensive. But it is, of course, a very superficial understanding of her life which makes the Wadsworth connection absolutely crucial— which says, in effect, that Emily Dickinson became a recluse because of her frustrated love for a married man, that she dressed in white in order to be the priestess at the altar of love, and that she became a poet in order to write a "letter to the world" conveying the interesting facts, in spiritual language, about her love life. However commendably "human" such an attitude toward Emily Dickinson may be, it involves a libel upon her, by underestimating her both as a woman and as a poet. It also involves a libel on poetry, by underestimating the complexity of experience out of which good poetry comes, the difficulty with which it is written, and the reasons why it is written. Emily Dickinson wrote poetry before she met Wadsworth; the path towards her ultimate seclusion already stretched before her. There is, to be sure, a measure of truth in the "frustrated love" theory, for she did make a kind of religion out of marriage, she did behave a little like a priestess, she did respond to the loss of Wadsworth with poetry. Yet when we try to estimate the effect of the Wadsworth connection we shall be right in thinking that it confirmed a way of life already taken and wrong in thinking that it was revolutionary, that it abolished Emily Dickinson's past and determined her future. Her life was narrow, straight, and deep. Wadsworth made it deeper but no less narrow and no less straight. Had she not, after all, *chosen* her way of life?

The new "Emilie," the "Emilie" of 1854-62, is the old "Emilie" without the insouciance and the facetiousness and without quite the same sense of youthful rebellion and aspiration after ideal experiences. The poet and the letter writer now exhibit the sense of maturity and assurance which comes from having all of one's deepest native characteristics confirmed and consolidated. She speaks with a new economy of language, the image of a life newly defined and delimited. Her aphoristic style begins in these years.

In a letter to Dr. and Mrs. Holland which may have been written as early as 1857, we read: "That you be with me annuls fear and I await Commencement with merry resignation. Smaller than David, you clothe me with extreme Goliath." This is very consciously—too much so, one may think—a literary style. Emily Dickinson's aphorisms remain one of the striking mementoes of American inventiveness, like Whitman's free verse or Melville's combination of American folk language with traditional English forms. On the whole it does not strike my ear as a very great style, though on frequent occasions a concentration or ellipsis of syntax produces a brilliant *mot* and on rare occasions an aphorism which even a Blake or a Pascal hardly surpasses.

The two sentences I have quoted above illustrate many of her characteristic devices. She delights in the subjunctive mood. She no doubt learned from her Amherst Academy courses in Latin that the subjunctive is volitive, optative, and potential. And in "Emilie's" opinion it is intellectually and spiritually admirable to be volitive, optative, and potential. (Did not Emerson advocate an "optative mood"?) "That you be with me" implies more than simple futurity. It implies "That it is your will and my will that you should be with me," "That you wish to be with me," "That you possess the possibility of being with me," and so on. Legal words like "annul" are common in her aphoristic style. But why should the visit of friends annul "fear"? Is it merely that, being shy of crowds, she will fear the Commencement exercises less if she can go in the company of the Hollands? Have they relieved her fear that they would not come by sending word that they would? Or is she referring to some more subjunctive realm of potentiality? Is she praising friendship, which is so much the substance of immortality, so much the solace of the soul in its precarious, its fearful path in this world? At any rate friendship makes one strong, clothes one "with Goliath," as she says, characteristically translating a proper name into an abstract word.

In the following sentence, she has used an abstract word, "south," as if it were concrete: "The lawn is full of south and the odors tangle, and I hear today for the first time the river in the tree." The river might suggest, to Emily Dickinson's epistolary friends, distant intimations of death,

of the remote, the vague but overwhelming action of nature which was death to human beings. She continues
by saying: "A woman died last week, young and in hope
but a little while—at the end of our garden. I thought since
of the power of death, not upon affection, but its mortal
signal. It is to us the Nile." She often speaks of the Nile or
rivers in general as representing death. (For example, in a
letter of about 1879 she writes: "I shall bring you a handful of lotus next, but do not tell the Nile. . . . He is a
jealous brook.") She makes death synonymous with nature. The Nile carries us along towards our appointed
merging with the sea (immortality); it has the paradoxical
function of nourishing and sustaining our lives even as it
inexorably bears us along to our destiny. One may quarrel
with the phraseology—why, for example, except to be consciously "literary," does she say "I thought" instead of the
more accurate "I have been thinking"?—but we see that
in the late 1850s "Emilie" is making the commendable attempt to invent a kind of personal shorthand language
which will have the advantage of being both concise and
capable of encompassing a rich complex of meanings. Undoubtedly we enjoy and admire such phrases as "Sisters
are brittle things. God was penurious with me, which
makes me shrewd with Him" and are ready to ignore such
stilted affectations as "I do not know of you, a long while.
I remember you—several times. I wish I knew if you kept
me?" It is clear that, however memorable some of her
phrases are, she had an exaggerated idea of what could be
accomplished merely by tinkering with syntax. This faith
in the efficacy of words, in a kind of word magic, is one of
the permanent acquisitions of the period we are considering.

In the later "Emilie" period the characteristic subject-matter of the letters becomes crystallized. From then on any single letter is likely to contain a string of more or less related sibylline utterances on friendship, immortality, death, and nature. Friendship for the later "Emilie" is rather different from its earlier form. A friend is now no longer merely a companion in unconventionality and in intellectual adventure. Friendship now clearly extends beyond the terrestrial bourn and partakes of eternity even while it is still hampered by the trammels of flesh. Friendship is the surest warrant of immortality, as it is the best consolation amid the injuries which nature inflicts upon us in this life. Friendship gives one wealth and status, and provides one with both the advantages and the duties of the rich and the ennobled. "My friends are my 'estate,' " she writes to Mr. and Mrs. Bowles. "Forgive me then the avarice to hoard them." Friendship raises one above the petty conventions and inhibitions of ordinary life. In a letter to the Hollands (probably 1861) she chides them gently for not writing to her and declares that she will allow no scruples to stop her from writing them. "I can't *stop* to strut in a world where bells toll." If her eagerness makes them laugh at her, she says: "*I* can't stop for that! *My* business is to love."

After a visit in 1861 from Mr. and Mrs. Bowles, she writes: "Though it is almost nine o'clock, the skies are gay and yellow, and there's a purple craft or so, in which a friend could sail. To-night looks like 'Jerusalem!' " According to Emily Dickinson's cult, the ideal experience is to sail off with a friend through a somewhat dubiously colored sky toward that new world which is promised in her favorite book of the Bible, Revelation. The language of mineralogy, as one might call it, is made familiar by her poems; it was a favorite form of metaphor, as we have noted, in the sermons of Wadsworth, as it is in other religious writings, including the Book of Revelation. In the poet's letters we frequently find ideas about friendship translated into the uneasy language of jewelry. For example, there is the letter of 1861 to Mr. Bowles in which (as she more than once had to do) she apologizes for not having seen him when he had recently called at the house, presumably because her shyness made her too dilatory about appearing before him. She then adds that "Friends are gems, infrequent. Potosi is a care, sir. I guard it reverently, for I could not afford to be poor now after afᵣfluence." It might understandably cause Mr. Bowles, that vigorous and hard-driving journalist, some difficulty to understand why he should regard a silver-mining town in Bolivia as his special care, or hers. But, if he was accustomed to his correspondent's habit of using exotic foreign names in this odd fashion, he perhaps would have understood her to say that friendship is a precious possession, rich in both the happiness and the responsibility it bestows.

Friends such as Samuel Bowles must have been a good deal mystified and possibly a little overwhelmed by Emily's protestations. To Mr. Bowles in Europe she wrote (in June of 1862): "I grope fast, with my fingers, for all out of my sight I own, to get it nearer." And she goes on with her curious subjunctives, her jewels, her exotic names and colors, her estates, and (in one or two places) her incomprehensible shorthand:

> How extraordinary that life's large population contain so few of power to us—and those a vivid species who leave no mode, like Tyrian dye.

Remembering these minorities, permit our gratitude for you. We ask that you be cautious, for many
sakes, excelling ours. To recapitulate the stars were
useless as supreme. Yourself is yours, dear friend, but
ceded is it not, to here and there a minor life? Do not
defraud these, for gold may be bought, and purple
may be bought, but the sale of the spirit never did
occur.

Be sure, dear friend, for want you have estates of
lives.

This is a fairly full example of the language of royalty or
courtliness which Emily Dickinson used in both her letters
and her poems to denote the different degrees of the status
of the soul in its quest for friendship and immortality, a
range of status which begins with the lonely, hungering,
friendless "little girl" and ends with the queen or empress
who has put on the purple robes of immortality.) In the
passage quoted above, she addresses Mr. Bowles as a courtier
his king. It is reminiscent of the poem in which she addresses
God as "Sir" and beseeches Him to enfold a "tiny courtier"
in His ermine robe. The democracy of central Massachusetts was strangely conducive to monarchies of the imagination. It produced, finally, a poet who could sign her letters
with the single word "Amherst."

Our poet's idea of nature changes somewhat during the
twelve or fourteen years of her "Emilie" period. In earlier
letters, such as the one on the "departed Humphrey,"
there was a kind of romantic graveyardism and melancholy
in her descriptions of nature. In the letter of 1850 which
reported to Abiah Root the great occasion of the knock on
the door and the ensuing crisis, the forest, one may think,
assumes a symbolic meaning very much like the forest in
The Scarlet Letter. It is the part of life—dark, vital, mys-

terious, threatening, erotic—which differs most radically
from life in the household wherein she is destined to remain—as, analogously, Hawthorne's forest symbolizes the
qualities of life opposite to those represented by the repressive morality of seventeenth-century Boston. Another
mood in which the "Emilie" of the earlier period perceived nature was distinctly Emersonian. Thus in a letter
of 1852 to Austin she can describe nature as joyful,
boundless, full of ministering and tutelary spirits, and instinct with a principle of resurrection and immortality.
Yet one must not strain too hard to discover the symbolic
meaning of nature in her earlier letters. Her general tendency is to use nature as a decoration for her moods, for
her spiritual or sentimental adventures.

In the later letters of the "Emilie" period—and this is
generally true of her poems as well as of the letters of the
last half of her life—nature appears in two basic modes: as
a symbol of the mysterious processes of death and as a
child's garden of flowers and birds. As for the latter, or
Christopher Robin, aspect of nature, a passage from a letter of 1861 to Mrs. Bowles will amply illustrate:

> How is your garden, Mary? Are the pinks true,
> and the sweet williams faithful? I've got a geranium
> like a sultana, and when the humming-birds come
> down, geranium and I shut our eyes, and go away.
> Ask "Mamie" if I shall catch her a butterfly with a
> vest like a Turk? I will, if she will build him a house in
> her "morning-glory."

Doubtless it is a matter for endless curiosity that the writer
of these words could speak almost simultaneously of "that
bareheaded life, under the grass" which "worries one like
a wasp"—for these are very memorable phrases and they

bespeak a vision of life and death and nature belonging more to the greatest epochs of poetry than to the Anglo-American mid-nineteenth century.

The idea that "the gentian is a greedy flower and over-takes us all" is not typical of a time that tended to see soul-bracing transcendental or pantheistic ineffabilities in fringed gentians, rhodoras, violets, and flowers in the crannied wall. For Emily Dickinson the gentian is symbolic of man's voracious and inescapable enemy, nature. For the natural universe operates on inexorable principle: "Blossoms belong to the bee, if needs be by *habeas corpus*." Though in certain of her poems she could imitate the bathos of Emerson's "The Humble-Bee," she connected the bee with processes a good deal more darkly fated than did Emerson. The blossom is ravished and destroyed by the bee as the individual is by nature, or by that burglar-banker and beelike Father whose laws nature follows. Yet the proviso in this mainly disillusioned view is that nature kills us only as a part of the accession of the fortunate to immortality. The blossom perishes and is seen no more, but faith tells us that it has merely been translated into a higher and purer life, as the bee transmutes the dying flower into pure gold and stores it away in the chambers of his hidden mansion, the vaults of his mysterious bank.

The cult of "little women" which Emily Dickinson shared with several of her female correspondents, and especially with her cousins the Norcross sisters, had the advantage of justifying both of her views of nature. If one imagined oneself a helpless "creature," and indeed as a child, one could regard nature as a child does: either a timeless realm of beautiful toys and charming pets as alive and sentient as oneself or as a terrifying force which levied deprivations upon one or snatched one away to a hideous fate. Thus the same writer who says that "Heaven hunts round for those that find itself below, and then it snatches," and that "the terror of the winter has made a little creature out of me," protests that she cannot visit her cousins because "the geraniums felt so I couldn't think of leaving them, and . . . carnation pink cried." And the writer who speaks of her protracted sickness during the "curious winter" of 1859 and who was "amazed" by March can close her letter in this manner:

> Now, my love, robins for both of you, and when you and Vinnie sing at sunrise on the apple boughs, just cast your eye to my twig.
>
> Poor Plover

Her "Dear peacocks," it would appear, understood the idiom very well. For was there not a sisterhood of "little creatures" all over the world? "The Yorkshire girls" (authors of *Jane Eyre* and *Wuthering Heights*) were the "friends," as Emily declared, of both her cousins and herself. And other robins had fainted:

> That Mrs. Browning fainted, we need not read *Aurora Leigh* to know, when she lived with her English aunt; and George Sand "must make no noise in her grandmother's bedroom." Poor children! Women, now, queens, now! And one in the Eden of God. I guess they both forget that now, so who knows but we, little stars from the same night, stop twinkling at last? Take heart, little sister, twilight is but the short bridge, and the moon stands at the end.

We have the sense that during the winter of 1861-62 Emily Dickinson was energetically at work on her poetry.

It may have been the most productive period of her career, although the evidence does not allow more than speculation on this point. She herself accounted for her poetic outbursts by saying that they were responses to adversity. In a letter to Higginson (June 1862) she recapitulated her poetic career thus: "My dying tutor told me that he would like to live till I had been a poet, but Death was much of mob as I could master, then. And when, far afterward, a sudden light on orchards, or a new fashion in the wind troubled my attention, I felt a palsy, here, the verses just relieve." That is, Newton had urged her to her first concerted attempt to write poetry but after his death in 1853 Emily, saddened and at a loss for guidance and encouragement, had given up poetry, considering that it was all she could do to cope with the mere fact of the death of her tutor. But later she had become newly aware, aware with a kind of pain, of the color and action of nature and of the suffering of human beings and had found that writing poetry gave her relief.

A few facts, at least, can be adduced as background and provisional cause of the probable poetic activity of this period. In a letter of April 25 she had written to Higginson that "I had a terror since September, I could tell to none; and so I sing, as the boy does of the burying ground, because I am afraid." Mr. Whicher plausibly argues that the "terror since September" may well have been a crisis in her relation with Wadsworth. Whether he actually visited her in the late summer of 1861 is not unquestionably known. But it is likely that either by letter or in person he strongly impressed himself upon her at this time in his mythical and tragic way—as the "Man of Sorrow" who often seemed to be "almost overpowered by a spasm of gloom" and who palpably shivered as he told her that his life was "full of dark secrets" and that he was "liable at any time to die." We may conjecture that he had come to Amherst, or had written, to say that he was seriously thinking of leaving the East and of taking a new post in San Francisco. His admirer was "poor once more." As Whicher perceptively says: "Once before Emily Dickinson had gone through a parting with a man whom she held dear, and he had gone away to die. Now the inexorable nexus of circumstance seemed to be coiling back upon itself and displaying a similar pattern, even more huge and hopeless to conceive than before. She had reason to be afraid."

The specter of death, always the most powerful figure the poet's mind could entertain, often visited Amherst in the early 1860s, as it visited the whole country. "Sorrow seems more general than it did," she writes in 1862, "and not the estate of a few persons, since the war began." And again: "The hearts of Amherst ache tonight—you could not know how hard." Her letters concerning Frazer Stearns, the handsome and promising son of the president of Amherst College, are (with some of the entries in Whitman's *Specimen Days*) among the classics of their kind and period:

> Christ be merciful! Frazer Stearns is just leaving Annapolis. His father has gone to see him today. I hope that ruddy face won't be brought home frozen. Poor little widow's boy [son of a Mrs. Adams] riding tonight in the mad wind, back to the village burying ground where he never dreamt of sleeping! . . . Austin is chilled by Frazer's murder. He says his brain keeps saying over "Frazer is killed"—"Frazer is killed," just as father told it to him. Two or three words of

lead, that dropped so deep they keep weighing. . . . I had read of those [the "minie-ball"]—I didn't think Frazer would carry one to Eden with him. Just as he fell, in his soldier's cap, with his sword at his side, Frazer rode through Amherst. Classmates . . . to guard his narrow face.

Emily Dickinson had grown acquainted with anguish both in her personal life and in the village around her. She had learned, as she says, that "to all except anguish the mind soon adjusts." And she had learned that the writing of poetry was one way of making the difficult adjustment. But of course the mere writing of poetry would not in itself preserve one's balance and one's sanity. And this was indeed a period in which just such an extreme question as the question of one's sanity came up. It was a time when childhood fears rose up afresh and threatened the very foundations of one's being. We catch the palpable sense that extremities have been reached by 1863 from the following words:

> The nights turned hot when Vinnie had gone, and I must keep no window raised for fear of prowling "booger," I must shut my door for fear front door slide open on me at the "dead of night," and I must keep "gas" burning to light the danger up, so I could distinguish it—these gave me a snarl in the brain which don't unravel yet, and that old nail in my breast pricked me; these, dear, were my cause.

Emily Dickinson, can one doubt it? had been profoundly shaken. The motions of neurosis and insanity were alive in her soul. The disposition of her being was achieving, with some violence, its final character. Her personality was being refined in anguish, settled in pain, and rendered energetic by the release of her deepest emotional resources.

For her suffering had its rewards: "I noticed that Robert Browning had made another poem, and was astonished [for Mrs. Browning had died in 1861]—till I remembered that I, myself, in my smaller way, sang off charnel steps. Every day life feels mightier, and what we have the power to be, more stupendous."

Emily Dickinson began sending her poems to T. W. Higginson in April of 1862. She knew him only as an eminent man of letters whose opinion she would most certainly honor and for whose advice she would be grateful. The odd note which asked: "Are you too deeply occupied to say if my verse is alive?" and which, though unsigned, was accompanied by her card was the distant beginning of the long-delayed publication of Emily Dickinson's poems.

The Economy of Poetry

IN SPEAKING of the "economy" of Emily Dickinson's poetry I intend to emphasize the limitations and exclusions of substance and means which the poems make, and then to take note of the abundance, such as it is, which the poems offer. The economy of Emily Dickinson's poetry is, to use one of her favorite words, frugal. It does not do this admirable poet any service, and some of the criticism she has received shows that it may do her harm, to speak as if she wrote great poetry in abundance. Of the fifteen hundred or so poems which she wrote, only about fifty have the substance and the fineness of manner which urge us to accord them equality with much else that is excellent in the literature of lyric poetry. And to my ear at least only a dozen or two urge one to use the word "great."

It scarcely matters whether readers of Emily Dickinson's poetry agree on the exact number of her poems which they wish to call great. But it is of pre-eminent importance to establish a general idea of the range of her poetry. The extraordinary and proliferating abundance discovered in the Dickinson canon by some writers will seem, when we have understood her poetry and her mind, to consist largely of the half-successes left by repeated failures to reproduce her few characteristic insights.

Emily Dickinson regarded poetry as one of the strategems by which she was empowered to endure life until the time came to assume the "estate" of immortality. And these stratagems—others were stoic fortitude, intuitive vision, redemption through love and friendship—she typically speaks of in terms of the limitations of what can be done with them. "Existence" itself, she says, "has a stated width." Her conclusion after hearing a clergyman preach on "breadth" was that "the broad are too broad to define." And again,

> The soul with strict economy
> Subsists till Paradise.

Her estimate of the richness of subsistence out of which her poems sprang similarly stresses a frugal economy. The lot was "bleak," as she says, on which she strove to raise her "bloom." The grape and maize yielded by her "acre of rock" came late and sparsely. Her life itself she describes as a "sumptuous destitution" and a "banquet of abstemiousness."

In its profound reaches the mind of Emily Dickinson moved with the power of resolute decision. With the Calvinist sense of the narrow chance of salvation and of the absolute distinction between the saved and the damned, she asserted that she was ready to "venture all upon a throw." Her success as a poet, her redemption as a woman, her entrance into "bliss" or "heaven" was to be a wager, a "hazard" of the soul, which tossed its single coin. She was like David with his single pebble:

> I took my power in my hand
> And went against the world;
> 'Twas not so much as David had,
> But I was twice as bold.

The laws of chance are against the wagerer, victory comes late if it comes at all, the sustenance of life and art is meager. No wonder then that once the wager is made, once the conditions of success are decided upon, the mind clings tenaciously to the "stated width" of its existence. No wonder that

> The soul selects her own society,
> Then shuts the door,

and no wonder that the soul should strategically

> close the valves of her attention
> Like stone.

In Emily Dickinson's poetry, taking it by and large, there is but one major theme, one symbolic act, one incandescent center of meaning. Expressed in the most general terms, this theme is the achievement of status through crucial experiences. The kinds of status our poet imagines are variously indicated by such favorite words as "queen," "royal," "wife," "woman," "poet," "immortal," and "empress." The kinds of experience which confer status are love, "marriage," death, poetic expression, and immediate intuitive experiences which have the redemptive power of grace. We have here the basis of a fairly complex and various poetry. Yet we must observe that the view of life which our poet has taken for her central theme is based even more severely than it at first seems on a series of sharp and definitive exclusions. Each "estate" involves its own renunciation, except for one: immortality. And each of the crucial experiences which confer the different kinds of status is a type and emblem of one of them: the coming of death.

This is not to imply, of course, that she has no topic but death and immortality. But it remains true that we cannot see her work very clearly until we perceive that her best and most characteristic poems proliferate from one center of energy and that many of her lesser poems either try to issue from this center and fail or else do not issue from any center at all and remain random gnomic observations or incidental experiments and notations. The fact that many of these random observations display great charm, wit, and even the visionary power of genius should not lead us to blur the edges of her fine power of self-limitation. We know life mostly by thirsting for it, as she repeatedly states. And we know freedom largely by being prisoners. To slake the thirst with too much wine, to enfranchise the prisoner too abruptly or too completely is to invite surfeit and extinction. These are not the sentiments of a freely ranging and widely various mind. They are the sentiments of a mind which instinctively inclines to its characteristic bias.

"Experience" in Emily Dickinson's best poetry is narrow and profound. Typically it takes the form of a sudden illumination, an appalling pause in the motion of things, a seizure of an unspeakable power, an ecstatic influx. Her favorite images for the typical experience are a bolt of lightning, a brilliant light, the sun, the eruption of a volcano, the unannounced arrival of a lover in his coach, the surprising knock of his hand upon the door, the confrontation of some threatening or overwhelming natural or psychic phenomenon. Experience at its lower and less decisive intensity tends to be the reverberation, the afterglow, or the diminishing memory of the few forcibly revelatory experiences. This is the warrant for her fanciful idea of the simultaneity of experience—for her idea, to take one example, that she was

> Born—Bridalled—
> Shrouded—
> In a day.

It is her warrant for assuming the typicality of experience, an assumption which leads her to the sometimes questionable conclusion that she perfectly knows what it is to be married or to die.

When she speaks specifically of experience as if all limitations might be easily transgressed, she leaves the privilege to God. For God, each morning may be new, unique: "the Experiment of our Lord." But if we consider the possibilities of experience open to human beings we merely gain a new sense of its closure. In "Experience is the angled road" she calls it a testimony to the "complicate" discipline of man that experience always compels him to choose "his pre-appointed plan."

If we assume from such a poem as "Water is taught by thirst" that Emily Dickinson is propounding an open universe in which knowledge is freely derivable in the pragmatic or empirical manner, we are brought up short by the realization that, according to this poem, everything man learns from is represented by some emblem of disintegration or death: thirst, oceans (usually a symbol of eternity in her poems), throe, battles, memorial mold, and snow.

And if we assume that this poem, and the several others which deal with opposites like "water" and "thirst," is evidence of a widely ranging system of tensions or of a dialectical cast of mind, we are investing Emily Dickinson's work with meanings it does not have. She has, as we shall note, an admirable vein of "Stoicism." But this does not mean, as some writers have seemed to think, that she produced a philosophy of tensions. She had certain visionary qualities in common with Blake, and she invented a poetically imagined eschatology. But this is no evidence that she developed a dialectic of contraries.

An "experience" means an emptiness newly filled or informed or enlivened—or a fullness made empty. One of the aphorisms of her letters reads: "Nature is a haunted house, but art a house that tries to be haunted." And she distinguishes from nature in this respect not only art but human existence itself. One may discern two sources for this idea of experience. The first is the Puritan tradition, with its characteristic notion of grace. As Perry Miller says: "Regeneration was the receiving by man of 'the fulnesse of the infinitenesse of all perfections which are in the Lord,' who alone is 'able to fill up all the empty chinks, void places, the unsatisfied graspings & yawnings of the spirit of man. . . .' Therefore grace is to be understood as something inward and spiritual, and when it has wrought upon a man in regeneration 'it leaves an impression upon the most inward motions of the soul, as they meet with God in the most retired and refined actions thereof.'" In Emily Dickinson's accounts of how her spirit yearns for the fulness of infinity and of how it is "fathomed" by the emanations of a mysterious power she remains a true daughter of her New England ancestors.

The second source of her idea of experience is simply her reaction to the culture of provincial America. Tocqueville, after delineating the emptiness, the monotony, and tenuousness of this culture, predicted that American poetry would derive a mythology of universalism and abstraction from its cultural habitat. His prediction was amply justified by the appearance of Walt Whitman. He neglected to imagine the appearance of such writers as Hawthorne and Melville and Emily Dickinson, who were more interested in the haunting of the house than in singing the song of the open road. For these writers existence was an emptiness to be filled by the imagination.

It has often been remarked that American, and particularly New England, writers have to be read in the light of their relation to experience. Experience, that is, has been a problem, something to conjure with, to American writers as it has not typically been for Europeans. The particular qualities of experience could not be assumed among Americans as known and identifiable, because of the newness of the New World and because of the Puritan ideas of sin and renunciation which, in conduct if not always in theory, placed the individual in opposition to his experience and forced him to question it. Emily Dickinson shares this American tendency of opposing the individual to his experience. But her idea of what experience is differentiates her from some writers and puts her in the company of others.

She differs from Emerson in the separations she makes. Emerson is often tempted to assert a too easy correspondence between man, cosmos, and God, and too easy interflux of consciousness, nature, and spirit. But experience for Emily Dickinson is not the act of dilating and expanding into harmony with a loosely conceived cosmos or deity. It is the dramatic action of one thing upon another, the influx of power or illumination from nature or God which is received by something radically different from either, man.

She has moments remotely reminiscent of Whitmanesque intoxication and singing of oneself. But Whitman's myriad perceptions of natural experience were certainly beyond her, and one may well conclude that she and not Whitman gains by the contrast. Whitman's mind, despite the voracious setting down of facts, was strongly transcendental and abstract. Emily Dickinson's grasp upon reality was narrower, but within its limits it could often be a good deal more firm.

Among the romantic poets of the early part of the century, her mind was perhaps closest to Wordsworth's. But the closeness is not very marked, consisting largely in the formal coincidence that both poets tend to subsume experience under the revelatory moments when the "gleam," to use Wordsworth's term, suffuses the mind and to stress the importance of memory, whose function it is to recapture and retain the experience of the "gleam." But Emily Dickinson expresses, for example, no idea of the development of man from childhood to maturity of the kind one finds in Wordsworth, and for her the revelation of truth through experience has a much more abrupt and definitive quality, in the Puritan manner, than it has for the English poet. Again she sees no such correspondence of mind with nature as does Wordsworth. She differs from most romantic poets and from the American Transcendentalists because, as she sees it, nature not only fails to give daily support to the life and reason of man but actively threatens him with extinction.

The rather stark simplifications of Emily Dickinson's view of human experience rule out the possibility that she should develop a complex or subtle psychology. In this respect she is like Hawthorne rather than Wordsworth or Melville. Reality and truth have for Emily Dickinson and Hawthorne so much the quality of something finally given to the clairvoyant mind once and for all that they do not easily take to ideas of evolution and unfolding. Wordsworth may trace the development of man's personality with the greatest scrupulosity and ingenuity. Melville may delineate in the figures of legend the gradual emergence of his Ishmael. But for Hawthorne and Emily Dickinson reality tends to appear hard and fast, emblematic and typical. Truth is given, not evolved.

But the psychology which she reveals in her poems, though narrow, is both profound and convincing. She thought that the soul of man, to remain healthy and sane, must subject itself to a "strict economy." To establish and preserve its integrity, the soul must be ready to close the valves of its attention, to seek its "polar privacy" and remain immovable and proud. Yet within its established confines the soul has a double character. A hunting, pursuing, watchful function of the soul is seen to be separable from the soul itself.

> Adventure most unto itself
> The Soul condemned to be;
> Attended by a Single Hound—
> Its own Identity.

In this poem the object-finding or externally operative part of the mind while recognized as separate is paradoxically said to be identical with the mind's self-generated moralizing guardian. But in poems such as "My soul accused me" and "Me from Myself to banish" the moralizing part of the mind is said to be autonomous and imperial. Of the soul in its accusatory aspect, she writes that it is easier to endure fire than the soul's disdain. What may happen when the "single Hound" part of the soul lapses in its vigilance is described in "The soul has bandaged moments." Here the soul is said to be transfixed when confronted by a ghastly apparition which strokes, with its long fingers, her freezing hair. Or the temporary abeyance of the "single Hound" may result not in fright at some eruptive sexualized image but in pure euphoria, the sense that the soul has burst "all the doors" and "dances like a bomb abroad." The watchful hound may have the quality of destiny or of the Puritan conscience but its reign is precarious, the soul it guards being subject to eruptions of uncontrollable energy.

Emily Dickinson considered sanity, one might say that she considered existence itself, to be just barely possible. Reason, she repeats in her poems, is hemmed in and threatened by madness. It is a frail bark on a profound and imminently tumultuous sea. It is the quiet momentarily imposed upon Etna or Vesuvius. Its path through the abyss is a narrow "groove"; once let it swerve and it is exposed to the terrors of the deep. In the psychological scheme of her poems, Emily Dickinson regarded all consciousness as derivable from and as typified by the consciousness of death and immortality. Fortunately, as she says in "I never hear that one is dead," the "daily mind" does not "till" the abyss of death, for if it did it would go mad. Consciousness guides the soul. Yet it is a measure of man's desolation and the precariousness of his existence that consciousness, fully understood as consciousness of death, appears to us as an "awful stranger."

If we wished to pursue a Freudian analogy, we should

say that her fine poem called "As one does sickness over" (with its account of how "one rewalks a precipice" and "whittles at the twig" that had barely saved one from extinction) can be fruitfully read as a poetic treatment of the realms of psychology which extend "beyond the pleasure principle." Like Freud, she sensed the quality of destiny in the human mind that makes it recapitulate in fancy or hallucination the occasions of its suffering. There is as little nonsense in her idea of dreams as in Freud's. "Dreams are a subtle dower" but they clearly set themselves apart from "reality" by flinging us back into "the precinct raw/Possessed before." She knew the relation of neurosis with creative efficiency: "It is easy to work when the soul is at play."

In Whitman's house of the soul there are no doors, and hardly any house. But Emily Dickinson believed that if sanity was to be preserved and a meaningful existence made possible, the soul must indeed be a house with a door, a door which is left "ajar." This is one of her most revealing images, by which she imagines not only the mind but also nature. In the following poem we encounter one of those apparently vague personifications ("the heaven") which tend to weaken even some of her best poems—"the heaven" here means, one gathers, "the revelation of truth under the aspect of death":

> The soul should always stand ajar
>   That if the heaven inquire,
> He will not be obliged to wait,
>   Or shy of troubling her.
>
> Depart, before the host has slid
>   The bolt upon the door,
> To seek for the accomplished guest—
>   Her visitor no more.

The ambiguities of "the accomplished guest," which include God, death, grace, a "tutor," a lover, are a topic for later consideration. Here I am speaking only of the "strict economy" the poet attributes to the mind, and wish to emphasize the severity with which she presents the precarious possibility that the soul can acquire (what she elsewhere calls) its royal diadem through the reception of ineffable experience, "the accomplished guest."

"Doom is the House without the Door," wrote Emily Dickinson. For Whitman, houses themselves were doom. A house for Thoreau was not considerable by spiritual man if it was more complex, structured, and intricate than a shack by the pond, every nail and slab of which was known personally by the builder. There was no house through the walls of which Emerson's soul might not be expected to dilate. For though he wrote (in a manner that must have interested Emily Dickinson) that "every spirit builds itself a house; and beyond its house a world; and beyond its world a heaven," the building of the house was less remarkable than the speed with which its confines were transcended. But the American writers with whom Emily Dickinson has her closest kinship have all made profoundly symbolic use of the house, as we recall from Poe's "Fall of the House of Usher" and "The Black Cat," Melville's *Pierre*, "I and Chimney," and "Jimmy Rose," Hawthorne's *The House of the Seven Gables*, and Henry James's "The Jolly Corner," among several other of his fictions.

A house is one of our poet's favorite symbols of the mind. In such poems as "Remembrance has a rear and front" and "One need not be a chamber to be haunted," we discern her idea that consciousness presents itself to us as a dual discourse, having a latent content behind the manifest content; that the garret of a house is like the abode of the mind's ego-functions and that the cellar is symbolic of the unconscious; that the "prudent" who carry a revolver to ward off external enemies are misguided if they do not also guard against the "superior spectre" who may be stalking the corridors of their own minds.

The critic who tries to explicate Emily Dickinson's ideas cannot help making her sound more speculative and theoretical than she actually was. The reader must discount and translate as he judges proper. One must agree with the emphasis, at least, of Mr. Allen Tate's remark that she "cannot reason at all. She can only *see*," so long as we remember that Mr. Tate is speaking of "reasoning in verse form" as this is done, for example, in the lesser poems of Tennyson. She had great intellectual power and her poetry is eminently considerable, so Mr. Tate notes, as a "poetry of ideas." But part of the economy of her mind was her own clearly expressed knowledge that she could not "organize." She was incapable of systematic abstract thought, just as she was incapable of organizing a closely knit poem of any but the shortest length. Her intellectual bent is intuitive and radically realistic. Her greatness as a poet issues from the fact that, though she had little power of systematic speculation and little enough aptitude for poetic coherence, her mind instinctively moved towards those severe separations and exclusions and that closely limited vision of things which she called the "strict economy" of the soul.

There are several reasons, some obvious, some difficult to get at, for the desire many critics have had to find in Emily Dickinson a universal genius, or—if not a universal genius—then a kind of Puckish or Ariel-like creative spirit which roved with joyous inspiration or with sharp, irreverent ironies throughout the range of human experience. Feelings of patriotism have doubtless played their part in this estimation. More important, one suspects, have been certain attitudes associated with modern liberalism: the idea, for example, that excellence in a woman poet is to be measured by her success in having escaped the confines of her environment and its narrow and backward conventions, by her success (we must suppose the argument to be) in having overcome the unfortunate circumstance of being female. Poor Emily, we have thought—hemmed in by an unenlightened Victorianism, threatened by Calvinist superstition and provincial reaction, doomed to disappointment by a cruel, narrow-minded father, by prudery, and by illiberal divorce laws. One does not of course condone any of the circumstances which were actually repressive in their influence on Emily Dickinson. But neither does one condone the automatic assumptions some writers have made upon perceiving them. These writers have concluded that since Emily Dickinson's background is narrow, repressive, and reactionary her poetry (how else should such a poet succeed?) must be a triumph of broadness and variety, freedom and gaiety, experimentalism and progressivism.

Now all this has a color of truth. But the "free" Emily Dickinson remains extraordinarily confusing in our minds, and we have not known how to discriminate within the body of her work. With a few exceptions, her critics have neglected to see the poems with objectivity and to grasp the idea that history is not always to be understood as something evil from which writers must free themselves but that it may be a complicated force which works both good and evil.

Constance Rourke (in her *American Humor)* did a great deal towards establishing Emily Dickinson as a universal American genius—a genius, that is, whose characteristics are freedom, adventurousness, inspired improvisation, vigorous creativity, humor, irony, resilience, an ever-renewing Promethean inventiveness. In her brilliant and sensitive way, Miss Rourke stressed the poet's "elastic and irreverent rebellion"; her quizzical eye; her subjectivity, which made even her glances at the outer world the property of her "indwelling" poetry; her tendency toward "swift turns of inner drama" and yet her sheering away, in the American manner, from pure drama; her bold, humorously and defiantly experimental language. Miss Rourke was content to stress American qualities of spirit in the poet. She did not suppose that the poetry was always of the first order of greatness and she spoke of its "hasty anarchy" of meaning and expression.

Miss Rourke concluded that Emily Dickinson "was in a profound sense a comic poet in the American tradition," adding that she had seen the universe in the profoundly comic manner—as a shifting ground of being towards which one's attitude must be part reconciliation and part "knowledge of eternal disparity." It seems to me that this is fundamentally true, but that the feminine Prometheus whom Constance Rourke calls "Emily Dickinson" does not really exist.

The trouble comes when Miss Rourke (alluding to "I taste a liquor never brewed") remarks of our poet that "seraphim tossing their snowy hats on high might be taken as her symbol." The inescapable reply to such a proposition is that if this is Emily Dickinson's symbol, why should not the reader think himself forced to reject both it and her? Can we take so awkwardly facetious a poem as "I taste a liquor never brewed" as evidence that Emily Dickinson is in the company of the authors of *Moby-Dick, Huckleberry Finn,* "Mr. Higginbotham's Catastrophe," and *The American?* Miss Rourke's few pages on Emily Dickinson are among the most brilliant we have, and they epitomize (in their special way) the general attitude of many critics. But there is a radical weakness in Constance Rourke's argument. She did not read the work apart from her methodological preoccupations. She did not, furthermore, consider Emily Dickinson's historical situation. If the same may be said of Miss Rourke's reading of Melville, Hawthorne, James, and others, one can only remark that these cases were such that her method performed its office with a more ready efficiency.

Reading "I taste a liquor never brewed" without critical preoccupations, one finds coy, childish, and awkward jollification, but one hardly discovers "elastic and irreverent rebellion" or "swift turns of inner drama." If we are at first inclined to see in such a poem an ever-fresh inventiveness and energy, do we not soon come to sense a thinness of emotion, a straining after ecstatic release and a failure to achieve it, a conscious playfulness within the meager confines of a rather oppressively contrived private poetic convention? Is there not an inescapable air of decadence in precisely those poems where we are asked to behold the fresh improvisations of the American spirit? Do we not, indeed, find a version of rococo, where we had been led to expect American humor?

We have noted the vein of genuine American humor in

Emily Dickinson's writings of the early period. But if we are to discover how this humor found its best expression in later years, we must not look to her much admired "humorous" poems. We must look to her poems on death and the personification of death which emerges from them. It is there, in that genteel visitor who comes in his fine carriage, that we discover the only image of American humor which places her in the company of Melville, Twain, Hawthorne, and James.

Having said so much by way of delineating the "economy" of Emily Dickinson's verse, one feels it necessary to recognize its considerable variety. There is nothing within her purview towards which, in different moods, she is not able to entertain two or three various and even contradictory attitudes. She was entirely free of the idea of sin; she was, almost, an immoralist. And this was considerable warrant for her freedom of manner. How, then, are we to reconcile this variousness, ostensible and real, with our account of her narrow profundity? We can do this by reflecting on a truth about all severe and renunciatory minds —that they have a center of meaning and a source of energy to which, however far they may wander, they return again and again. Mr. Whicher, though his account of the poet's mind is not the one here expressed, speaks very acutely of the power of "psychic reconnaissance" which Emily Dickinson inherited from her Puritan ancestors. That is exactly the phrase, implying as it does a curious, searching, ingenious interest in the things of the mind but implying also a center, an established base of operations, from which the searching imagination sallies and to which it returns.

Having perceived these basic facts, we may safely admit

that Constance Rourke's idea of Emily Dickinson has its element of truth. One may even imagine Miss Rourke going on, with some show of discovery, to compare our poet with another daughter of the Puritans: Pearl in *The Scarlet Letter.* Wondering if we do not catch sight of a "fiend peeping out . . . from the unsearchable abyss of her black eyes" (but Emily's were the color of sherry), we are moved to inquire, with Hester Prynne: "Child, what art thou?" And we hear the child's answer, full of diablerie, mock innocence, and hidden meaning: "Oh, I am your little Pearl!" Like Pearl, Emily Dickinson can sometimes strike us as an embodiment of purely magic power and an unprincipled but endlessly searching and ingenious imagination mysteriously in touch with the forces of the universe. Like Pearl, she is the only person in her milieu totally lacking in reverence for respectable society and its institutions, and, like Pearl, she embodies the newly creative energy released by the collapse of the Puritan theocracy. Like that of little Pearl, her life runs out into those ranges of fairy tale wherein we behold her as "the richest heiress of her day" and finally, as the lady of a great nobleman.

In short, there is a sense in which we are right to entertain our ideal vision of Emily Dickinson as a kind of marvelous *ignis fatuus* which flits here and there through the universe lighting up various facets of human experience in its quick and brilliant way. We are right to see in her a kind of searching and (as everyone says) gallant mind playfully snatching the appointments of a meaningful existence from a society and a cosmos which she saw as chaos and disintegration. And we are right to find this spectacle both moving and inspiring. But we must remember that this ideal vision has approximately the same dispensation of great truth and great falsehood as Edmund Burke's vision of Marie Antoinette, an Elizabethan poet's image of Gloriana, or (coming closer to home) Henry James's myth of the American heiress of all the ages. Our ideal vision should not keep us from bringing what disinterested assessment we can to the particular contemplation of Emily Dickinson's poetry. The more we are determined to discover a beautiful success in every poem she wrote, the less likely we are to have any clear conception of her mind and her work.

A Poetry of Ideas

THE pervasiveness of the idea of status is clear, though its significance is not, from almost any random reading of Emily Dickinson's verse. The fact that death is the fate of all living creatures may be conveyed in a number of ways without speaking of the "estate" death confers. But Emily Dickinson, in treating this theme, characteristically calls death "the common right/ Of toads and men," the "privilege" of all. The poem beginning "Did the harebell loose her girdle" asks, in terms of a rather confused nature allegory, whether female creatures (the category seems extensive) lose caste by yielding to their lovers, and also whether the lovers lose caste (for "Eden" read "the innocent sexuality of women," and for "earl" read "lover"):

> Did the paradise, persuaded,
> Yield her moat of pearl
> Would the Eden be an Eden,
> Or the earl an earl?

There is no specific idea of sin in this poem. The specification is of status, though the exact kind of status in question is, as frequently happens, not very clear.

In "The child's faith is new" the poet, wishing to speak of the self-delusion of children, does so by saying that the child imagines himself to be a mightier sovereign than Caesar. Disillusion comes when the child perceives that men are men and not kings. If we take "My worthiness is all my doubt" to be a love poem (though as in several of the "love" poems it is disconcertingly difficult to separate the image of God from the image of the lover), we see that such terms as "worthiness," "merit," "qualities," "lowlier," "chiefest," and "elect" are preferred to the more usual vocabularies of the love lyric. Her love poems show a persistent impulse to establish lover and loved in a kind of legalized hierarchy, instead of picturing the ecstatic fusing of souls or weeping at the swift passage of time.

In nature she finds many and diverse analogies of the kinds of status she discerns among human beings and between human beings and God. There are the sovereign Alps and the meek daisies bowing at their feet. There are the queenly moon and the docile sea. There are the diamond and the coal, the alabaster, topaz, or ruby and the lowly stone; there are the regal butterfly and the vulgar buttercup.

Some of Emily Dickinson's best poems involve an idea of status. For example:

> Presentiment is that long shadow on the lawn
> Indicative that suns go down;
> The notice to the startled grass
> That darkness is about to pass.

This poem, like Marvell's "To His Coy Mistress," defines the inevitability of solar motion in terms of the fated coming of death. Yet this idea, presented in the first two lines, finds a new specificity in the second couplet, where "darkness" is imagined as a king whose heralds have already announced to a startled populace the approach of the royal entourage.

The beautiful poem beginning "There's a certain slant of light," to say no more about it here, conveys an impression that the "imperial affliction" of "despair" which enigmatically comes to us from heaven on winter afternoons endows the recipient with a kind of *noblesse oblige*—the fortitude and compassion of those who are royal but troubled and wounded.

Such a poem as "I died for beauty" does not directly pose a metaphysical problem of the relation of truth to beauty, as does Keats in the "Ode to a Grecian Urn." The emphasis is on status. It is not only in the realm of metaphysics that truth and beauty are congruent. They are equal, as two queens or dukes are equal, according to an imaginary order of rank, analogues of which may be seen throughout the universe.

Status, as we noted in the last chapter, is conferred by an influx of divine or at least mysterious energy. The poem called "The sun just touched the morning" may be taken as expressing, at a rather low level of intensity, the essence of Emily Dickinson's trope of "estates." The "morning," newly instinct with the ray of the sun, is blissfully "raised." She feels "supremer" and innocently ventures forth on her gay holiday in pursuit of her "wheeling king." Yet the "haughty" sun in its appointed course not only bequeaths the joy of queenly rank but also leaves "a new necessity." This new necessity is the renunciation of her crown, which "the morning" now loses as she flutters and staggers back to her lowly estate. The central trope of Emily Dickinson's poems could be said to be similar to the myth of Cinderella, if in the fairy tale the marriage of the heroine with the prince meant marriage with death and "living happily ever after" referred to eternity.

In her fictional use of status, as in her psychology, Emily Dickinson is akin to Melville, Hawthorne, and James rather than to Whitman, Emerson, and Thoreau. Whitman does not make much of the idea of status. For Emerson and Thoreau the soul of every man is rather too expandable and retractable ever to allow him to dispose himself into orders of rank. But Melville, though politically democratic, worked out an extensive myth of the human lot in the new world which he derived from his own secularized idea of the fall of man, and this gave him an imaginative order of spiritual, moral, and intellectual rank which occurs throughout his work. In Hawthorne the idea of status is an almost purely moral order of relation among men according to their involvement with other men or their estrangement from them. And James, the novelist of manners and morals, deals intricately with the question of status within American and European society and within the international scene, evolving finally a far-reaching mythical order of redemption in the late novels, in which the intrepid investigator might find interesting parallels to ideas of redemption entertained by our poet.

Nearly everything in Emily Dickinson's personal, cultural, and historical background brought home to her the question of status. Although certainly not a feminist, in the public, crusading, nineteenth-century meaning of the word, she shared with other intellectual women of her time an interest in "the position of women." The romantic English society novels by women authors which she avidly read in her early years were intensely conscious of rank.

Mrs. Child and Margaret Fuller—not to mention that ardent crusader for women's rights, T. W. Higginson—were strikingly on the American scene, posing to the thoughtful the problem of woman's position in a society which had abandoned the social structure of aristocracy and along with it most of the certainties as to women's rights and duties. Mrs. Browning and George Eliot, whom Emily Dickinson read and admired, were concerned with the status of feminine intellectuals as well as with that of working women. The Brontës dealt with the problem even more radically than Mrs. Browning or George Eliot, understanding the lot of women not only from the social point of view of feminism but from the point of view of their deepest biological and spiritual characteristics as these were threatened by the overbearing force of men like Rochester and Heathcliff or the inscrutable power of the universe which seemed to find special instrumentalities both for enslaving or destroying women and for providing them with the basis for their ascendancy in society, intellect, and spirit. Inevitably, Emily Dickinson's poems on Charlotte Brontë and Mrs. Browning confer royalty upon these writers. Once a plain bird, Charlotte Brontë enters heaven as a nightingale. To read Mrs. Browning's poems is to witness a general promotion among the ranks of nature: the bees become butterflies, the "low inferior grass" is newly resplendent. And Mrs. Browning's poetry impels one to place a diadem on a head already too high to crown.

Coming closer to home, we may note that although Emily Dickinson did not have to struggle for social position, she would certainly have been made aware that she already had it by the tradition of the provincial pre-eminence of the Dickinson family and also, doubtless, by her father's somber affirmations of respectability. There was indeed a tradition of spinsterhood and even poetry-writing among New England women. But though her father seems never to have pressed Emily unduly either to marry or to remain a spinster, she must nevertheless sometimes have regarded spinsterhood as a status to be explained and established. With the exception of her sister nearly all of her young women friends were married.

I would suggest, however, that these considerations are of minor importance compared with the mere fact of the existence of such a father and such a daughter within the isolated family circle. Edward Dickinson does not appear to have been an ogre of any kind; he was certainly no Patrick Brontë nor even an Edward Barrett. Yet to a "little girl" he must have seemed formidable enough, with his solemnity and his terseness, with the rigidity and anxious remoteness of his being, with his long silences and his grave legislative disposal of family matters. And Emily Dickinson, so she says, remained a "little girl" all her life; as we have seen, she often expressed her desire, particularly in the letters of about her twentieth year, to be really and exclusively a little girl. In the family circle, in short, there was status, real and symbolic. Her father was "imperial," she was "low." Yet Emily had a good deal of her father's temperament, his integrity and independence, his willingness to be outspoken, something of his austerity and of his impatience with incompetence, weakness, and confusion. Both the similarity and the dissimilarity of father and daughter compelled her to the consideration of her "estate."

If Emily Dickinson's imagined hierarchy contains only

two classes, the nobility and the commoners, we may well look to the family relationship for one influence upon this dispensation. If the lowly achieve status through ravishment by unspeakable power, we may again remember, without specific psychoanalytic intent, the relation of father and daughter. If the poems in which Emily Dickinson is most inarticulate and confused tend to divide themselves most strikingly into a series of inexplicable abstractions on the one hand and an inert substratum of concrete words on the other, we may again be justified in recalling the relationship of father and daughter. A major technical flaw in Emily Dickinson's poetry is the lack of perspicuity in her abstract words. We shall have occasion to note several ways of accounting for this failure. But the account would not be complete without recalling the possibility that the first sense of abstraction a child attains is derived from its father, a mere "presence" as compared with the palpable reality of the mother. And we should want to recall too the abstraction of myth and idea with which the daughter endows her father in response to the feelings of guilt which rise between them. The father, beheld as an aggressor, is more easily admitted to the mind of the daughter as a speechless or ineffable abstraction than in his human reality. After early childhood Emily doubtless discovered that in the passive and ineffectual Emily Norcross Dickinson she had, as she said in later years, "no mother." The defection of her mother made her relationship with her "pure and terrible" father even more exclusive than it might otherwise have been.

One might add that her father's profession undoubtedly helped to confirm the idea of status in her mind. As

Tocqueville pointed out, with its practice and theory of status, the legal profession was one of the few real analogues of aristocracy in nineteenth-century America.

And certainly of great importance is the heritage of New England Calvinism, the most legalistic of religions. There is considerable warrant in the Covenant Theology for ideas of legally defined position, since this theology was an attempt to clarify the relation of man to a capricious God by coming to an agreement with Him on where, under different conditions, He stood and where man stood. Calvinism, of course, implies a severely simple two-class order, first in its doctrine of salvation and, second, in its stress on the immediate relationship of man with God. The doctrine of justification through faith urged perpetual attention to one's status in relation to God. And as she uses it in her poetry Emily Dickinson's idea of status may be regarded as the doctrine of justification translated into a private language of romance.

The fall of man and man's sinfulness, as we have seen, play almost no part in Emily Dickinson's poetry. She does not, as Melville does, characteristically picture an Eden in which in the past the individual has lived and from which he has fallen. Nor does she, like Hawthorne, describe the ravages of sin upon the human personality. She has so much the sense of loss and desolation that she regards them as almost exclusively the quality of life. When she speaks of Eden as apart from "home," she usually means heaven, the heaven which lies in the future. She has not fallen. She *is* fallen. Her idea of sin is almost entirely confined to "conscience" and to the abdication or guardianship of the moralizing part of the mind. But even the few poems which treat of these matters show that our poet was more interested in psychology, or possibly the fated and limited quality of human action, than she was in moral judgments. She was a realist and a seer. No moralist can delve such abysses in the universe.

We have yet to specify exactly what kinds of "estate" Emily Dickinson adumbrates, and I am not sure that this can finally be done with perfect clarity. In very general language, the queenly or upper status meant to her the following things: 1) the condition of being blissfully "domestic," of enjoying a redemptive sense of fulfillment or vitality of spiritual health, a condition which may be achieved through immediate visitations of grace; 2) the achievement of mature womanhood or the involvement of oneself in the sacramental occasions of a woman's life through love and "marriage"; 3) accession to the absolute ground of immortality through death; 4) the achievement of seerhood and the station of prophetic poet, and ultimately of immortality, through beauty and truth. The lower status is simply the opposite of the upper. When one is not regal or an "Empress of Calvary," one has either missed the great transmuting experiences or, having had them and achieved regality, one has had to renounce them. Renunciation is the condition of earthly life, since the only absolute status is immortality.

For the Puritans, Perry Miller writes, regeneration was subject to only one interpretation. "It was the act of communion in which the infinite impinged upon the finite, when the misery of the fragmentary was replaced by the delight of wholeness." Grace is not likely to come to the recalcitrant soul of miserable man in any mild or contemplative moment. It is more likely to "pursue the soul, forcibly seize upon it," and, if the soul be stubborn, "violently reverse the will." As one Puritan divine said, grace is "a holy kind of violence." It does not work by "morall perswasion" but by God's "powerfull operation, and omnipotent hand put forth for such a purpose."

In her moments of what she called "rapt attention" Emily Dickinson, though late upon the Puritan scene, was capable of the ecstatic experience of grace. In the usual Christian manner, she makes "light" or "glory" the symbol of this experience:

> Glory is that bright tragic thing,
> That for an instant
> Means Dominion . . .

"Dominion" in Emily Dickinson's poetry is a resonant word. Its emphasis is particularly Puritan, since the Puritans stressed, above all God's attributes, His sovereignty. By derivation the word is related to "domestic," and in the words "dominion" and "home" one discerns the particular kind of regeneration which our poet conceives as being immediately bequeathed by grace. Thus a poem whose subject seems to be an annunciation to Eve reads as follows:

> Not when we know
> The Power accosts,
> The garment of Surprise
> Was all our timid Mother wore
> At Home, in Paradise.

In its combination of sexual imagery ("accosts") with the imagery of supernatural grace, this poem approaches the subject matter of Yeats in his poems dealing with the annunciation to Leda and to Mary. Aside from obvious differences, the basic difference between these two poets is of course that Emily Dickinson is totally unconcerned with the historical and cultural implications of the divine ravishment. The "impingement" of Zeus upon Leda is the impingement of "knowledge" and "power" upon "beauty," and the issue is Helen—that is, Greece and the Greek cycle of history. For Emily Dickinson, to be accosted by "the Power" is purely a matter of personal regeneration.

The most complete statement she made about the immediate bequest of grace is the uneven poem called "The farthest thunder that I heard." In the thunder she hears "life's reverberation" and she understands that the "explanation" of life—its meaningfulness—is to be seen in "that waylaying light" of which the reverberation constantly reminds the fortunate recipient. The "lightning," as she says, "struck no one but myself," and she

> would not exchange the bolt
> For all the rest of life.

The "waylaying light" allows us to understand the world because "every clamor bright" is "but the gleam concomitant." Yet the most precious gift of the divine visitation is that

> It founds the homes and decks the days.

Eve, we would gather, wore a gown more regal than the "garment of Surprise" after being accosted by the Power. Her days grew as opulent as is possible in this world. "Home" is the residence of bliss; it is Eden and Paradise domesticated. And "home" is the place of "dominion." In short, redemption by the immediate reception of the divine regenerative experience gives a status to domestic life—it "founds the homes"—and, as she says in a related poem, it gives a queenly dominion and imperial furnishings to the "dazzled Soul" of her whose "room" would otherwise be "unfurnished."

To Emily Dickinson, then, the idea of grace entailed the rare moment of exalted, intuitive experience which conferred a redemptive status upon her personal and domestic life. Among her contemporaries—and, I should think, over the whole range of history—only the Brontës rival her in their attempt to "domesticate myth"—to invest the domestic lot of women, that is, with a structure of imaginative meaning. And here again Emily Dickinson is typically "frugal" and Puritanical, whereas the imaginatively derived status of women presented in the Brontë novels is copiously grounded in the traditions of English tragic drama, English romanticism, and European folklore. The distinction is pointed up in Jane Eyre's rejection of the Calvinistically inclined curate St. John Rivers in favor of Edward Rochester, whereas, though she might find intimations of Rochester in him, Emily Dickinson worshiped the Calvinist Wadsworth above all men.

Our poet shares with the Brontës their sense of the desolation of women before nature, before man, and before God. But for Emily Dickinson the means towards woman's redemptive status is a personally imagined version of the Puritan idea of grace, whereas the Brontës sought to establish the status of women by marshaling the forces of domestic life on a large tragic and mythical scale in such a way as to give woman the power to combat the destruction with which nature and society threaten her.

If the reception of brilliant intuitive experiences makes life meaningful and "reverberative," there is still the need for more concrete experience. Grace, that is, must come in some bodily or actual form in order to establish a more nearly perfect communion between the fortunate recipient and the transcendent source of light. Only in this way can existence be formulated and its meaning subsumed under the few sacramental crises of one's life. Emily Dickinson does not think of her life as unfolding through all of the traditional sacramental moments of the Christian belief. There are only two important sacraments: the ceremony of "marriage" and the ceremony of death—an idea she perhaps means to convey when, in one of her letters, she remarks that "Gethsemane and Cana are still a travelled route." Though there are only two sacraments, even these two tend to be identified in some of the poems, so that the lover is unmistakably death and commitment to the grave a marriage in Heaven.

The attempt to read the poet's "love" poems in relation to any particular man whom she may have loved will always be precarious. Many of the poems speak of her passionate love for an unspecified man, of the impossibility of fulfilling this love, of the parting, the renunciation, and the making of "the white election" in the hope of meriting entrance into heaven and reunion with the loved one. Such poems as "I never lost so much but twice," "There came a day at summer's full," and "I envy seas whereon he rides" probably refer specifically to meetings and partings with Wadsworth. And Wadsworth is undoubtedly the inspiration of many other of her poems which deal with love. Yet even if all the love poems referred to a specifiable man (and most plainly do not) and even if we could in each case identify the man, we should be very little advanced toward understanding the poems. We must take seriously the statement to Higginson that the female person referred to in the poems was "a supposed person." We are rather underrating Emily Dickinson as poet and woman if we suppose this to be a mere timid disclaimer. Poets make fictions, and in fictions we meet "supposed persons." Emily Dickinson was committed to her poetry as a way of spiritual and emotional salvation. Her poetry was, then, not a mere confession of biographical facts thinly concealed by fancy. It was a large symbolic construction. Her love poems have as one of their purposes an imaginative treatment of how a woman's life may be established through its sacramental occasions.

Emily Dickinson divided the Ages of Woman into three. The first is childhood, a time of fear, deprivation, and hunger only partially brightened by a naïve sense of the preciousness of the gift of life. From the biographical evidence we gain some sense of the poet's adolescence; but the "supposed person" of the poems has no adolescence. Childhood, though it is never entirely abandoned, outwardly ends (legally ends, one might almost say) when one finds the great love of one's life. The second age ensues upon the renunciation of all the fleshly and worldly components of this love. Death is the entrance to the third age, to that immortality for glimpses of which one seeks during life. As she says in one of her poems, the "first act" is "finding"; the second is "loss"; and the third is the expedition in search of the "golden fleece." In the poems which refer to nature, such as the "Cinderella" poem called "The sun just touched the morning," the three times of day—morning, noon, and night—refer with varying degrees of specification to the three ages.

Emily Dickinson departs from the poets of her century in her idea of childhood. She does not share Wordsworth's idea that the child is a "mighty prophet." Nor does she speak of the child's creative vision in the manner of Blake. Her emphasis is usually on the child's sense of deprivation and suffering (though the romantic poets spoke of this too). Wordsworth might depict the child leaping up on his mother's arm as a mighty emperor, free and clairvoyant until the shades of the prison house closed down upon him. Blake might speak of the small fiend in a cloud who almost as soon as he leaped up in his new-born exultation sank down on his mother's breast dismayed by the repressive forces of life. But for Emily Dickinson no such great issues are involved in childhood. The overwhelming facts about childhood are weakness, fear, and the attempt to find love. As late as 1883 she wrote in one of her letters: "The ravenousness of fondness is best disclosed by children. . . . The bird that asks our crumb has a plaintive distinction." And again, in 1882, "No verse in the Bible has frightened me so much from a child as 'from him that hath not, shall be taken even that he hath.' "

We remain children in later life in so far as we are weak and deprived of life, in so far as our being is uncompleted, our consciousness not fully developed, and our power of elective decision still hampered. In no sense do we redeem or advance our adulthood by returning to either the innocence or the poetic wisdom of childhood. The romantic poets tended to regard the three ages of man as being characterized by innocence, experience, and, finally, the wisdom brought into being by a dialectic interplay of each upon the other. These poets made a fairly abrupt transition between innocence and experience, but the third age was, in its genesis at least, a turning back to the first two. Emily Dickinson, with her usual resoluteness of mind, carries out the series. For her the third age cannot finally arrive until a second abrupt transition is made, the transition to immortality, to the final revelation of truth which comes with death.

What strikes the poet about her adulthood is that "I'm different from before," that "my gypsy face" has been transfigured, and that becoming an adult is such an "eclipse" of childhood that we have difficulty remembering the actual woe that threatened "childhood's citadel." The "gypsy face" of childhood is a suitable image because it brings to mind the child's deprivation and his wandering quest for love. It brings to mind, also, his outlandishness in a world of adults, the aching sense of rejection which, we would guess from such a poem as " 'Tis true they shut me in the cold," the poet had herself sufficiently felt. Her poems express the terrible helplessness and dependence of the child who fears that the sky may tumble down on her and who waits with such unspeakable joy—mixed, it would seem, with vague apprehension—for the return of her father from a trip: she listens for the approaching train and then the coach, which takes so long to arrive that time seems to have been transfixed; then with violently beating heart she hears the footsteps in the hall, timidly greets her father, and creeps away unnoticed.

In the poems of childhood (the most instructive of which were first made available in *Bolts of Melody*), Emily Dickinson makes hunger figure prominently as a symbol of the child's powerful but undirected demands on life. She writes of the "finer famine" the child knows, comparing the child with the "starved maelstrom" which "laps the navies," with the vulture, and with the tiger whom every morsel makes a "fiercer thing." In a poem of metaphysical wit, which reminds one of Donne's "Flea," the poet plays upon the resemblance between herself and a gnat. The "living child" had subsisted on such fare as would have starved a gnat. Though "food's necessity" was on her "like a claw," there was no escape, for unlike the gnat she could not fly away, nor seek sustenance other than what was given to her. Nor had she even the art, as the gnat had, to "gad" her life out by flying into the window pane. In "Alone and in a circumstance" she contrasts herself with a spider who crawled upon her "reticence" and complains that there is no legal redress against the spider's criminal behavior, which consists in insulting her by being more at home in the universe than she is.

In "A loss of something ever felt I" she pictures the child as looking back nostalgically to the "delinquent palaces" from which she believes she has come. She says that the first emotion she can recollect was the emotion of bereavement; a "mourner," she "lurked among the children" and bemoaned "a dominion" from which she had been cast out. The idea of pre-existence, however, does not commonly occur in Emily Dickinson's poetry. The imaginative embodiment of the child's sense of loss and bewilderment was amply suggested to her by such physical facts of childhood as hunger, cold, smallness, gnats, spiders.

Though the predominant characteristics which she attributes to childhood are its weakness and its kinship with the animal and vegetable world, and though she has no such consequential notions of the child's imaginative powers and their continuation into adult life as do the romantic poets, she does not suppose that childhood is ever entirely abandoned. Indeed, she regarded herself as a "little girl" throughout her life and she made a cult of child-ishness both in her poems and (as we have noted) in her letters to such "little creatures" as the Norcross sisters. We have suggested in a previous chapter that her strangely divergent views of nature—which allow her to picture it as a kind of pretty nursery in which little creatures both animal and human are free to frolic and then again to regard it as the hostile force which imposes the hard conditions of man's tragic existence—can be reconciled in only one way: by observing that to the child's imagination both of these views are true. The real facts of nature in the mind of a child are that it is a playful world of equally sentient creatures and that it may at any time erupt into a hostile force which devours and destroys.

The most remarkable of Emily Dickinson's poems on the transition from childhood to adulthood through marriage is "I'm ceded, I've stopped being theirs." The "supposed person" exultantly proclaims herself through with the name given her at baptism (Emily herself was never baptized); her name, she says, can now be put away with her dolls and the string of spools which she has now finished threading. If we are in search of sexual symbolism (and we sometimes have to be to keep up with the poet), we may easily see in the doll a virginal woman and in the threading of the spools a ritualized sexual act. The second stanza must be quoted:

> Baptized before without the choice,
> But this time consciously, of grace
> Unto supremest name,
> Called to my full, the crescent dropped,
> Existence's whole arc filled up
> With one small diadem.

She has used here the conventional symbol of the full moon, which is related to the crescent moon as womanhood is to childhood. She adds her special image of the diadem, by which she usually means to signify the queenly estate conferred upon her by the sacramental event. Not usually a very compelling or exact image, it has in this poem at least the merit of suggesting a crown, and thus a completed circle, and of reinforcing the moon image. Perfectly typical of much of her love poetry is the representation of an experience which is both the spiritual reception of grace and union with the lover. If there had always been an ambiguous sexual component in the imagery of grace as the Puritans used it, Emily Dickinson has of all poets surely made the most consistent and determined capital out of the ambiguity.

But one must not neglect the striking affirmation of consciousness and the new power of making choices which womanhood confers. In the concluding stanza it is this which is most heavily accented. She has found her first "rank" too small. "Crowing on my father's breast," as she writes, she had been but "a half unconscious queen." The bird imagery of "crowing" is a charming relegation of the child to the animal world, to the world of semiconsciousness. The reference to the father states her new independence of him. She is now "adequate, erect" and has the power of decision:

> And I choose—just a throne.

As she says in another poem, love has given her (or the "supposed person") vision and veto. Marriage makes her a queen—that is, a woman in the second age of existence who has gained a full emotional experience, consciousness, and the power of election. Like every great event, marriage is decisive and consequential. There is nothing dubious about its influence. It confirms every tendency the woman has to emotional conservatism. "Alter? When the hills do," she exclaims. Is it possible to "rearrange" a wife's affection? she asks. And the answer is that it is possible only by expunging her femininity root and branch, by dislocating her brain, by amputating her freckled bosom, by making her bearded like a man.

So consequential is marriage, as she says in "Title divine is mine," that it implies every other great experience. On the day when she became "Wife" or "Empress of Calvary," she was simultaneously born, bridalled, and shrouded. She was born into the second age of woman, and she was shrouded, in the sense that no event of comparable significance was left to her except death, which will be, furthermore, a "new marriage" and also a new birth.

Emily Dickinson had a strong sense of the sardonic, and this is to be seen in her poems of marriage as well as elsewhere. She is not, strictly speaking, an ironic poet. Her mind has too much "economy" for that, irony being dependent upon the flexibility and variousness of mind which we find in such different writers as Sophocles and Nietzsche. She has the sardonic quality of the wry New England mind. It issues in part from the strong strain of Dickinsonian independence which always existed in her despite her constant desire to be somebody's scholar or somebody's "gnome." We are assured by her love poems that she feels no passive dependence upon the lover. The lover is rather ghostly. Very little appears to happen to him; she possesses him and the experience he brings her, and she makes the "marriage" an integral part of her life. She certainly suffered from lack of masculine love, she certainly suffered in being separated from Wadsworth. Yet we need to notice such a poem as the following to round out the picture:

> Of all the souls that stand create
> I have elected one.
> When sense from spirit flies away,
> And subterfuge is done;
>
> When that which is and that which was
> Apart, intrinsic, stand,
> And this brief tragedy of flesh
> Is shifted like a sand;
>
> When figures show their royal front
> And mists are carved away,—
> Behold the atom I preferred
> To all the lists of clay!

The fine quality of this poem, the stoical steadiness of vision, the felicity and congruence of imagery, the absence of vague abstraction make doubly forceful the magnificent sardonic realism of the idea conveyed. It is wry, realistic, unsentimental, but not contemptuous. The lover is an "atom" no doubt, but that is the tragedy of flesh. Her election of an atom is as much a witty comment on the strict limitations of human possibility as is the atom himself. And however much one may be impressed by the regality or even the divinity of human beings, they have after all only one status: they belong, every one, to the lists of clay.

But in her poems of love and marriage, as elsewhere, Emily Dickinson displays her habit of maintaining two or more very different attitudes towards the same idea. The poem just quoted is perhaps technically the best product of her strain of Stoicism (to which we shall return later). A quite different attitude toward the elected union of souls and the "new marriage" they will achieve after death is to be discerned in such a poem as "There came a day at summer's full." This poem, conjecturally referring to a visit by Wadsworth in 1861, ends with a passionate avowal that a love so consecrated that "each was to each" a "sealèd church" can be finally beatified only "At supper of the Lamb." Their bond in this world is

> Sufficient troth that we shall rise—
> Deposed, at length, the grave—
> To that new marriage, justified
> Through Calvaries of Love!

Her references to the supper of the Lamb and the "new marriage" she owes to the Book of Revelation, a frequent source of her ideas about the future life and its relation to the great events of life in this mortal world. Such poems as "My worthiness is all my doubt," "I live with him, I see his face," "A wife at daybreak I shall be" express her idea that the earthly marriage implies a heavenly marriage, that love proves the existence of immortality, that the day of the death of one who loves is also the day of his new marriage. In its true and ultimate significance the queenliness of a "wife" is a "title divine."

It is certainly not surprising that, living as she did, Emily Dickinson should have regarded the coming of a visitor as among the most striking of experiences. As an heiress of Puritanism, she was accustomed to expect visitations of the divine. As a recluse, she could not help attributing an extraordinary importance to the occasions when someone visited. Poor Higginson was rendered all but speechless by the consecrated ceremony with which she greeted him in the parlor at Amherst, gently laying a flower in his lap and speaking to him in hushed accents heavily fraught with meaning. The strange gentleman who comes to call becomes a favorite theme of her poetry. It was a theme which she tried to invest with enormous significance. The caller is sometimes death, sometimes the lover, sometimes both at once. In one or two poems he seems to be a personification of consciousness. As we should expect, the coming of the visitor confers regality upon her. She wrote a very great poem on this theme: "Because I could not stop for Death." Kindly stopping by for the poet, Death, an accomplished and well-mannered gentleman, takes her into his carriage. They enjoy a leisurely ride, noting as they ride the schoolchildren playing in a ring, the "gazing grain," and the setting sun. They pause beside a house which is also a grave. And then she puts on Death's "civility"—that is, the status of immortality.

I shall mention only three other poems of the many which either are built around or contain the theme of the mysterious visitor, in order to suggest the range of meaning which Emily Dickinson attributes to it: "A bee his burnished carriage," "The wind tapped like a tired man," and (one we have noticed already) "I think the longest hour of all."

The intent of the visiting bee is exclusively erotic. He drives boldly to the rose; he alights gallantly from his carriage; the rose withholds from his cupidity no "crescent"; their moment consummated, it remains only for him to flee and for her to be content with the "humility" of rapture. Clearly this visitor is in no sense death, but merely lover.

In "The wind tapped like a tired man," the visitor is bodiless. He enters the poet's "residence" like a ghost. She hears his "speech," which is "like the push/Of numerous humming-birds." His fingers play delicate music in a ghostly mode upon a cluster of glass pendants (of the kind which a generation ago were still to be seen in many New England houses). Then he leaves with a timid flurry. I should think that in this poem the visitor is consciousness, "that awful stranger, consciousness," to whom the poet refers in "I never hear that one is dead"—or "the accomplished guest" of "The soul should always stand ajar," if in that poem we may take this personage to mean the consciousness which the soul ought to keep itself ready to receive. The timidity and tiredness of the bodiless visitor perhaps indicate that we have to do with consciousness as a delicate or precariously surviving motion which plays in a minor mode over the hard realities of the world. Consciousness as the awful stranger has the force of revelation by grace. Consciousness as a tired musician is more akin to the neo-Platonic or pantheistic spirit which the romantic poets heard strumming delicately upon the Aeolian harp.

We might be tempted to suppose, from Emily Dickinson's conjunction of love, death, and consciousness in the "mysterious visitor" poems, that she adopts from the romantic poets an idea of personality or heroism or even, in the manner of Freud, genetically relates consciousness to erotic and death instincts. But to attribute to her thought either a myth of romantic heroism or a genetic psychology would be a mistake. The intellectual justification for making the mysterious visitor represent love, death, and consciousness is not a romantic myth or a principle of psychology but her belief that love and death are revelatory experiences through which we become conscious of the profoundest meanings of life and which confer upon the fortunate recipient a redemptive status. Clearly her allegiance in this matter is to her ancestral Puritanism rather than to more modern modes of thought. For though nineteenth-century romantic literature had its doctrines of experience and its related conceptions of the hero, it did not regard heroism as directly conferred by experience. Heroism was a distinction to be achieved through *the evolution of personality* in its experience of such phenomena as love and death, through pitting the personality against the natural universe or receiving into the personality the warlike or the benign forces of nature. Though in her personal life she tended to make a romantic hero out of Wadsworth, in her poetry she imagines no Heathcliff nor Rochester—no hero whose traffic with love and death, whose superior consciousness, have given him superhuman power and the magical personality of a figure in myth. The Puritan mind stressed experience very heavily, and when it grew imaginative or speculative rather than merely moralistic it tended to rely on experience rather than on reason. But it was not interested in "personality." The excellent or "new born" man was one who exhibited signs of redemption through those forms of experience that hinted of divine grace, one who became the "focus of experience." Emily Dickinson imaginatively donning her queenly diadem is not so much the desolate woman becoming a heroine to the romantic hero as the desolate woman sacramentally restored, the empty vessel newly replete with the redemptive effulgence. Not of course that our poet, on the whole an unbeliever, wrote conscientiously in the Puritan manner. But in her love poems, as elsewhere, Puritanism is the type and source of her imagination in its deepest and most characteristic quality.

Generally speaking, Emily Dickinson presents man, nature, and God as radically distinct. She does not share the forms of nineteenth-century naturalism which attempt to reconcile the claims of human nature with the claims of cosmic nature. She does not regard cosmic nature as in itself beneficent or health-giving or as containing primitive forms which emerge in unbroken evolution into human life. Nor does she share any of the nineteenth-century transcendental religions which deify nature by making it an emanation of God or which naturalize God by deifying nature.

> Nature and God, I neither knew,
> Yet both so well knew me
> They startled, like executors
> Of an identity.

Man is seen by the eye unafraid of fact to be passive before God and nature. Like a couple of executors—doubtless lawyers—who are managing an estate according to an inviolable will, they determine one's very identity. The poem continues by pointing out that these lawyers observe strict professional ethics:

> Yet neither told, that I could learn;
> My secret as secure
> As Herschel's private interest,
> Or Mercury's affair.

Although she is unable to understand the secrets of the cosmic executors, they easily understand hers: that God and nature have conferred upon her the right to die at their hands and that God holds out the promise that she will inherit the estate of immortality, once nature, as God's agent, has carried out his task. The reader will perceive that in imagining a world in which status is so important (is connected indeed with the idea of grace), in which there are mysteriously secretive legalistic divinities, and which is riven throughout with comic or tragic incongruities Emily Dickinson was adumbrating the work of Kafka.

The three realms of being, then, are separate but not absolutely closed and self-contained; they remain "ajar" and, in so far, open to each other. They may join forces, as when nature becomes the agent of God's will that man shall die and when (if faith does not mislead) the human soul becomes the agent of God's will that nature and death shall be transcended by immortality.

In this life it appears to us that man is a desolate pilgrim; that nature is the objective mode of death; and that God is impersonal, absolute, eternal:

> Our journey had advanced;
> Our feet were almost come
> To that odd fork in Being's road,
> Eternity by term.
>
> Our pace took sudden awe,
> Our feet reluctant led.
> Before were cities, but between,
> The forest of the dead.
>
> Retreat was out of hope,—
> Behind, a sealèd route,
> Eternity's white flag before,
> And God at every gate.

At some crucial point in our lives—perhaps it is when we have loved, renounced, and made the "white election"— we realize that the sole purpose of life is to achieve immortality. We perceive the final resting place in God, the whiteness of whose flags waving over the citadel bespeaks His unconditioned stasis, His existence outside of time and change. But first we must pass through the vicissitudes of nature: "the forest of the dead."

Emily Dickinson often represents nature as a pageant or a symbolic pantomime. The motions of nature in summer, for example, make her think of "priests" adjusting symbols or of "the far theatricals of day." Yet it would be a mistake to say that she makes nature into a mere bodiless drama, shadowing forth divine things. Nature does not symbolize God. It is true that in the sun or the lightning one may see a mode of His action, as in darkness one may see a simulacrum of His leisure or as in the ocean one may sense His width and depth. But on the whole one does not see God in nature. So far as one can perceive it, the essence of nature, beheld in relation to human life, is impermanence, anxiety, and disintegration. The essence of God is His absolute changeless repose. So striking to Emily Dickinson is this difference that she does not easily imagine any natural phenomenon to be symbolic of Deity. Except for His very general quality of repose God remains inscrutable. But nature is aggressively a fact—so consequential and inclusive a fact that it symbolizes itself. Its "theatricality" is the ritual of its destructive encroachment upon human life. Thus nature is both symbol and reality. This paradox, together with the irreparable estrangement between man and nature, renders nature unintelligible in its final essence, though there is no doubt about its function in relation to man.

> But nature is a stranger yet;
> The ones that cite her most
> Have never passed her haunted house,
> Nor simplified her ghost.

> To pity those that know her not
> Is helped by the regret
> That those who know her, know her less
> The nearer her they get.

Nature is both reality and symbol, both house and ghost. The "simplicity" of nature consists not in its essence but in its function, which is to act as the condition of man's death. We cannot know nature by getting close to it, because the closer we get to nature the closer we get to unconsciousness and death.

The transcendental doctrine of correspondences doubtless made an impression on Emily Dickinson's thinking, and it may have given her some warrant (beyond her inherited Puritanism) for talking about the symbolic and typifying function of nature. But she differed from Emerson in never doubting the estrangement of man from the cosmos. "Correspondence" was hardly the word for the sense of bereavement, alienation, and dread which man feels when he confronts nature. She could not believe in what Emerson called "that wonderful congruity which subsists between man and the world," though in fairness one must add that Emerson did not always believe in it either.

In her view of nature Emily Dickinson is more easily

compared with such a writer as Jonathan Edwards than with Emerson or the romantic poets. In speaking of Edwards, Perry Miller has said that he "went to nature and experience, not in search of the possible, but of the given, of that which cannot be controverted, of that to which reason has access only through perception and pain. . . ." If she had formulated her view of nature, Emily Dickinson would have written something a good deal like this. She was not much given to speculative thought. But there is obviously considerable philosophic activity in her verse. And this is some warrant for saying that when she reflects upon nature, she does so in the manner of Edwards and that at those moments in her poetry when "reflects" is too uncomplicated a word to describe what is going on, her imagination works with what T. S. Eliot would call the "emotional equivalent" of Edwards's theological naturalism.

Many readers will remember Emily Dickinson's treatment of nature in the spirit of light verse, her picture of the oriole or bee as this or that kind of madcap. Others will remember the little tippler and the debauchee of dew who appears to find nothing in nature but delight and gaiety. And to these readers it will seem wrong to treat the "nature" of her poems as a hostile monolithic power which she regards with dread. But there can be no doubt that she entertains both views and that she finds them mutually necessary. We have already noticed in what way this double view may be said to belong to the childhood imagination and we have pointed out that more than most poets (poets, for example, who made no cult of "little women") Emily Dickinson was likely to cling in certain special ways to her childhood perceptions. We are now in a position to observe that she found warrant both in Transcendentalism and in her inherited Puritanism for reaffirming her early sense of nature, for continuing to see nature on the one hand as an outward show of gay and delicate objects with more or less symbolic value and, on the other hand, as a hostile and awe-inspiring power. The two ideas are explicit and distinct enough to allow us to isolate them for examination. Yet she hardly ever speaks of nature in one mode without at least implying the other. And indeed, as I shall suggest in later pages, her poems can best be judged according to their success in rendering structurally interdependent two aesthetic modes—the "rococo" and the "sublime"—which are respectively analogous to the two modes in which she sees nature.

If, therefore, we look into Emily Dickinson's poems expecting her to say that nature is merely frolicsome and harmless, we shall be disconcerted at every turn. Even in such a poem as "Nature, the gentlest mother" in which nature's government of her household is "fair" and "mild," one notices that her tenderest office is to put "her golden finger on her lip" and to "will silence everywhere." The most poignant and beautiful moment of the day is evening or sunset or the return of the robin to its home or the extinction of the butterfly and the hay makers in the sea of night. And one notes too that the oriole, though beautiful, is not beneficent; he is a pleader, a dissembler, an epicure, and a thief. The bee, rapacious in his lust, visits the rose to cheat and bereave and escape. Poems such as these are written more or less off the top of the poet's mind, and so the sense of the presence of death in nature, always remarkable in the deepest levels of her imagination, is only dimly mirrored.

More profoundly conceived are the poems which stress the passivity of man before the universe, the incongruity of the relationship of man to the cosmos, the loneliness man feels in being separate from nature, and nature's cold indifference or its active hostility. The interesting but imperfect poem called "I dreaded that first robin so" expresses the agony of the newborn motion which the coming of spring forces upon the dormant soul:

> I thought if I could only live
> Till that first shout got by,
> Not all the pianos in the woods
> Had power to mangle me.

Here indeed is nature "given" as Mr. Miller writes, nature to which "reason has access only through perception and pain." And here too is the dread of recognizing one's estrangement from nature:

> I dared not meet the daffodils,
> For fear their yellow gown
> Would pierce me with a fashion
> So foreign to my own.

The dismay human beings feel at the indifference of nature, and its active hostility, is relieved only by death. Safety consists in being beyond the touch of nature:

> Safe in their alabaster chambers,
> Untouched by morning and untouched by noon,
> Sleep the meek members of the resurrection,
> Rafter of satin, and roof of stone.

Outside the tomb, the breeze laughs and the birds sing

in "ignorant cadence." The mindless process goes on through the cycles of time.

The sense of cosmic loneliness, in which, for the moment, nature herself seems to partake of the loneliness felt by man, is finely conveyed in the following poem:

> Farther in summer than the birds,
> Pathetic from the grass,
> A minor nation celebrates
> Its unobtrusive mass.
>
> No ordinance is seen,
> So gradual the grace,
> A pensive custom it becomes,
> Enlarging loneliness.
>
> Antiquest felt at noon
> When August, burning low,
> Calls forth his spectral canticle,
> Repose to typify.
>
> Remit as yet no grace,
> No furrow on the glow,
> Yet a druidic difference
> Enhances nature now.

We see nature, that is, under its most ancient, truest, and most moving aspect when in a kind of requiem it celebrates the unpassable abyss between itself and the mind and being of man. Our perception of the universe is enhanced, is rendered most exact, by "difference." For the moment, nature is not seen as actively hostile. "No ordinance is seen" appears to mean that in its present mood nature does not display her fundamental decree or law: death. The "grace"—that is, the coming of death and the immortality it bestows—seems "so gradual" that the positive thought of nature as death can be briefly suspended. In this moment of poignant loneliness, we need pay no immediate or ostensible homage to death—such may be the purport of the unintelligible: "Remit as yet no grace." The idea of nature as death need not blemish—put "no furrow on the glow"—the pure contemplation of loneliness. One may easily agree with Mr. Yvor Winters that the "intense strangeness" of this poem makes it one of Emily Dickinson's most interesting. But the lack of perspicuity in some of its particular phrases and the awkward jingle of sounds one hears in "Antiquest felt at noon" and "Repose to typify" somewhat injure this poem.

It must be said that Emily Dickinson found the gradual coming of "grace" or death the most resonant and moving of all possible poetic themes. It is present even in such a poem as

> 'Tis little I could care for pearls
>   Who own the ample sea;
> Or brooches, when the Emperor
>   With rubies pelteth me;
>
> Or gold, who am the Prince of Mines;
>   Or diamonds, when I see
> A diadem to fit a dome
>   Continual crowning me.

The reader who has understood the characteristic quality of the poet's mind will see that in this poem her subject is death. For the poem says in effect: "What need I care for earthly wealth and earthly position who am dying and who in death will be crowned a queen?" For the "ample sea" is immortality; the rubies are missiles from whose wounds we slowly die. It is the theme implicit in most of Emily Dickinson's verse. She uses it in her unsuccessful poems, like the one just cited, and in her best poems, like the following:

> There's a certain slant of light
> On winter afternoons,
> That oppresses, like the weight
> Of cathedral tunes.
>
> Heavenly hurt it gives us;
> We can find no scar,
> But internal difference
> Where the meanings are.
>
> None may teach it anything,
> 'Tis the seal, despair,—
> And imperial affliction
> Sent us of the air.
>
> When it comes, the landscape listens,
> Shadows hold their breath;
> When it goes, 'tis like the distance
> On the look of death.

Regarding human life as so precariously poised in the universe and seeing in every external event a power which wounds and destroys man as well as all merely human values, Emily Dickinson became the poet of anxiety. She confesses that "I lived on dread," and she writes that "suspense is hostiler than Death" because it does not "conclude" but merely "perishes to live anew." In the poem beginning "While I was fearing it, it came," she defends anxiety as a necessary discipline; we must continually "try on the utmost" since to put it on once and for all

> Is terribler than wearing it
> A whole existence through.

The permanent cumulative harm of small injuries, the "processes" of "dilapidation," the small "leech on the vitals," one "anguish in a crowd," the unrelenting whips that finally slay the heart—these are the substance of life. Yet she thought it still possible, barely so, to endure life and to make it meaningful. Man's cosmic position is like that of a mouse with which the cat plays—so Emily Dickinson invites God to observe in the poem beginning "Papa above!"

Nevertheless the process of disintegration has its "economy": "Ruin is formal." Within this economy, nature still allows room for various forms of human well-being and fulfillment, various royal "estates," such as are achieved by those who receive an ineffable intuitive experience, by the woman who loves, or by the poet who creates—though these estates involve great renunciations, are merely temporary, and gain a good deal of their value by being preliminary experiences of the final and absolute estate of immortality.

> After great pain a formal feeling comes—
> The nerves sit ceremonious like tombs.

Pain enlightens us as to the inexorable law, the form, by which we live and die; it opens out before us the vista of things as they are; it shows us the meager economy of our lives, which includes, however, certain "ceremonious" occasions, though these take their character from the final accession to immortality.

While we live, Emily Dickinson seems to say, a kind of *noblesse oblige* requires that we should not be craven or paltry. Feeling oneself struck, maimed, and robbed, even though one has never been the "foe of any," one must still accord "beloved recognition" to a cosmos which slays in order to enthrone. So she says in different imagery in the following lines:

> Magnanimous of bird
> By boy descried,
> To sing unto the stone
> Of which it died.

The mingled dread and delight of being the mouse with which the cosmic cat plays or the bird at which the boy throws the stone is among the most basic of our poet's emotions.

At this point, if at any, we find ourselves in a position to grasp Emily Dickinson's "philosophy." Apart from all images, symbols, and personifications, death, she seems to say, is the underlying principle of the universe. In her universe, death all but replaces God. For death is a free agent, itself beyond the necessity it imposes on human and natural life. Larger than man or nature, it transcends the boundaries which separate them. The patterns of ruin and disintegration are the archetypes of form. The gradual encroachment of death upon living beings imposes the only philosophically meaningful relationships between man and nature, the soul and the body, the forms of spiritual value and the forms of material value.

> Death is a dialogue between
> The spirit and the dust.
> "Dissolve," says Death. The Spirit, "Sir,
> I have another trust."
>
> Death doubts it, argues from the ground.
> The Spirit turns away,
> Just laying off, for evidence,
> An overcoat of clay.

The inconsistent point of view, which makes death first a dialogue and then synonymous with one of the terms of the dialogue—which makes death, that is, both a dialectical principle involving spirit and matter and identical with matter—will suggest to the reader a final philosophical incoherence. The unphilosophical tone of this poem cannot be missed. The tone is legal, as if the case were being argued in court. It is also playful, as if some kind of game were going on.

"Death is a dialogue" is a crucial poem in any discussion of Emily Dickinson. For a good deal more clearly than most it adumbrates what we may call the dialectic of death which would have been the basis of her philosophy had she developed a philosophy at all. And just as clearly this poem shows why her cast of mind is not consistently philosophical—namely, because it is incorrigibly both legalistic and playful, because, in other words it preferred as the substance of poetry an elaborately contrived private convention of status to a system of coherent ideas.

The principle of death is, however, Emily Dickinson's most strikingly characteristic and original theme. It is the idea upon which her mind most often turns. It is the idea which illuminates better than any other her most particular as well as her most general poetic statements. Philosophically considered, this principle of death is not supportable by logic. But poetically considered, it is her indispensable leading idea.

We may say that, in the manner of Jonathan Edwards, Emily Dickinson turned to nature in search of the given and the incontrovertible rather than the possible and that, for her, reason has access to nature only through perception and pain; but it would be wrong to attribute to her an elaborately conceived "idea of nature" such as we attribute to Spinoza, Wordsworth, or Edwards himself. If one sees nature as the condition of human disintegration, and as little or nothing else, one cannot be much of a naturalist, though one may have a tragic and moving and poetically fruitful sense of nature.

If fundamentally she is unable to accept nature in any of its aspects but one, the same may be said of her idea of God. Though she pictures God in a variety of ways, there is usually a note of sardonic reservation unless she pictures Him abstractly, as stasis or repose. This is the single image of God which calls forth her passionate assent. Nature is process; God is not.

It must be recognized, however, that though Emily Dickinson nearly always maintains her distinction between man and nature, and though there is no doubt about her ultimate distinction between nature and God, God does seem sometimes to be identified with nature. He is to be seen in the sunset or heard in the wind. In one poem we find the striking phrase,

> For in the zones of paradise
> The Lord alone is burned.

Yet though such poems make their bow to pantheism, few nineteenth-century poets are so little pantheistic. If pressed to make a formal statement of her idea of God (which she never did), Emily Dickinson might well have said something like this: God is the unmoved mover; He wills that we should die; He sends the imperial afflictions which gradually call us to His bosom; He moves nature, which is the concrete expression of His action and

His will; yet He remains distinct from nature because nature is perpetual process and God in His essence is perpetual "leisure." To the human being, nature seems almost entirely hostile, but God, in so far as He can be conceived as a Person, is both an "Inquisitor" and a beneficent Monarch, is both hostile and friendly.

The poet had, however, small respect for God in any of His personal guises. In a letter to Higginson she informed him that her family were "all religious, except me, and address an eclipse, every morning, whom they call their 'Father.'" She refers to God as "the father in the skies," Papa, a marauder, a burglar, a banker, and a swindler. She coyly calls herself His naughty girl and His tiny courtier. In some poems He seems indistinguishable from her lover. In "'Heavenly Father,' take to thee" she demands that God take back the Evil which He Himself created in a "moment contraband," chides Him for not trusting mankind, and apologizes to Him for His own "Duplicity." In short, she blames God for the existence of sin and Adam's fall. Even though writing playfully, she appears sincerely to find the whole idea of sin a dreary and hypocritical notion of those "faded men" who composed the "antique volume" known as the Bible. What is sin?—"a distinguished Precipice/Others must resist." A distinguished Precipice indeed! This must surely have pleased Samuel Fowler Dickinson—as also must Emily's idea that Orpheus' religion was superior to Christianity because "it did not condemn" on moral grounds. The fact is that she entirely rejected the idea of original sin. In the last year of her life she could write (lines that may remind us again of Kafka):

Of God we ask one favor,
That we may be forgiven.
For what, He is presumed to know.
The crime from us is hidden.

This strain of wry satire, however, is not directed against God so much as against conventional *ideas* of God and the hypocrisy of religion and morality. Emily Dickinson is not a moralist. She is not continuously interested in the moral condition of man or the choice of modes of conduct. Like a true visionary, she is interested in reality. Her blasphemy and satire issue from her impatience with those who allow timid conventions to misrepresent the reality of the human plight. She has no idea of sin except perhaps her instinctive assent to Edwards's tendency to think that since salvation is achieved through experience, sin consists in being obtuse to experience, or afraid of it, as are the gentlewomen of Amherst whom she describes in "What soft, cherubic creatures"—women whom one would no more "assault" than one would "a plush." The conventional ladies of Amherst are sufficient images of sin. One needs no theology in this matter, no doctrine of the fall of man. It is part of sin, as we see, to be ashamed of Deity. Those who do not fear to confront reality will leave room for the idea of God, will leave the soul this much "ajar," however ridiculous they may find Him in His personal guises.

Yet there is more than satire in Emily Dickinson's personifications of God. In His essence God is eternal repose, but the imagination, when it conceives the fate of human beings, pictures God as a Father. Her phrase "Burglar, banker, father" indicates that she imagined God to be a

Father who behaved like both burglar and banker. In His bank, one may suppose, is love, redemption, grace, and of course above all, immortality. Like a prudent New Englander, He bestows His wealth parsimoniously upon man during man's earthly existence. He displays His "duplicity" in robbing as well as disbursing. His victim is robbed of the very gifts which have been bestowed upon him and finally he is robbed of life itself. Yet it is understood between man and God that this painful cat-and-mouse game, this anxious "subterfuge" of life, is to end with the final disbursement of God's wealth: immortality. The "duplicity" or double character of God is no longer apparent or relevant to the immortal soul, which is finally united with God in His essence. The pain of life as well as the preliminary "estates" one has achieved are "guaranties" or "certificates" of immortality. Emily Dickinson's poetry is a contract or covenant with God.

Our poet's custom of dressing exclusively in white in her later years—the years of her "white election"—was her symbol of the final queenly estate, to which she would accede on the fulfillment of her covenant with God, when she passed through the "forest of the dead" and entered the city at whose gates the white flags of God were to be seen. If this accession distantly reminds us of the pilgrimage of Poe's A. Gordon Pym and of Melville's Ahab in pursuit of the white whale, or even of Henry Adams gazing with nervous astonishment at Mont Blanc after the sad death of his sister, it is partly because Emily Dickinson, like her most imaginative countrymen, was stirred more profoundly by whiteness than by any other color. For her, whiteness signified the Absolute, the final transcendence of time, change, and nature. To go "White to the White Creator" is to "adjust" oneself to the essential condition of God, who fulfills His part of the agreement by "removing" the "relative."

As we have observed, Emily Dickinson had no systematic philosophy. The substance of her intellectual life was a complex of imaginatively possessed ideas, most of which arose from her historical relation to New England Calvinism and the Romanticism and Transcendentalism of the nineteenth century. Two further tendencies of her thought were her peculiarly personal version of Stoicism and a fanciful eschatology which was partly gnostic and apocalyptic.

Although there is undoubtedly a vein of Stoicism in Emily Dickinson's mind, the critics who have noticed it most directly have probably overemphasized it. There are general affinities between Puritan and Stoic: the sense of personal innerness, the search for salvation within one's own heart, the immediate relation of the individual to God, the severe ethic, the resignation in the face of suffering, the sense of the evanescence and worthlessness of the flesh. Was not unreflecting Edward Dickinson a Stoic by nature, with what his daughter called his lonely life and his lonelier death, with his "pure and terrible" heart? Was he not, even, a latter-day Roman, with his austere earnestness, his obtuseness in matters of art, metaphysics, and theology, his legalistic turn of mind?

But there is very little in the poet's thought which belongs to the Stoic cosmology—no philosophical materialism, no consistent monism or pantheism, no doctrine of dynamic tension (though there is a poetic echo of this latter in her poems which stress the individual's sense of anxiety and dread). Her Stoicism is a part of her personal vision of the conditions of life. Occasionally she feels the Stoic's cosmic fear, as when she speaks of the mouse who

> pricks his ear
> Report to hear of that vast dark
> That swept his being back.

Sometimes she tells us that the admirable human being is he who can bear the most suffering, as in "Fate slew him, but he did not drop." Yet the truth is that the concrete detail of Emily Dickinson's imagination is very far from classical Stoicism and that the abstractions of her poetry move a good deal less toward the cosmos of Cleanthes and Marcus Aurelius than toward the occult formulations of Gnosticism.

"Consciousness," she remarks in one of her letters, "is the only home of which we *now* know. That sunny adverb had been enough, were it not foreclosed." The decisive event in time, she seems to say, is the destruction of the present and the mysterious opening out of the future. "Not what the stars have done, but what they are to do, is what detains the sky." Accordingly her mind is continuously eschatological, much more so than the Stoic philosophy will allow. It is true that throughout her adult years she entertains doubts about immortality. "Do you think we shall 'see God'?" she asks in 1858. In 1859 she asks, "Does God take care of those at sea?" And again, in 1883, "I cannot tell how Eternity seems. It sweeps round me like a sea." "Are you certain there is another life?" she asks, also in 1883. "When overwhelmed to know, I fear that few are sure." Yet despite these hesitancies it remains true that whatever residual religious belief Emily Dickinson retained was directed towards the future life. "I believe we shall in some manner be cherished by our Maker," she writes in 1882, "that the One who gave us this remarkable earth has the power still farther to surprise that which he has caused. Beyond that all is silence. . . ."

Intimations of the future state Emily Dickinson constantly felt. Almost any moving experience might summon immortality to her mind. After Higginson's first visit to her in 1870, she wrote him that "Abroad is close tonight and I have but to lift my hands to touch the 'Heights of Abraham.'" If her friend Mr. Bowles seemed somehow magnificent to her, it was because he already lived in eternity. "You have the most triumphant face out of Paradise, probably because you are there constantly, instead of ultimately." And again: "Immortality as a guest is sacred, but when it becomes as with you and with us, a member of the family, the tie is more vivid. . . ." This extraordinary generalization of immortality, outside of history, church, and dogma, clearly has the quality of Gnosticism. For, like the Gnostic believer of all ages, Emily Dickinson makes of immortality an almost omnipresent magic power, a generalized force which is "sacred," "vivid," "triumphant," and so on, and which may be mysteriously attendant upon any striking event.

Also in the Gnostic manner is her occasionally indulged habit of obscuring the fact of death by speaking as if through suffering or receiving revealed truth the fortunate individual may already possess immortality in this life. But the most strikingly Gnostic strain is to be seen in her constant insistence that immortality is a form of knowledge. It is the fullest illumination—"the illumination that comes but once"—and the knowledge of truth which one receives through revelatory experiences during mortal life is merely a dim, preliminary shadowing forth of the truth immortality vouchsafes to us. And finally there is a certain kinship in her position to Gnosticism's peripheral relationship to Christian belief, which makes it possible for her to accept some of the myths of Christianity without accepting the dogma. Her rejection of the dogmas of original sin and redemption through Christ (whom she regards merely as a type of sufferer and as a sort of companion en route to immortality) allows her to affirm that "Paradise is of the option." This implies a kind of thought-magic which is like the Gnostic's overestimation of the efficacy of "knowing." In these purlieus of spiritualism she came uncomfortably close to adumbrating Christian Science.

Though Emily Dickinson's religion of immortality may be loosely described as "mystical," she was surely not a mystic in any closely defined sense of the word. On this point one must agree with Mr. Yvor Winters who writes that, although such a poem as "Great streets of silence led away" is concerned with the mystic experience of immortality, it is not itself a mystic poem. Her poems on immortality, as Winters says, dramatize an idea of salvation, and they do so in such a way that the idea is poetically presented but that the experience is not immediately possessed and rendered, as in a genuine mystic poem it must be. Our poet understood the mystic experience, the totally engaged contemplation of the eternal, beatific light, and she sometimes wrote about it as an idea—as when she speaks of the "rapt attention" to immortality.

But she never tries directly to render the experience itself. She is no St. Catherine, no John of the Cross. A true product of New England Puritanism, her vision of the Godhead never entirely transcends the gross facts of experience and never entirely eludes the intervention of ideas. And if Emily Dickinson was not in the strict sense a mystic, she was not, in any significant sense, a Catholic. The argument that her poems show her to have turned toward the Catholic religion is not supported by the evidence.

Emily Dickinson's love of the Book of Revelation may seem odd in a poet so little given to elaborate myths and allegories. It is her eschatological tendency, of course, which makes Revelation her favorite book of the Bible. "Fabulous to me are the men of the Revelations who 'shall not hunger any more,' " she exclaims. And: "I have read of home in the Revelations, 'Neither thirst any more.' " Was not this marvelous book written specifically to appeal to the poor, the humble, the deprived, the desolate, the solitary soul who lived in the remote corner of a heartless heathen empire? Did it not hold out a vision of "new marriage" to the disappointed soul? of the ascendancy of the humble as kings and priests unto the splendid regal court of God? of the blessed life in store for those who wear white raiment? of power, riches, wisdom, strength, honor, and glory? of rich food? of living waters? of gold, silver, and precious stones? of jasper and onyx, of emerald and amethyst? of fine linens and scarlet silk? of cinnamon and odors, ointments and wine? Our poet was always enough of a "little girl" to fear hunger and privation and inferiority and to regard with wide-eyed wonder such fantasies of wealth and regal splendor as she found in Revelation. Nor did this Book trouble her with the dogmatic morality or the command of faith which Christianity elsewhere levied. It promised, simply, to bestow fitting rewards on the worthy. The pre-eminent act of Christ for John, as for Emily Dickinson, was his death. For these reasons, she turned to a book which, had the reasons not been compelling, she must surely have found a flamboyant and possibly ridiculous fantasy. Her "littleness" and her weakness and her frustration inspire her dreams of the royal estate of the future:

> God made a little gentian;
> It tried to be a rose
> And failed, and all the summer laughed.
> But just before the snows
> There came a purple creature
> That ravished all the hill;
> And summer hid her forehead,
> And mockery was still.
> The frosts were her condition;
> The Tyrian would not come
> Until the North evoked it.
> "Creator! shall I bloom?"

Emily Dickinson's eschatological cast of mind, on the whole a departure from New England Puritanism, was entirely a personal vision of life and has no direct historical or social implications. Yet it places her in distant spiritual kinship with those revolutionary movements within Christianity which have justified social radicalism by their vision of future things. If she does not have their program of social revolution she does have their iconoclasm, their general lack of reverence for the institutions and conventions of the world they live in. Her irreverence extends to God in all His personal guises, and the poet who juxtaposes the words "burglar, banker, father" has as little conventional respect for the eminent personages of heaven as of earth.

So much one may say about Emily Dickinson's thought. In her imaginative life she lived with a loose and sometimes mutually contradictory complex of ideas historically akin to Calvinism, Romanticism, Transcendentalism, Stoicism, Gnosticism, and even revolutionary Futurism. Philosophically considered, it is a hopelessly confusing creed. Considered as the background of a body of poetry, her complex of ideas helps to account for the extreme unevenness of her poems and for the vague, obscure, and fragmentary quality many of them have. The strongest influence on her thought was undoubtedly Calvinism and to her historical relation to this religion we must attribute much of what is pre-eminent in her work. Had not Calvinism been so much stronger than the other elements of her thought, it is inconceivable that she would have been the poet whom we now remember.

With this curious mixture of ideas Emily Dickinson constructed her private poetic convention of redemptive status. Having observed somewhat how an "imperial" status comes to the woman who domesticates grace, to the "wife" who loves, and to the justified soul which puts on immortality, we must turn to the question of the poet and his poetry.

The Idea of Poetry

POETRY is one of the "estates" to which those who are capable of seeing the truth may aspire. Through his poems, the poet, while still in mortal coils, wears the crown and assumes the throne of those who accede to immortality. Like a number of Emily Dickinson's other poems, the rather absurd "God made a little gentian" (quoted in the last chapter) may be read as the biography of a modest candidate for the heavenly accolade who, despite the contumely of public opinion, achieved the royal purple of immortality through death, or as the biography of a modest poet who tries to bloom in a magnificent flowering, is mocked, but becomes immortal through her poems. The poet, to whom above all men truth is revealed through intuitive experience, has the same grandeur and the same claim upon our reverence as the grace-inspired, the lover, and the dying.

Emily Dickinson's views on art and the artist are not without subtlety and insight. But they are more conventional than her views on other matters. It has been well said that with some few exceptions American writers have traditionally shown themselves to be intensely interested in every craft but that of writing. She did concern herself with the nature of poetry, and the technique of her verse has been of interest to later poets. Yet no more than Melville and Emerson and Whitman did she ever conceive of the kind of professional interest in poetic technique which has been part of the equipment of later writers like Yeats and Joyce. The final publication of a variorum edition may show her to have been more of a technician than she now seems. But one supposes that whereas her experiments were often bold and sometimes brilliant, they were hardly made on the basis of any consistent or elaborate aesthetic theory.

Her idea of the poet was thoroughly conventional. Mr. Emerson had said that the poet was a seer. And Emily Dickinson, in "This was a poet," tells us that the poet is a "discloser." He has, furthermore, an "hermetic mind." The revealer of truth, he is the greatest of mortals. The artistic genius is not fundamentally distinguishable from the religious prophet. Poetic utterance is an upwelling or outpouring of the soul, and the poet is as capable of receiving sublime revelatory experience as he is of uttering its message. Emerson spoke of the outpouring of genius as "that redundancy or excess of life which in conscious beings we call *ecstasy*." Genius, according to Emerson, also involves the openness of man to profound experience. If this influx-efflux theory, as it might be called, seems to make of the poet a kind of cosmic pipe or bellows, it at least has the advantage of stressing the quality of possession by some apparently automatic higher power which critics from Socrates to Santayana have attributed to the process of poetic creation. Emily Dickinson believed that the poet was indeed possessed at the moment of utterance by that "spectral power in thought that walks alone." Her belief that every great mental experience is received as grace is received and that the poet is a truth-teller whose poem attempts to render revealed truth is fundamentally no different from Emerson's idea of genius.

She perhaps differs from Emerson in stressing the difficulty of receiving and uttering poetic truth, in the struggle and agony of the soul which the process may involve. In one of her letters she refers to Jacob as "pugilist and poet," and she seems to be thinking of Jacob as she did in her poem called "A little over Jordan," wherein she speaks admiringly of the wily and determined "wrestler" who will not let go of his divine adversary until he has been subdued and has granted Jacob his blessing. The union of the human agency with the divine revelation which results in the genuine poetic experience is arduous and difficult. Melville used the same myth in his short poem called "Art." Though his point of view was somewhat different, his theme was also the difficult struggle the poet has in making "unlike things . . . meet and mate,"

> . . . fuse with Jacob's mystic heart,
> To wrestle with the angel—Art.

Melville would also have agreed that the artist is a teller of truths, the blackest as well as the brightest.

Of greater interest than her ideas about the poet and genius are Emily Dickinson's notions about the origin or impulse of poetry. She thought that poetry issued from pain, from the suffering involved in personal relationships or in beholding the naked threat of the cosmos to human existence. Poetry was a kind of creative agent for suffering. "I sing," she told Higginson, "as the boy does of the burying ground, because I am afraid." Or she sings because her verses "just relieve" a "palsy" which she feels when her attention is troubled by a "sudden light on orchards, or a new fashion in the wind." If such apparitions from the purlieus of nature bring the mind close to insanity, this also may be the occasion of poetry. For poetry is a form of divine madness. "A wounded deer leaps the highest," and to the "discerning eye," "much madness is divinest sense."

Song is universal among living creatures, from the inspired utterances of man to the humming or singing of those "patient laureates" the insects and birds. All of sentient life joins in a hymn in praise of the cosmos which destroys it, as the magnanimous bird sings to the stone of which it dies. Poetry, she seems to say in "One joy of so much anguish," is an extended "inquiry" into why her spirit is "ravished," an inquiry which, however, can never receive a complete answer short of the death of the inquirer. Poetry originates, then, in the most urgent personal dilemmas, and in so far as it is not a purely automatic process, its purpose is to relieve suffering, to make pain bearable, and at most to suggest to the suffering soul the final purpose of its travail. It would never have occurred to Emily Dickinson that a poem might have a primarily metaphysical origin, or that anyone would write a poem out of a desire to create a finished and formal object of art.

As for the poem as a formal object, Emily Dickinson gave her assent to such Emersonian pronouncements as: "It is a proof of the shallowness of the doctrine of beauty as it lies in the minds of our amateurs, that men seem to have lost the perception of the instant dependence of form upon soul. There is no doctrine of forms in our philosophy." It was almost inevitable—and it is hardly a matter for regret—that she should have followed so unquestioningly the Transcendentalist conventions of her time in aesthetic theory. Her Puritan tradition sometimes modified her thinking for the better. But it was hardly equipped to do so in poetics, since it had always regarded poetics with suspicion and had preached plain speaking as well as plain dealing.

Accordingly, the first question she asked of Higginson when she sent him her poems in 1862 was not Is my verse intelligible, coherent, and beautiful? but Is it "alive?" If the reply had been that her verse was an organism vibrant with universal spirit, she would have considered herself a poet. Higginson told her that her poems were indeed alive but that they were metrically "spasmodic" and "uncontrolled"—which was true but not profound. Later she sent more poems with the question whether these were more "orderly" and the confession that "when I try to organize, my little force explodes and leaves me bare and charred." Her best poems belie her confession, though the majority do not. In her best poems she achieves the formal perfection which it would never have occurred to her to describe abstractly or to adopt as the goal of composition.

Her lack of interest in the purely theoretical formulation of ideas is nowhere so striking as in the disparity between her best poetic practice and her few statements about it. In a letter to Higginson she speaks of poetry as if it were made by taking a suitable thought and then putting it in the "gown," though anyone can see that in her successful poems something more complicated has happened than the mere fanciful decoration and embellishment of an idea. Her own method of distinguishing poetry from non-poetry was entirely simple. "If I read a book and it makes my whole body so cold no fire can ever warm me, I know *that* is poetry. If I feel physically as if the top of my head were taken off, I know *that* is poetry. These are the only ways I know it. Is there any other way?" Such a view is by no means contemptible, for though there are other ways and though one ought to employ them, poetry is something which is either experienced along the nerve or not experienced at all. One cannot wish that Emily Dickinson had forsaken her kinaesthetic ecstasies and devoted herself to the pretty meters Higginson offered her as an ideal or even to the Whitmanesque free verse he seems also to have offered her. No purely technical formality or informality open to her could have notably improved her verses. For coherence she tended to substitute a dogged Puritan severity which gave her utterances coherence only up to the point where it began to be unable to encompass all that she wished to say—at which point she was accustomed to take refuge in her vague, aspiring, abstract words. There was in fact remarkably little either in her temperament or in her background which made the theory and practice of coherent form available to her.

In asking Higginson whether her verse was "alive," she was implicitly subscribing to the doctrine current during her impressionable years which held that nature and spirit were superior to poetry, and that poetry ought to be measured against them rather than against principles belonging to the realm of poetry alone. Consequently her opinion of the relation of poetry to nature may help us to discover what she thought about poetry as a form, in so far as she thought about it at all. Her famous aphorism that "Nature is a haunted house, but art a house that tries to be haunted" clearly suggests that she took poetic form for granted, as if it were something sufficiently given or implied by the mere attempt to write a poem. The form—the "house"—was in some unexplained way already provided; the task of the poet was to breathe spirit, life, and beauty into it. This aphorism, which is one of Emily Dickinson's very few explicit utterances on poetic form, agrees with the transcendentalist doctrine of the congruence between the forms of nature and the forms of thought. And it also has a striking similarity to the traditional Puritan metaphor which pictures unregenerate man as an empty vessel longing to be filled by the ravishment of grace.

Emily Dickinson's idea of beauty is the most impressive aspect of her aesthetic credo. She derived it directly from her central vision of man's suffering and his redemption, and accordingly it is a good deal more substantial than most of her other ideas on poetry. Her idea of beauty is closely derived from her New England ancestors, though it also has broad origins in traditional Christianity. Jonathan Edwards, writes Perry Miller, developed the thesis that the visible universe was "an emanation of God for the pure joy of creation, in which the creatures find their justification by yielding consent to the beauty of the whole even though it slay them." As she did with every idea of her religious background Emily Dickinson took imaginative possession of this one, ignored the theological dogma involved (for she had no notion of the universe as an emanation of God), and added to it her personal eschatological myth. Beauty is the name she gives to the joyful ecstasy with which we perceive that nature is slaying us towards the consequent working out of redemption. Thus she often connects the idea of beauty with the inexorable encroachment of nature, as in "Beauty crowds me till I die." Even the gayest flower takes some of its gaiety from the poetic perception that beauty is an "affliction." Like everything else man cherishes, like everything else that gives him his redemptive status, the experience of beauty is won through the anguish and struggle which end only in death. "Delight becomes pictorial" when it is "viewed through pain." And

> Essential oils are wrung:
> The attar from the rose
> Is not expressed by suns alone,
> It is the gift of screws.

Beauty is involved in the universal fate of man; like truth it is directly revealed to anyone who can behold it, to anyone who "yields consent to the beauty of the whole." To behold beauty and to partake of its redemptive power one must consent to the disintegrative process of nature, to the destructive action of God against man: "How vast is the chastisement of beauty, given us by our Maker!"

One of Emily Dickinson's best poems brings up the familiar question of how beauty and truth are related.

> I died for beauty, but was scarce
> Adjusted in the tomb,
> When one who died for truth was lain
> In an adjoining room.

> He questioned softly why I failed?
> "For beauty," I replied.

"And I for truth,—the two are one;
We brethren are," he said.

And so, as kinsmen met a night,
We talked between the rooms,
Until the moss had reached our lips,
And covered up our names.

We have already suggested that this equating of beauty and truth implies no metaphysical relationship, but that it does imply a kind of legalized status. We may now add that beauty and truth are focuses of experience, intensified moments of our perception of the universe and man's destiny in it. They produce such similar ecstatic emotions in the percipient soul as to be indistinguishable. They are nothing but the moments in which we experience with the greatest intensity and joy the full sense of our destiny. These moments of experience have a place in the poet's hierarchy of redemption which puts them above all other experiences: they are "royal" or "Tyrian" or "emerald."

It will be noted that in the poem I have quoted above, she does not write that she died *by*—through the action, that is, of the destructive power of nature which is beauty. She says that she died in the name of or in pursuit of beauty, whereas the gentleman died in the name of or in pursuit of truth. In other words, she is identifying beauty and truth with "immortality," and this is the only sense in which she may be said to have tried to give beauty and truth a metaphysical meaning. But it is hardly more than one of her Gnostic assertions. And the great power of the poem lies in the remarkable feeling of the impotence and limitation of the human condition and of man's consciousness and the inevitable engulfment of man in the natural world.

There is, to be sure, another order of truth and beauty in Emily Dickinson's aesthetic credo, though it takes all of its larger meanings from the relation to nature, death, and immortality which we have just been examining. I refer to the factuality, the clear and unillusioned perception of ordinary natural things for which she has often been justly praised. It is part of her notion of poetry that the poet

> Distills amazing sense
> From ordinary meanings,
> And attars so immense
> From the familiar species
> That perished by the door . . .

Wordsworth had certainly shown that much could be done with "ordinary meanings." And had not Emerson written that "the invariable mark of wisdom is to see the miraculous in the common"? Few poets, at any rate, have excelled Emily Dickinson in the deployment of common objects to convey the awful pathos of ordinary life suddenly seen in relation to death. For example, the thimble, fly, and cobweb in the marvelous poem called "How many times these low feet staggered":

> Stroke the cool forehead, hot so often,
> Lift, if you can, the listless hair;
> Handle the adamantine fingers
> Never a thimble more shall wear.
>
> Buzz the dull flies on the chamber windows;
> Brave shines the sun through the freckled pane;
> Fearless the cobweb swings from the ceiling—
> Indolent housewife, in daisies lain!

Emily Dickinson is wonderfully perceptive of fact, a good deal more precisely so than is Whitman, for all his sensory voraciousness. Yet the humble order of fact, when she begins to think of it as truth or beauty, becomes resonant of something beyond itself, of death and immortality. She can sometimes feel that

> Faith is a fine invention
> For gentlemen who see;
> But microscopes are prudent
> In an emergency!

but one may conjecture that if the poet looks through her microscope, she is sure to see a microbe putting on immortality.

> I like a look of agony,
> Because I know it's true;
> Men do not sham convulsion,
> Nor simulate a throe.
>
> The eyes glaze once, and that is death.
> Impossible to feign
> The beads upon the forehead
> By homely anguish strung.

It is inescapably an article of Emily Dickinson's belief that however beautiful or exciting familiar things are, the poet's function is to represent them not only as they are in themselves but as they are in their relation to the "attars" (that is, the intimations of death and immortality) which may be distilled from them.

Though she never phrased it fully, Emily Dickinson's practice of poetry shows that at its best it was an ecstatic notation, tenacious and precise, of her personal observation of death and her personal hope of salvation. But at its worst, her practice of poetry might be described as the monotonous, fragmentary, and vague verbalization of an uncertain mind in breathless pursuit of meaningless abstractions. Her poetic credo leaves ample room for the indulgence of her spiritualistic tendencies. Her declarative mood is certainly the one we admire, her subjunctive mood the one with which we feel uneasy. She often thought of poetry as a place where anything can and should happen, as distinguished from prose, which was more limited and more ordered. This attitude, which is directly in contrast to the more profound part of her mind and is the convention of a debased romanticism, must be taken into account if one is to gain a complete idea of her imagination. In her cultivation of poetry as "Possibility," she of course had the entire support of the admired sage of Concord, who had written such sentences as this: "The perception of real affinities between events, (that is to say, the *ideal* affinities, for those only are real), enables the poet thus to make free with the most imposing forms and phenomena of the world, and to assert the predominance of the soul." She was capable of taking such fatuous platonizings to heart in support of her Gnosticism.

Emily Dickinson makes free with the most imposing form and phenomena of the world by her unique manipulation of words, which she tended to regard as magic counters capable of doing anything. Her cultivation of language is, to be sure, her strength as well as her weakness. One must agree with Richard P. Blackmur that in Emily Dickinson's verse, as in Whitman's, the only technical "weapon constantly in use is . . . the natural aptitude for language." She made constant use of her lexicon. And to a very good purpose, her vocabulary being undeniably rich, subtle, and strikingly original. But the ever-present lexicon promised too much, and the poet who consulted it was often too eager to find within its covers some marvelous word, like attar, extrinsic, cochineal, plush, or phosphor, which would body forth a complicated range of meaning. There was much in the Transcendental doctrine in support of her faith that there could be no radical disjunction between verbal discourse and non-verbal reality. For though she was capable of writing that "The broadest words are so narrow we can easily cross them, but there is water deeper than those, which has no bridge," in practice her assumption was that there was a word for everything except, perhaps, the reality imperfectly rendered by "immortality":

> I found the phrase to every thought
> I ever had, but one;
> And that defies me. . . .

One might also say that her poetry was written in the hope of some day finding the magic phrase, some revelatory fusion of such words as noon, blaze, mazarin, circumference, and recess. And however often she might remind herself that some waters cannot be verbally bridged, she never doubted that every "broad word" allows us to make some sort of crossing. The truth is that many of her broad words are not bridges but merely vague and meaningless gestures of the aspiring soul. The following poem may be taken as one of her least successful ones; it is an exceptionally bad poem, an examination of which will indicate a fundamental weakness of her work:

I can wade grief,
Whole pools of it,—
I'm used to that.
But the least push of joy
Breaks up my feet,
And I tip—drunken.
Let no pebble smile,
'Twas the new liquor,—
That was all!

Power is only pain,
Stranded, through discipline,
Till weights will hang.
Give balm to giants,
And they'll wilt, like men.
Give Himmaleh,—
They'll carry him.

The "broad words" here are *push, drunken, liquor, power*, and *Himmaleh*. These words are used differently from *grief, joy, pain*, and *balm*, which though "broad" in the sense of being general or abstract do not have quite the quality the poet means when she calls a word "broad." They are used, that is, to evoke nothing much beyond what is usually evoked by any writer who uses them. They are not being used as magic gestures, they do not have the air of throwing bridges out into space in the confident hope of crossing abysses. She uses the word *push* to suggest the act of ravishment such as is experienced by those who receive influxes of joy from beyond the flesh. The person in the poem is *drunken* in the sense of being ecstatic with love, grace, immortality or whatever this "new liquor" may be. *Power* is simply a vague honorific term for some unspecified superior ability of those who are in touch with infinity. *Himmaleh* is synonymous with *liquor*, which is synonymous with such words as *Arabia*, *Potosi*, *emerald*, *blaze*, *Eden*, *firmament*, *Apennine*, *sea*, and *circumference*.

The poem is certainly incoherent as a rational statement and as a system of images. The pools of grief are bathetic, especially if the person in the poem insists on wading in them. "Breaks up my feet" is inconceivable. It will hardly do to tip the drunken person into the pools of grief, if that is what happens. "Let no pebble smile"—which means "let the drunken person not be mocked by the vulgar, the unfortunate, the unredeemed"—is inadequate to what it wishes to say, and the pebble is imperfectly established in the metaphorical realm of discourse it implies.

In the second stanza the person is no longer in the pool and is perhaps not being referred to at all. The poet begins here to speak of what is true of all men. Man is imagined, apparently, to be stranded on earth, as a fish might be on shore, and struggling to escape into the sea of immortality. As he gradually stands up, or takes off, the weights, no longer pinning him to the ground, will swing free, as from his shoulders. Even giants, if given balm—that is, merely earthly medicaments—will wilt. But give them a draft of Himmaleh and they will carry him, or them—at any rate they will be no longer stranded or wilted.

No great poet has written so much bad verse as Emily Dickinson. It is nearly incredible that she who wrote "Safe in their alabaster chambers" and "All circumstances are the frame" could also have written "I can wade grief." Yet though few of her poems are so bad in detail as this one, perhaps two thirds of her work is flawed by the weaknesses this poem so graphically displays.

Emily Dickinson's habit of shuffling oddly disparate words like *Himmaleh, liquor, blaze,* and *infinite* into her poems as if they were synonymous, or at least generally suggestive of the same thing, is analogous to her similarly free shuffling about of crucial or sacramental experiences. Convinced that death and the putting on of immortality constituted the one great and typical experience, she accordingly felt no compunction about treating other experiences as if they all had the same quality as this great and typical one. A visionary to whom truth came with exclusive finality, she assumed that every experience in life was typical of every other, in so far as it was an analogue or "reverberation" of the truth revealed by grace to the dying. Is it possible to say what the following poem is about?

> He fumbles at your spirit
>   As players at the keys
> Before they drop full music on;
>   He stuns you by degrees,
>
> Prepares your brittle substance
>   For the ethereal blow,
> By fainter hammer, further heard,
>   Then nearer, then so slow
>
> Your breath has time to straighten,
>   Your brain to bubble cool,—
> Deals one imperial thunderbolt
>   That scalps your naked soul.

Mr. Whicher plausibly suggests that this poem may describe how Emily Dickinson felt while listening to one of Wadsworth's sermons. Yet "he" might be God bestowing the ravishment of grace, a lover consummating their love, the cosmos encroaching upon her unto death, or even Death himself. The poem certainly implies her aesthetic belief that ecstatic moments identify poetry as poetry.

The trouble with this poem is that though its verbal texture is very good, very eloquent and moving if considered by itself, the poem does not refer to anything more specific than a generalized experience. When we begin to wonder what exactly the poet is talking about, we perceive that we are dealing with "ambiguity." But this poem is ambiguous in the bad sense. The implied meanings are shuffled around too easily and within too ill-defined a context. A poem must display a certain amount of resistance to being taken ambiguously in order to generate the feeling of excitement and the sense of complexity and wonder derivable from a poem which makes successful use of ambiguity. Emily Dickinson's use of disparate orders of abstract words and proper nouns as if they were all suggestive of the same thing and her similar use of different orders of experience represent that basic failure of resistance in ambiguity which is one of the flaws in her poetry. I do not mean to imply that all good poetry must make use of ambiguity. But the fact is that given her particular cast of mind, her work offers many opportunities for this device. And so one's demand upon her must often be for good ambiguity as against bad. Again, I do not mean to imply that this question is necessarily pertinent to each of her poems.

Emily Dickinson was like her Puritan forebears, severe, downright, uncompromising, visionary, factual, sardonic. Within her vision of things there is room for considerable complexity. But when she attempts to widen the purview of that narrow vision, all is more than likely to be lost in a featureless generality. The ecstatic notation of personal existence could often become a vague aspiration of mind toward Gnostic ineffabilities. Her economy of mind was in itself a kind of warrant for her enormous generalities. "*One* is a dainty sum!" she exclaims in a letter. "One bird, one cage, one flight; one song in those far woods, as yet suspected by faith only." To which might be added: one father, one mother, one brother, one sister, one house, one room, one garden, one dog, one love, one life, and one death. Her private experience led her as inexorably as Whitman's public and generalized experience led him to the practice of what Tocqueville predicted would be the generality and abstraction of American poetry.

Neither in her thought nor in her style is Emily Dickinson influenced in any particularly demonstrable way by literary sources. Her style is a tissue of words from her lexicon, from the hymns and sermons she had heard from childhood, and from the legal terminology of her father's profession (Miss Taggard has listed well over two hundred legal words from the letters and poems). She might on occasion take such words as "circumference" from the essays of Emerson or possibly from Sir Thomas Browne. She might be indebted to "Ik Marvel" for the word "anthracite." In some of her "nature poems," she could occasionally echo the verses of Emerson. Dr. Henry Wells has noticed that "When I see not, I better see" is a deliberate paraphrase of Shakespeare's sonnet beginning "When most I wink, then do mine eyes best see." The body of her work contains evidence of a few other specific influences. But generally speaking, her verse is not literary in its reference. On one occasion she apologizes for a line in a poem she had sent Higginson because she had later realized that the line had been unconsciously imitative of something she had read. It was a part of her independence and of her poetic credo to avoid particular verbal or stylistic influences; she would, as she declared, "never consciously touch a paint mixed by another person."

Yet she read considerably, a good deal more so, we may suppose, than can be determined from her references to reading in her letters and poems. She must surely have read better, with more seriousness and ingenuity, than one might gather from the tone in which she often speaks of her books. Her poems on the subject are not commendable, content as she is to compare books with frigates and pages of poetry with prancing horses. Again she writes with a kind of "Ik Marvel" luxury of sentiment that books are those endearing companions to whom one turns after tired days; one's "small library" promises "banquetings to be." She hears bells delightfully ringing when she gazes at the "countenances bland" of "these kinsmen on the shelf." Such poems were written, doubtless, under the impression that there was a necessary convention, a particular literary style, in which one must write about literature.

Besides the books she read in her teens and twenties in connection with her schooling and in company with such intellectual companions as Leonard Humphrey, Benjamin F. Newton, and her brother Austin, her father's library was always available to her—the books which she described (perhaps because Edward Dickinson read them) as "*lonely* and *rigorous*." In this library she would have found the histories of Hume, Macaulay, Motley,

Bancroft, and Prescott; such sound essayists as Jeffrey, Carlyle, and Sydney Smith; as well as political books by Hamilton, Webster, and Jefferson; travel books, a complete Shakespeare, Washington Irving, the standard English poets—the books, in short, which a conservative mid-century American lawyer might possess in firm contradistinction to these "modern literati" who fell so far short of the old authors.

Of ancient literatures, Emily Dickinson makes scarce mention. The one exception is of course the Bible ("The Bible dealt with the Centre, not with the Circumference"). Her favorite Book is, as we have noted, Revelation. But she knew the whole Bible intimately; she speaks several times of Moses, for example—for whom she has a partiality because he spent his life looking forward to the Promised Land and smashing graven images. In the New Testament she favored Paul, after Revelation: "The sunshine almost speaks this morning," she writes in a letter, ". . . . and Paul's remark grows graphic, 'the *weight* of glory.'" Of classical antiquity she knows little and speaks less. In one of her poems on reading she refers (with dubious chronology) to the time

> When Plato was a certainty,
> A Sophocles a man,

but her classical allusions are sparse indeed. There is almost no use of Greek myth in her verse, though she might have found much there relevant to the characteristic tropes of her imagination. One of her few allusions shows that she pronounced Amphitrite without the final syllable.

There are one or two references to Dante, and, as Mr.

Whicher has pointed out, one of her poems shows that she pronounced Beatrice in the Italian manner. But there is no sure proof that she ever read Dante or that she knew Italian, or any language but English. Shakespeare she seems to have read with the greatest devotion, and it would be wonderfully enlightening if one could trace the influence of Shakespeare on her work as one can do in the case of Melville. But there were elements in Melville's view of things which found such ready relationship to elements in Shakespeare that the lesser man was able to make a series of striking and useful appropriations from the greater. This possibility was not so much open to Emily Dickinson. The direct influence of Shakespeare upon her work remained peripheral and verbal if also continuous. "Beloved Shakespeare" was a staunch companion. "Touch Shakespeare for me" she implores her friend Mr. Bowles as he embarks for England. On the occasion of his first interview with her, Higginson wrote in a letter: "After long disuse of her eyes [this was in 1864-65] she read Shakespeare and thought, 'Why is any other book needed?'" And once she sententiously wrote that "While Shakespeare remains, literature is firm." Mr. Whicher has shown that the plays she most frequently cites are *Othello*, *Macbeth*, and *Antony and Cleopatra*. *King Lear* she does not mention, and it is indeed curious that "Cordelia" did not become for Emily Dickinson one of the "broadest" of words. And what of the queenly Hermione and her transfiguration?

Aside from Shakespeare and the Bible, our poet's reading was confined preponderantly to her own century, though she clearly had some knowledge of Milton, Sir Thomas Browne, Bunyan, and Herbert. In her earlier years the German authors were cultivated in Amherst and she had heard at least of Schiller, Lessing, and Goethe. The English romantic poets she knew but hardly mentions in any illuminating way. She is fond of citing Keats; one reason for this fondness is suggested by a remark she made upon the death of her literary friend Helen Hunt Jackson: "Ah, had that Keats a Severn!" She read most of the Victorian worthies: Tennyson, Browning, Ruskin, and "dear Dickens."

Pre-eminent among the Americans, of course, was Emerson. She read the Essays, and found a good deal there of direct use in her thinking and writing. There is no evidence that she ever met Emerson, but he visited Amherst several times and spent one night at her brother's house. She had read Theodore Parker, Longfellow, and Bryant. Her comments on other American writers are tantalizing but their import is not clear. "Of Poe I know too little to think," she writes to Higginson in 1879; "Hawthorne appalls, entices. . . . Mrs. Jackson soars to your estimate lawfully as a bird, but of Howells and James, one hesitates." Of Higginson himself she wrote: "That it is true, Master, is the power of all you write"—which perhaps approaches the mixture of badinage and seriousness which Higginson deserved.

But of course it was the "little creatures" of Victorian literature to whom she gave her closest attention: the Brontë sisters, Elizabeth Barrett Browning, and George Eliot. Miss Taggard has ingeniously discovered a series of interesting parallels between Emily Dickinson and the Brontës. Our poet and Charlotte Brontë were similar in appearance, both unusually small, both plain and pale, both with reddish hair and striking eyes, both nearsighted. Like Emily Dickinson, Charlotte worshiped a moody and sensitive "teacher," her Professor Heger. Like Emily Dickinson she sent her work unheralded to a reigning literary power of her time, Wordsworth.

Aside from her name, she had resemblances to Emily Brontë (the name of Emily *Elizabeth* Dickinson also gave her a sense of mystic kinship with Mrs. Browning). Like Emily Brontë, she cherished a large dog, found housework tiresome, stayed at school but a short time, suffered from precarious health, and loved solitude. And there are resemblances more profound. For though no poet is really "like" Emily Dickinson, Emily Brontë is more like her than anyone else. They both tend to regard nature as death, even though there is more vitalism in the English poet's idea of nature; they both tend to regard crucial personal events as steps in the gradual release of the soul into eternity; both regard death as the final illumination; both maintain a childlike attitude toward life compounded of innocence and a sense of radical weakness and deprivation—

> Weaned from life and torn away
> In the morning of her day—

as Emily Brontë writes; both are able to make of this childlike simplicity a fearless vision of the world in all of its hostile actions; both record as their most memorable experience their reception of grace or illumination from beyond the natural world. Such a poem as Emily Brontë's "Ah! Why because the dazzling sun" is remarkably Dickinsonian—with its account of how the fierce arrows of the sun struck "my brow," how she buried her face in her pillow to escape the heavenly ravishment, but how

It would not do—the pillow glowed,
   And glowed both roof and floor;
And birds sang loudly in the wood,
   And fresh winds shook the door.

Also Dickinsonian is a later stanza in the same poem:

The curtains waved, the wakened flies
   Were murmuring round my room,
Imprisoned there till I should rise,
   And give them leave to roam.

There can be little doubt, one may add, that Emily Dickinson is a greater poet than Emily Brontë. She held to her central vision of things much more closely and tenaciously, and amid the repetitive imperfections of her verse, found ways of expressing herself more fully, with more technical variety, and with a steadier grasp of reality than did her English counterpart.

Yet from her comments upon them, one would never gather that Emily Dickinson's kinship with the Brontës was any more remarkable than her kinship with Mrs. Browning and George Eliot. One would simply gather that all these English "girls" were spiritual sisters and that they were all extremely admirable. That Mrs. Browning "fainted" she knew from *Aurora Leigh*. The "Anglo-Florentine," as our poet honorifically calls her, was always a source of wonder and solace. Mrs. Browning's picture, along with those of George Eliot and Carlyle, adorned the wall of her bedroom. Of George Eliot she exclaims "What do I think of *Middlemarch?* What do I think of glory—except that in a few instances this 'mortal has already put on immortality.'" When George Eliot died, Emily Dickinson wrote that she is "now *my* George Eliot." And she adds revealingly: "The gift of belief which her greatness denied her, I trust she receives in the childhood of the kingdom of heaven."

Emily Dickinson never mentions Christina Rossetti, though there are several circumstances in their lives which might have recommended to each an interest in the other. They were both born in December of 1830, both renounced men with whom love appeared to be a possibility, both became more and more reclusive, devoting themselves to poetry and the cultivation of a personal relationship with eternity. Yet the truth is that of all the Victorian women writers Christina Rossetti was least likely to capture the interest of Emily Dickinson. Morton Dauwen Zabel has reminded us of the great difference between the cultural settings in which the two poets lived: Christina Rossetti practicing her impassioned and mystical Anglicanism in an artistic context heavily weighted with both an Italian heritage and the English tradition of poetry and religion—Emily Dickinson, the irreverent daughter of a vanishing Calvinism, annotating the results of what Mr. Zabel calls her "searing introspection" in the face of a world of "moral obscurantism and tyranny" and "aesthetic and creative apathy." It is a pity that the only comment on Emily Dickinson by a Victorian woman of letters is Christina Rossetti's notice of her first published poems: "a very remarkable work of genius—though I cannot but deplore some of the religious, or rather irreligious pieces."

A poet who has left so many of her verses in a fragmentary state and who herself brings to our attention her uncertain power of poetic organization continually forces us, as we read her work, into comparisons with other poets who have done what she attempted with more perfect co-

herence and with firmer constructive strategy. A dozen or
two of Emily Dickinson's poems are unrivaled; perhaps
fifty can claim a kinship with the best of English lyric
verse. We are not in danger, then, of treating her unjustly
in speculatively seeking out certain comparisons, since our
purpose is to study the real qualities of her poetry and
not to deride it.

Thinking of her in relation to other poets who have
treated some of her characteristic themes, we are struck
by how persistently she acted upon her belief that poetry
is the inspired utterance of revealed truth. This was the
theoretical warrant for the fugitive quality of her imagination, for its tendency to leap from one intuition to another without stopping to develop and to elaborate. Her
fine poem beginning "Farther in summer than the birds"
is remarkable for the way in which she seizes upon the
idea of the loneliness of man in the universe. But a poem
about snow ("It sifts from leaden sieves") which seems
headed in the direction of the same theme evaporates into
superficiality. There are good lines:

> It makes an even face
> Of mountain and of plain,—
> Unbroken forehead from the east
> Unto the east again.

There is an enticing reference to the effect of the snow
on "Summer's empty room." But the poem runs out into
two of her common symbolic modes—garments and royalty—which are as poetically dubious here as on most
other occasions. If one recalls Robert Frost's "Desert
Places," the fault of "It sifts from leaden sieves" becomes
clear. The poet's intuition of the loneliness of man in

the universe has been alluded to but not held in steady contemplation as it has in Frost's poem. Frost writes:

> The woods around it have it—it is theirs.
> All animals are smothered in their lairs.
> I am too absent-spirited to count;
> The loneliness includes me unawares.

Instead of grasping the real movement of her poem Emily Dickinson has allowed it to be countered and denied by her symbolic clichés. The snow

> ruffles wrists of posts,
> As ankles of a queen . . .

and we are left with the impression of having discovered in the snow which she describes only an uninteresting decorative effect.

Though Emily Dickinson constantly wrote about eternity and though she gives us many striking insights into her sense of what it is, she never produced a fully structured image of it. Verging upon a full vision, she writes:

> And still within a summer's night
> A something so transporting bright,
> I clap my hands to see;
>
> Then veil my too inspecting face,
> Lest such a subtle, shimmering grace
> Flutter too far for me.

The instinctive response to the tremendous imagery which seems about to come before her mind is too delicate, too unsustained to allow any such rendering as that of a poet like Vaughan:

> I saw Eternity the other night
> Like a great *Ring* of pure and endless light,

> All calm, as it was bright,
> And round beneath it, Time in hours, days, years
> Driven by the spheres
> Like a vast shadow moved. . . .

Emily Dickinson's mind contained all the properties of Vaughan's vision, but they never came together in anything like Vaughan's large construction. In picturing eternity she characteristically confined herself, in her successful poems, to such a quick, concrete image as

> Eternity's white flag before,
> And God at every gate . . .

and, in her less successful poems, to the use of her "broad" words.

Such a poem as "The luxury to apprehend" clearly shows her inability to elaborate one of her most common symbols, food and hunger. In this poem she presents herself as an Epicure who longs for the luxury of a "banquet on thy Countenance." Presumably the person addressed is her departed lover, though it could be Christ or God. The idea of the poem is moving, as it applies to the poet's personal life. But it is not a good poem because she has hardly known what to do with her metaphorical equipment beyond merely stating informally the idea that has occurred to her. Compare this poem, for example, with Herbert's "The Odour," which begins:

> How sweetly doth *My Master* sound! *My Master*!
>   As Amber-gris leaves a rich scent
>   Unto the taster,
>   So do these words a sweet content,
> An orientall fragrancie, *My Master*!
>
> With these all day I do perfume my minde,
>   My minde ev'n thrust into them both,

> That I might find
> What cordials make this curious broth,
> This broth of smells, that feeds and fats my minde.

This poem does a great deal more than merely state the idea and adduce thereto a variety of loosely related words and phrases. It gradually evokes a totally imagined version of its idea.

The following phrases occur in the poem beginning "There came a day at summer's full":

> The symbol of a word
> Was needless, as at sacrament
> The wardrobe of our Lord.

The last five words are resonant and one pauses over them with a question, which, however, the poet does not answer. What is the symbolic range of "wardrobe"? Does it mean "flesh" or "garments" or both? How involved is the conception? Crashaw, indeed, has used the same symbolism with the amplitude which our intuitive poet has merely suggested (did she herself think of these lines?):

> They have left thee naked, Lord, O that they had!
> This garment too I wish they had deny'd.
> Thee with thyself they have too richly clad;
> Opening the purple wardrobe in thy side.

Emily Dickinson's poem beginning "I had no cause to be awake" expresses the longing of a person whose friends have died to know the conditions of their existence and to join them in eternity. Her poem concludes:

> So choosing but a gown
> And taking but a prayer,
> The only raiment I should need,
> I struggled, and was there.

There is a certain fine poignancy here, but there is also more than a little of the inveterate coyness which thins out the imaginative texture of so many of Emily Dickinson's poems. Vaughan is again pertinent to our question as to what can be done with this theme. The first lines of his unnamed poem are:

> They are all gone into the world of light!
> And I alone sit lingering here;
> Their very meaning is fair and bright,
> And my sad thoughts doth clear.

And after a series of brilliant elaborations it concludes:

> Either disperse these mists, which blot and fill
> My perspective (still) as they pass,
> Or else remove me hence unto that hill,
> Where I shall need no glass.

Emily Dickinson was almost entirely incapable of the shaping, constructive play of mind with the optical facts of light and vision which give so much imaginative substance to Vaughan's poem.

Tennyson's "Crossing the Bar" is not great verse but it is very good. The particular theme relates this poem to at least two of Emily Dickinson's poems: "Exultation is the going" and "On this wondrous sea." Characteristically she attempts to make her verses culminate in a feeling of blissful exultation conveyed to the reader by "broad" words: "intoxication" in the first poem and "Eternity" in the second. Tennyson has a good deal more carefully selected and deployed his familiar images: the sunset, the evening star, the clear call, the pilot. Speaking more generally of these two poets, however, one must surely conclude that in the close, imaginative observation of death, at which both are unusually adept, Emily Dickinson is clearly superior to Tennyson, as to nearly everyone else.

Emily Dickinson has often been compared to Blake. Hart Crane, for example, commonly linked them as "mystics" and visionaries and spoke of them as equals. Their aphorisms are sometimes similar, and some of the brief obervations which appear in the letters are easily equal to the aphorisms of *The Marriage of Heaven and Hell*: "Blessed are they that play, for theirs is the kingdom of heaven." "This is but a fragment, but wholes are not below." "Till it has loved, no man or woman can become itself." "Home is the definition of God." "To all except anguish, the mind soon adjusts." "Valor in the dark is my Maker's code." "Ecstasy is peril." "Maturity only enhances mystery, never decreases it." "Candor . . . is the only wile."

Not only the style but also the purport of some of Blake's sayings are similar to Emily Dickinson's. Blake writes, for example: "One thought fills immensity." "He whose face gives no light, shall never become a star." "The hours of folly are measured by the clock; but of wisdom no clock can measure."

Emily Dickinson never wrote an aphorism so profound as "Eternity is in love with the productions of time," or so brilliant as "The tygers of wrath are wiser than the horses of instruction." And she never produced a body of aphorisms with the intellectual coherence and range of those in *The Marriage of Heaven and Hell*, though it is hardly fair to press this comparison since she intended no more than to write her aphorisms informally.

It seems curious at first that Emily Dickinson, who lived

with one eye on the beyond, was not the equal of Blake in describing the poignant longing of natural organisms for eternity. Yet the few poems in which this may be said to be her purpose, such as "Longing is like the seed," fail to catch more than a little of the magnificence of "Ah! Sun-Flower." But we must recall that Blake's pantheistic tendencies made it easy for him to attribute human emotions to nature (since God is in man as well as in nature); whereas Emily Dickinson, who delves a deep abyss between man and nature, does not usually invest nature with powerful human emotions. This may be one reason why leopards and tigers in Emily Dickinson's verse—see "Civilization spurns the leopard" and "A dying tiger moaned for drink"—though they assume some of the mythical force they have in Blake do not symbolically subsume so much of the relation of man to nature as do Blake's tigers. One or two of her poems seem to have been written in imitation of Blake—for example, "There is a morn by men unseen" (a very good imitation of "The Echoing Green") and "How much the present moment means." The latter poem, which relates how the dog, the tramp, and the atheist stake their entire store

> Upon a moment's shallow rim,
> While their commuted feet
> The torrents of eternity
> Do all but inundate

is Blakeian in language, meter, and thought, as well as in poetic excellence. If we conclude that Emily Dickinson is more like Blake than she is like any other poet except Emily Brontë, we must not forget the difference between the motions of her mind—irregular, downright, intuitive —and the smoother, the more rapid, the more musically tactful mind of Blake, nor the fact that Blake is to be understood against a background of European history and politics whereas, however relevant her historical situation, Emily Dickinson's poems are resolutely, even sternly, private.

One might extend at length the comparison of Emily Dickinson's verse with that of others in the hope of gaining a clear sense of her poetic affinities and then of her particular limitations and her particular virtues. Yet in such an enterprise the law of diminishing returns soon sets in, and one is left with a renewed sense of Emily Dickinson's uniqueness. Our sense of this uniqueness can perhaps be enhanced by considering more closely than we so far have the metaphorical properties on which her poems rely.

The images which are usually selected for discussion are those associated with the poet's "broad" words. But they may be dealt with briefly, for the fact is that though they were the preoccupation of a lifetime, they are a good deal less endemic to a discussion of Emily Dickinson's poetic skill than to a discussion of the general qualities of her mind. Bees, blossoms, jewels, diadems, plush, bonnets, exotic geographical names, alcohol, and so on are her poetic stock in trade. But the motion her mind takes in passing from her bad poems to her good ones enforces a rigorous subordination of these troublesome images to the whole context of the poem, and sometimes it enforces their total suppression. We have had several occasions to glance at the private conventions of her "broad" symbolic paraphernalia, and one or two further examples will suffice.

A poem such as the following contains or implies the

whole range of what might be called Emily Dickinson's imagery of private redemption:

> Talk with prudence to a beggar
> Of "Potosi" and the mines!
> Reverently to the hungry
> Of your viands and your wines!
>
> Cautious, hint to any captive
> You have passed enfranchised feet!
> Anecdotes of air in dungeons
> Have sometimes proved deadly sweet!

The poem states that it is imprudent or irreverent to speak too lavishly of riches to beggars, of food to the hungry, or of freedom to prisoners, since death may ensue. Obviously the words *beggars, hungry*, and *captive* are being used with general reference. The beggar begs not for money but for love, wealth of experience, esteem, marriage, regality, and immortality—in short, for spiritual fulfillment or redemption. And so with the hungry. The captive is imprisoned in a number of unspecified ways: by circumstance, by renunciation, by the flesh. Being set free involves "air" and sweetness—that is, spirituality or immortality (air as opposed to earth) and bliss or (again) immortality. Having discovered that the poet is as usual speaking of this life in relation to the next, we perceive the one element of the poem which is of any real interest as poetry: the implication that wealth, food, and freedom are so tempting that not only may the deprived die according to physical law, by partaking too suddenly, but that having discerned the complete fulfillment of desire to be unattainable short of eternity, they will die in order to find fulfillment.

To the initiate in Emily Dickinson's private convention, "Potosi" will evoke the whole range of her language of jewelry and geography: silver, diamond, gold, ruby, emerald, amethyst, chrysoprase; Teneriffe, Tunis, Zanzibar, Africa, "Chimbarazu," Burmah, San Domingo, Apennines, Brazil. In one way or another (and it is scarcely profitable to wonder which way) all of these words signify the unusual, the precious, the exotic bliss of every experience in life which can be regarded as consecrated by being a type of eternal bliss, by being a "moment of preface." The viands and the wines exist in the same symbolic milieu.

The idea of the captive and his freedom invokes a far more complex range of symbolism—the symbolic modes of action and rest. But no considerable use of these modes is made in the poem under examination. The idea of captivity and freedom is related to her symbolism of doors and houses. She uses this symbolism primarily to convey her idea of separation: the separation of lovers and of friends, of man, nature, and God. The norm of experience for her, as we have noted, is symbolized by the image of the prison or house with its door "ajar." Separation is the natural condition of all life and of the cosmos itself; yet also natural is the modicum of access to that which is longed for across the abyss of separation. "Doom is the House without the Door." She also uses the house to symbolize the mysterious complexity of nature, heaven, and the mind.

Feet, and less frequently wings, are a constantly recurring symbol. Almost anything may have feet: a little brig, water-lilies, wheels. An ankle may pant. In short, like all of her imagery of redemption, the image of feet frequently ventures into coyness and sentimentality. The general intent of the image is to evoke the idea of the pilgrimage to immortality. Occasionally it is unobtrusively felicitous and even powerful:

> How many times these low feet staggered,
> Only the soldered mouth can tell.

She makes constant use of cloth and clothes. Frequently she arranges fabrics into a rather vague hierarchy, as she does with jewels and liquors, to indicate the difference between the impoverished and the wealthy, the commoner and the queen. Occasionally she will use a fabric with clearer intent, to suggest a quality of character or sensation, as when she says that one would as soon assault "a plush" as violate one of the gentlewomen of Amherst, or when she speaks of the sound of a dog's feet as "intermittent plush." Her habit of speaking of natural scenery as a gown or of trees, flowers, or hills as taking off or putting on gowns may have found some warrant in the Carlylean and Emersonian idealism, but her intent is decorative rather than philosophical:

> Till summer folds her miracle
> As women do their gown. . . .

Very often the putting on of robes or gowns signifies the royal estate of immortality.

Emily Dickinson's imagery of natural objects is usually nothing more than decoration or, at best, imagism (several critics, including Amy Lowell and Miss Marianne Moore, have remarked that her nature poems anticipate imagism and that like many imagist poems they show an affinity with Chinese and Japanese practice). The bee-blossom imagery has rather more resonance than anything else in her decorative nature poems. It gains in complication and interest by being associated with the cluster of images related to death. But one can hardly demonstrate that Emily Dickinson's paraphernalia of phoebes, leontodons, Indian pipes, orioles, and robins ever issues in major poetic statement.

There are limits to the utility of comparing Emily Dickinson with Shakespeare, yet her preference for Shakespeare above all writers lends plausibility to the comparison. One has only to read through Miss Caroline Spurgeon's treatment of Shakespeare's imagery to see afresh how Emily Dickinson failed to explore the implications and possibilities of her private convention. The imagery of hunger and food in *Troilus and Cressida*, of clothes in *Macbeth*, of animals and nature and the sea in *Othello*, of the firmament in *Antony and Cleopatra*—these and many other images Shakespeare employs organically with the central meanings of his plays. What Emily Dickinson might have learned from Shakespeare, or from any great poet (she might have learned it from her own best poems), was the poet's task of involving his images intricately and solidly with the intellectual meaning, the emotional tone, and the dramatic movement of his poem.

We have been so accustomed to thinking of Emily Dickinson's verse as a fresh and primitive invention full of the vigor, in however limited and feminine a way, of the American spirit that we forget how much this is true of her use (when it succeeds) of language and how little it is true of the other properties of her poems. In the midst of the raw vigor of nineteenth-century America though it was, Amherst was not exempt from the large operations of history. The poet lived in the last decadence of a religious culture. And hers was the last generation of her branch of the Dickinson family. Paradoxical though it seems in the burgeoning, progressive America of her time, the sense of last things, the sense of death, the sense of a future which is entirely confined to the supernatural world—these are strongly impressed on her mind. The vein of Stoicism, no less than that of Gnosticism, bespeaks, when it is not purely a personal utterance, the isolation and desuetude of a culture in decay. It is no wonder that (as we have noted) she felt "a cleavage" in her mind of the kind produced by a strong and coherent culture behind and a disintegrating culture before. No wonder that the gap could not be perspicuously bridged and that "sequence" ravelled "out of reach / Like balls upon the floor." No wonder she complained that the world she lived in had grown dull, colorless, and undramatic.

It seems to me that the historical view gives us the necessary insight into the real qualities of Emily Dickinson's poetic convention. As I have suggested, this poetic convention is a unique American version of the rococo style. Her style differs from the European rococo of the eighteenth century, the main difference among many being the stress on redemption and grace—to be accounted for, of course, by the fact that Emily Dickinson's style is a late offspring not only of Renaissance and Baroque art but also of New England Puritanism. One may grant that a great rococo style is possible. But one is struck by how rarely Emily Dickinson's rococo style (if we can conceive it by itself) achieves greatness. She remained too much the Puritan always to give license to her intoxications and her wantonness and the playful gambits of her feminine wit—not, one may add, because of moral scruples but because of a certain heaviness and downrightness of spirit. And when she does appear to grow wanton, who does not, as a general rule, feel the rough awkwardness of the Puritan mentality, which refuses, finally, to be banished and succeeds in making the playfulness misfire? We must look to this perpetual combat between wantonness and reserve, playfulness and somberness, "air" and "prison," in order to account for the element of strain, the incapacity for relaxation, which many readers have noted in Emily Dickinson. One of her most famous poems will illustrate:

> I like to see it lap the miles,
> And lick the valleys up,
> And stop to feed itself at tanks;
> And then, prodigious, step
>
> Around a pile of mountains,
> And supercilious peer
> In shanties by the sides of roads;
> And then a quarry pare
>
> To fit its sides, and crawl between,
> Complaining all the while
> In horrid hooting stanza;
> Then chase itself down hill
>
> And neigh like Boanerges;
> Then, punctual as a star,
> Stop—docile and omnipotent—
> At its own stable door.

This poem might be justified on the score of its coherence of imagery, its perspicuity of language, the felicity of its rhythms. Yet in that larger element of style which is called tone the poem fails. The phrase "punctual as a star" is successful on every possible count, but that is because it entirely escapes the tone of the rest of the poem, and has in fact nothing to do with the poem at all. The trouble is that the grace, the quickness, the fancy, or even the metaphysical wit which the poem is supposed to convey cannot be achieved by straining after them, as this poem does. These verses were written by a woman who had a large capacity for play and who played, in fact, almost on principle, but who had also a final incapacity which usually, though not always, made inspired poetic play impossible for her. It was an incapacity which differed only in degree from the analogous incapacity of her father, and indeed of the whole Puritan tradition.

Another famous poem (which we have mentioned already) is more purely rococo:

> I taste a liquor never brewed,
> From tankards scooped in pearl;
> Not all the vats upon the Rhine
> Yield such an alcohol!
>
> Inebriate of air am I,
> And debauchee of dew,
> Reeling, through endless summer days,
> From inns of molten blue.
>
> When landlords turn the drunken bee
> Out of the foxglove's door,
> When butterflies renounce their drams,
> I shall but drink the more!
>
> Till seraphs swing their snowy hats,
> And saints to windows run,
> To see the little tippler
> Leaning against the sun!

Like her poem about the train, this one is on several technical grounds a fully created and successful piece of verse.

Again it is the tone, the attitude the writer displays, which makes one uncomfortable. This is of course not a poem for children or about children; it is a poem for adults who like to play at being children but have not the relaxation or the sympathetic insight to succeed. One distinguishes as peculiarly rococo the emphasis on a sort of delicate epicureanism, the idea that a tankard ought to be of *pearl*, the assumption that aesthetic pleasure is to be found in smallness, feminine delicacy, capriciousness, coquetting with the masculine or bestial pleasure of drunkenness, and flirtation with death.

Egon Friedell has brilliantly summarized the characteristics of the rococo style. He describes it as issuing from a "last craving for illusion to carry one over the gateway of death" and as taking for its formula "loving and dying." The style is, as he says, feminine and affectedly "infantine." It is "forever ambiguously smiling . . . amusing, piquant, capricious, epicurean, witty, coquettish, full of anecdote, short story and point . . . with an atmosphere of comedy, theatrical and yet domestic." It stresses, above all, smallness, retirement, solitude, and fragile charm. It finds its forms in porcelains, delicately wrought gems, flowers, miniature china animals and birds. It seeks to decorate and enrich a blank or bored existence. It abandons literature and philosophy on the large scale and cultivates lyric, the epigram, the sharply phrased aphorism. It plays at love according to its particular convention of capricious mistress and chivalrous adorer; it eschews the grand passion of love for fear of spoiling the delightful playfulness of the game and dispelling the illusion of naïveté and childish innocence. It creates an illusion of agelessness by requiring a powdered whiteness of the hair.

One need not press the comparison very far to see the genuine elements of rococo in Emily Dickinson's elaborate poetic game of playing at being married or dead or at being an immortal queen or a child in a withdrawn miniature world capriciously embellished with jewels, robes, diadems, liquors, flowers, animals, and birds. Emily Dickinson is not Marie Antoinette and her private rococo is not that of eighteenth-century France. Yet, seen in relation to other rococo styles, the general purport of her convention becomes a good deal clearer. The historical view allows us to understand her imagery of clothes, for example, as a late rococo version of similar imagery in Shakespeare, or her imagery of intoxication as a rococo version of, let us say, Jonathan Edwards's imaginative theology of experience.

If we feel impelled to deplore the severe Puritanism which helps to create the element of strain in Emily Dickinson's poetic convention, we must still admit that the severer qualities of her mind are beneficially influential in the creation of her best poems and that these poems a good deal transcend any imaginable excellence her rococo convention, by itself, might have produced. In order to find our way towards her undeniable greatness we must steadfastly follow the image of death beyond the miniature world of rococo—the image which, however, that world strongly implies.

Not in all, but in the large majority of Emily Dickinson's poems, from the least impressive to the most, there are intimations of death. We have seen that she lived in a universe which she regarded as being sundered with cleavages between man, nature, and God. We have noted that there is but one free agent in this universe: death. God himself is so inscrutable in His perfect stasis that His emissary nearly usurps His place in our poet's vision of thing. For if the presence of God is dubious and hard to seek, there is no dubiety about either the presence or the efficient action of death. Nature is the actual condition of death, man is death's victim. If Emily Dickinson can hardly be called a pantheist, she often sees in nature a superhuman, personified power one might call Panthanatos.

She sees this divinity in the river that flows to the sea, or in the wind that blows through the trees like a river current. She sees him in the dark waters of a well. Occasionally he is the flowing tide: the encroaching darkness—

> Till sundown crept, a steady tide,
> And men that made the hay,
> And afternoon and butterfly,
> Extinguished in its sea—

or the ocean tide which all but overwhelms her as she stands entranced before "the mermaids in the basement" who "came out to look at me." The frost, one of her common symbols for death, is the "blond assassin" that "beheads" the "happy flower . . . at its play." Death is that icy "stranger hovering round" which the "flowers notice first" but which finally insinuates his way into human existence:

> Victory comes late,
> And is held low to freezing lips
> Too rapt with frost
> To take it.

Death may be seen in a slanting light on winter afternoons, in the wasp or bee that goads his victim but "will not state his sting," in the insect "menacing the tree":

> Bait it with the balsam,
>   Seek it with the knife,
> Baffle if it cost you
>   Everything in life.

The most impressive imagery in Emily Dickinson's poems is undoubtedly kinaesthetic rather than visual or auditory, and although she does of course invent some marvelous images of these latter sorts, they are likely, in her best poems, to be associated with images of motion, cessation, and rest. One of the major devices by which she subdues and transmutes her rococo style, depending almost entirely as it does on images of sight, sound, and taste, is by adducing kinaesthetic sensations. The following remarkable lines are a good example:

> I got so I could hear his name
> Without—
> Tremendous gain!—
> That stop-sensation in my soul,
> And thunder in the room.

One might almost say that at its deeper levels her typical experience is of motion—involving pain or terror—cessation, and an ensuing state of rest which either can be expressed by images or remains beyond perception. This fundamental trope tends to be the dramatic core of her best poems. One recalls the phrases of such a poem as "After great pain a formal feeling comes": the nerves "sit," the heart is "stiff," the feet go round a "wooden" way, the hour is of "lead," when pain comes it is like the experience of freezing persons who feel "first chill, then stupor, then the letting go." The striking phrase "quartz contentment" is basically kinaesthetic rather than visual, connoting as it does the crystallization of fluid substance.

All of her great poems on death display this kinaesthetic imagery. "Safe in their alabaster chambers" acquires its emotional tensions by contrasting the tomb with the cyclic motion of nature and human affairs (her use of the word "alabaster" here is a good example of how the imagery of her personal convention is controlled or transformed in her best poems; "alabaster" is not vaguely connotative and honorific; it expresses very precisely the idea of perfect motionlessness and coldness). "I felt a funeral in my brain" well represents the several poems in which she conveys her extraordinary perception of the kinaesthetic effects of New England funerals. Connected with this kinaesthetic imagery are her favorite tropes of the journey, as in "Our journey had advanced," and of the mysterious visitor, as in "Because I could not stop for Death."

At the heart of Emily Dickinson's vision of death, then, is the sensation of motion and rest. Almost any persistent motion, almost any condition of stasis, in nature or human existence, was likely to summon up in her mind this beautiful and menacing power.

Frequently she personifies death. In such a poem as "The only ghost I ever saw" he is held delicately halfway between a loose association of natural forces and a person. His chief qualities are his elusiveness, his silence, his quiet laughter diminishing with the breeze, his rapidity of gait, his grace, the lightness of his movements, his lace garment, his apparent shyness of human presence. He is, in short, a kind of gay but impalpable courtier. A figure in the rococo style, he suggests to us the only situation in which Emily Dickinson's playfulness achieves the pure grace of poetic perfection—when, with her severe vision, she beholds death.

When death is less shy, he is the visitor who knocks on the door and presents himself as one's "supple suitor." His persistence, though genteel, is not to be escaped. His "enamored mind" perceives all that one does; he "presides" wherever one may turn; he is "omnipresent" and lies in wait for his "impending bride." Whether he merely speaks in passing, like a cultivated Amherst acquaintance, or stands inexorably with "metallic face" at one's door ready to "drill" his "cordiality" in, he is polite, winning, and gracious. In his guise of "supple suitor" he is, like Melville's confidence man, one of the triumphant representations of American gentility. A shady character,

> Death is the only one
> You cannot find out all about
> In his native town:
> Nobody knew his father,
>
> Never was a boy,
> Hadn't any playmates
> Or early history.
>
> Industrious, laconic,
> Punctual, sedate,
> Bolder than a Brigand,
> Swifter than a fleet . . .

he goes about his business like the most respectable of small-town gentlemen, like Edward Dickinson.

Lover, genteel acquaintance, sober citizen, death is also king and emperor. This he becomes at the awful moment when it is alone possible to defeat him.

> The eyes around had wrung them dry,
> And breaths were gathering firm

> For that last onset, when the king
> Be witnessed in the room.

And in another poem:

> A triumph may be of several kinds.
> There's triumph in the room
> When that old imperator, Death,
> By faith is overcome.

Death is a protean divinity, a universal power whose insinuating presence is to be felt, seen, heard, touched, and smelled in nature and human life. As he appears in Emily Dickinson's poems, he is, as an image of nature, one of the most impressive concepts in English poetry since the seventeenth century and, as an image of man, one of the original and enduringly interesting characters of literature.

It may help us toward a more complete understanding of Emily Dickinson's poetry if we apply the word "sublime" to the order of experience generated by her images of death. The principles of her sensibility are thus reducible to the sublime and the rococo. Curious though it might at first seem, the best exposition and defense of this mode of sensibility is Edmund Burke's treatise on *The Sublime and the Beautiful.** Burke's idea of the "beautiful," though not close in detail to that of Emily Dickinson, is nevertheless a version of rococo—derived, as it is, from such qualities as smallness and delicacy. But his idea of the

---

* In most of its enduring significations the word "sublime" is both inevitable and unsatisfactory. It is clear that as far as Longinus's conception of the "sublime'" consists of his "doctrine of 'transport' and the 'lightning-flash'" (in Mr. Allen Tate's phrase), it is relevant to the present discussion. For the moment, I consider that Longinus's theories of rhetoric are irrelevant to Emily Dickinson (though actually they may not be) and use the word "sublime," in the manner of Burke, only where "astonishing" and "awful" would do nearly as well.

sublime is remarkably close to Emily Dickinson's idea of death. To be apprehended in such natural phenomena as oceans, lightning, dark mountains, stallions, and snakes, the sense of the sublime is produced by great power, pain, obscurity or ambiguity of outline and feature (as in images of Death), vastness, infinity, and terrifying privations (as of being suddenly bereft of light or human society). Yet as Burke understands it, the fundamental quality of the sublime is "astonishment"—"that state of the soul in which all its motions are suspended, with some degree of horror." "Astonishment" was well known to the poet who wrote so variously of that "stop-sensation in my soul" and who in fact placed this image at the center of her poetry. Emily Dickinson referred to her father as a "pause of space." She explained the origin of her most profound metaphor by saying that "Father's was the first Act distinctly of the Spirit." And we must therefore suppose that her father's image lingered at the background of her idea of the astonishing and the awful, and that she was herself the genesis of the idea of the playful and the delicate.

The most intelligible mode of relationship or tension within the poetry of Emily Dickinson is a relationship of the rococo and the sublime. There is hardly a poem in the whole canon which does not in some way exhibit both orders of experience. A thimble, a circling butterfly will appear even in those poems most consistently and powerfully evocative of the awful, just as in a predominantly light poem about tasting liquors never brewed there will be a hint of infinity and as in a poem about a gamesome train the underlying image of the horse will suddenly appear in an aspect of terrific energy. Her best poems are those in which there is a predominance of the sublime. In order to achieve a fine style in the light vein, says Burke, one must be able to conceive of pleasure as capable of existing positively and independently of pain. But the poet who found so many ways of saying that we know pleasure only through pain could not be perfectly successful in the purely pleasurable style, nor could she achieve so fine a balance of rococo and sublimity as, by not too remote analogy, we detect in the music of Mozart. In her best poems the rococo principle has been forced by the exigencies of the poem's structure to yield nothing but what is most admirable in it, its immediacy of pathos and its delicacy of form —the qualities with which, in these poems, the sublime must and does invest itself. This sustained imbalance constitutes the economy of Emily Dickinson's verse.

The haphazard manner in which, almost by necessity, Emily Dickinson's poems have been published has made the task of attentive and critical reading a difficult one. The chief advantage of the two volumes most generally read in recent years—the Bianchi-Hampson *Poems of Emily Dickinson* and Mrs. Bingham's *Bolts of Melody*—is that they contain very nearly all of the poet's verse. The disadvantages are that the poems have been arranged in confusingly vague categories, such as "Life," "Nature," and "The White Exploit," and there has been no attempt to winnow the wheat from the chaff. There is the further disadvantage that Mme. Bianchi and Hampson were very careless editors and that the original editors, Mrs. Todd and T. W. Higginson, made alterations of their own in the interest of rhyme, meter, or general decorum. And though this bowdlerizing has probably been less drastic than many people suppose, it is nevertheless true that at present there are only a few poems outside of *Bolts of Melody* of which we can be reasonably sure we have accurate versions. No wonder, then, that the poet's work leaves many readers perplexed.

One would give a great deal to know which poems Emily Dickinson would have chosen as her best. But we seem destined never to have a very clear sense of her choice, for, though she carefully bound some of her poems into paper "fascicles," these contain between eight and nine hundred poems, good, bad, finished, and unfinished. We know some of the poems she sent to Higginson, but we cannot always be sure whether she thought they were her best or whether she merely hoped they were nearer than the rest of her work to the conventional standards Higginson admired.

Emily Dickinson's critics have often expressed their choices; anthologists have made their selections; but aside from a recurrent core of both good and bad, these selections have varied widely. There is bound to be a subjective element in one's criticism of any poetry, and especially of poetry in the short lyric form. Accordingly, one offers one's own "anthology" of Emily Dickinson with a merely heuristic and not a legislative intent.

Although the poet will elude all such procedures as the attempt to categorize her poems according to style or subject matter, the attempt may at least have the value of a speculative exercise calcluated to lead the reader to the poems themselves. To begin with, there is the light verse. Emily Dickinson is certainly one of the great practitioners of this style, a fact easy to admit when we realize that "Because I could not stop for Death" is only somewhat less obviously a piece of light verse than such of her other poems on death as "The only ghost I ever saw." Remembering her poetic treatment of the elusive, the whimsical, the mock-gallant grace with which death performs his office, one does not need to advance such poems as "I like to see it lap the miles" in order to demonstrate her mastery of light verse.

Emily Dickinson's poems on childhood are among the most accomplished of her century—which is to say of all centuries. The best speak of the fear or deprivation which children know. "It troubled me as once I was" is a poignant and expert statement of the child's fear and bewilderment at the large spectacle of life. "A loss of something ever felt I" is one of the best renditions of a common nineteenth-century theme, expressed by Wordsworth and Emily Brontë: the child's sense of having lost some mysterious and unspeakably desirable felicity in the past and his feeling of homelessness in the present.

Emily Dickinson wrote on several occasions of the death of a child, a mode of poetry in which, among American poets, she is rivaled only by John Crowe Ransom. "She lay as if at play" is one of the perfect poems in English on this subject, as the last two stanzas will indicate:

> Her dancing eyes ajar
> As if their owner were
> Still sparkling through
> For fun at you.
>
> Her morning at the door,
> Devising, I am sure,
> To force her sleep—
> So light, so deep.

This poem brings to our attention again the marvelous lightness and deftness of which Emily Dickinson is capable when her central trope is death and when her poetic device is the clean-cut imagery of motion and rest. Here are no robins, no emeralds, no alcohols, but simply the immense mystery of a child's death expressed in the most efficient and most immediate terms. The poem is worth a dozen Victorian Requiescats. One may add that, as distinguished from the poems on childhood, the childish or childlike poems are not impressive. Lines such as

> Please to tell a little pilgrim
> Where the place called morning lies

are more suitably read by adult children, like the poet's cousins the Norcross sisters, than by children. The effort to extract from Emily Dickinson's writings a Child's Garden of Verses will hardly convince a large number of children.

The question of whether Emily Dickinson is a metaphysical poet is complicated. Yet certain limits to the discussion seem clear. Poems like "It dropped so low in my regard," "If you were coming in the fall," "I see the better in the dark," and "My life had stood a loaded gun" are close to the metaphysical style. But only in "The lightning is a yellow fork" does she succeed in uniting, what is strictly speaking, metaphysical imagery with her characteristic intuitive vision. This poem develops an extensive conceit according to which the lightning is said to be inadvertently dropped from tables in the sky; it is the awful cutlery of barely disclosed mansions; it is the apparatus of the dark. Like Donne and Marvell, Emily Dickinson is capable, as F. O. Matthiessen remarked, of "thinking poetry." Like them she uses the conceit. But the fact remains that she has too little of the elaborative weight and ingenuity of intellect of the seventeenth-century poets to allow us to apply the word "metaphysical," without radical qualification, both to them and to her. Her conceits issue from a Calvinist psychology and are the properties of a "rococo" style. They do not very closely accord with a style of English poetry which is, generally speaking, Anglican and baroque.

Emily Dickinson's original editors entertained strictly nineteenth-century attitudes towards literature, which accounts for the assumption that she must be a nature poet and for their consequent arrangement of some of the poems under that heading. We have already seen that she had an altogether impressive idea of nature and that it is admirably handled in a variety of poems. But she is not a poet of nature, if by that expression we mean one who observes the natural world closely and with devoted particularity and who employs his objective discoveries equally with his metaphorical or philosophical or religious sense of nature. So far as they find expression in poetry, Emily Dickinson's particular observations were few indeed. Mr. Whicher has carefully assessed the situation, noting, for example, that though Lowell mentions forty-two kinds of bird and Emerson about forty, Emily Dickinson mentions but twelve (though this count does not include *Bolts of Melody*, the proportions may be taken as correct). With insects she has done almost nothing, and she has hardly any trees. She is, to be sure, more widely allusive among flowers. Among her favorite images in fact are flowers, bees, and butterflies. To these she returns again and again, weighing them down, we may think, with an oppressive burden of ill-defined meaning. But even these are not so much observed as commandeered from the scenery and made to take their place in the rococo conventions of her private game of hierarchies. In selecting objects from nature and giving them a quasi-symbolic value, she was departing from the standard English and American practice of the time (for which she had the warrant of her Puritan view of nature) and was adumbrating the French symbolists and Yeats.

Her great insights into nature are not to be seen in the poems usually listed under that heading but in the "gazing grain" of "Because I could not stop for Death," the encroaching moss in "I died for beauty," the buzzing fly that hovers over the deathbed. There remain perhaps two poems which might reasonably come under the heading of nature poetry and which clearly belong with her superior work: "Farther in summer than the birds," and "The winds drew off."

Our poet wrote several fine love poems. The best is "I cannot live with you." It is her longest poem—fifty-one lines. On this occasion, her power of organization never flags, and she is able to unfold with consummate dramatic tact her idea of the different forms of separation which stand between her lover and herself. "She rose to his requirement" has a poignant dignity and a complexity of sense experience and intellectual meaning which distinguish it from most. Yet before one has read very far among these poems, one has the uneasy feeling that the public interest in the poet's alleged love affairs has led readers to expect more of her love poetry than is in fact there. She would not be of great eminence, surely, if her reputation depended solely on her love poems. They are weakened almost throughout by the inadequacies of her private system of imagery, her word-magic, and the general view of life that went with these tendencies. "There came a day at summer's full" is a very moving representation of the parting of lovers. Yet even this often praised poem may be somewhat weakened by a running analogy between the lovers and various phenomena associated with the Christian religion which tend to give a remoteness, an intangibility to the lovers and their feelings, and a diffuseness to the general movement of the poem. It reminds one uncomfortably of the precious religiosity of the love letters of Hawthorne and Sophia Peabody, in which Sophia is so often and with so little purpose confused with Christ.

If, as we have suggested, Emily Dickinson's poetry as a whole may be regarded as a running notation on her life, it is not surprising that scores upon scores of the poems are directly intended as versified comments on her personal experience or on her thoughts. One of the best of the personal poems is

> A solemn thing it was, I said,
>   A woman white to be,
> And wear, if God should count me fit
>   Her hallowed mystery.
>
> A timid thing to drop a life
>   Into the purple well,
> Too plummetless that it come back
>   Eternity until.

—even though the last two lines must be said just barely to have made the grade. The superiority of this poem over those like "Mine by the right of the white election" consists in the reserve of its language, the propriety of the symbolism, and its freedom from exclamatory verbalizations.

"I never lost as much but twice," which we have perhaps sufficiently discussed in a previous chapter, is easily equaled by the more famous poem on the same theme:

> My life closed twice before its close;
>> It yet remains to see
> If Immortality unveil
>> A third event to me,
>
> So huge, so hopeless to conceive,
>> As these that twice befell.
> Parting is all we know of heaven,
>> And all we need of hell.

"On the bleakness of my lot" is the best of those poems in which the theme is spiritual or artistic bloom in a sterile environment. If in such poems as "God made a little gentian" she is hampered by her verbal pedantries and her rococo convention, here she is concise:

> Soil of flint if steadfast tilled
>> Will reward the hand;
> Seed of palm by Lybian sun
>> Fructified in sand.

More numerous even than Emily Dickinson's notations on her personal life are what one might call her reflective poems. It is natural that many of these should also contain elements of personal confession. A large class can be paraphrased: "we perceive that in which we delight through the pain of being deprived of it." "To learn the transport by the pain" is perhaps the best of these poems, for here she has anchored the verbal level of the verse in her profound idea of nature as death. Of the poems dealing with the lonely soul and its strict economy, "The soul selects her own society" seems the most impressive. Emily Dick-

inson invented many less cogent ways of saying (what I
have quoted before):

> I've known her from an ample nation
> Choose one;
> Then close the valves of her attention
> Like stone.

There are at least four "Stoic" poems of great excellence:
"Superiority to fate," "Fate slew him, but he did not
drop," "Of all the souls that stand create," and "Patience
has a quiet outer."

It would be tedious to discuss too much in detail poems
which not only invite but necessitate a certain amount of
subjective bias and therefore a difference of response in
each reader. I shall therefore content myself with merely
listing those aphoristic or reflective poems which strike me
as clearly better than the large majority. These escape the
excessive verbalization, the verbal pedantry the lexicon-
minded poet so often displays in those scores of poems
which take the form of definitions (Faith is . . . Hope is
. . .) or in such mysterious word-shuffling verses as

> A nearness to Tremendousness
> An Agony procures,
> Affliction ranges Boundlessness.
> Vicinity to laws
> Contentment's quiet suburb—
> Affliction cannot stay
> In acre or location—
> It rents Immensity.

"As one does sickness over," "If pain for peace prepares,"
"Experience is the angled road," "Did our Best Moment
last," "Abraham to kill him," "Whoever disenchants,"

"Tell all the truth but tell it slant," "One anguish in a crowd," "How much the present moment means," "The things that never can come back," "To flee from memory," "Civilization spurns the leopard," "Of consciousness, her awful mate"—these are fine poems, clean-cut, neat, and terse in their enunciation of ideas. They are second-best in the Dickinson canon. Of first rank are two other poems of ideas: "After great pain a formal feeling comes" (despite the fact that the three stanzas come near to being three separate poems) and a poem hardly mentioned in Dickinson criticism, "All circumstances are the frame," of which the last stanza is:

> The light His Action and the dark
> The Leisure of His Will,
> In Him Existence serve, or set
> A force illegible.

This is, to be sure, one of the least original of her verses. Its appeal may consist in the close dependence on the best strain of language and meter in hymnology and on the majestic contemplativeness of the first and the second lines of the above, for which there is no adjective but "Dantean."

Emily Dickinson's poems on death are scattered in clusters through the two volumes which contain her poetic works. Drawn together in one of the several orders that suggest themselves, they constitute a small body of poems equal to the most distinguished lyric verse in English.

She is surely unparalleled in capturing the experience of New England deathbed scenes and funerals. Of this kind the three best poems are "How many times these low feet staggered," "I heard a fly buzz when I died," and "I felt a funeral in my brain." Her most successful device in these poems is her juxtaposition of the sense of the mystery of death with the sense of particular material stresses, weights, motions, and sounds so that each clarifies and intensifies the other:

> And then I heard them lift a box,
>   And creak across my soul
> With those same boots of lead, again.
>   Then space began to toll
>
> As all the heavens were a bell,
>   And Being but an ear,
> And I and silence some strange race,
>   Wrecked, solitary, here.

Few other writers have expressed such astonishing loneliness as this.

The objection has been made that no poet ought to imagine that he has died and that he knows exactly what the experience is like. The objection does not apply, at any rate, to "I heard a fly buzz," since the poem does not in the least strive after the unknowable but deals merely with the last sensations of consciousness.

> I heard a fly buzz when I died;
> The stillness in the room
> Was like the stillness in the air
> Between the heaves of storm.
>
> The eyes around had wrung them dry,
> And breaths were gathering firm
> For that last onset, when the king
> Be witnessed in the room.
>
> I willed my keepsakes, signed away
> What portion of me be
> Assignable—and then it was
> There interposed a fly

With blue, uncertain, stumbling buzz,
Between the light and me;
And then the windows failed, and then
I could not see to see.

I have quoted the whole in order to remind the reader of the textual difficulties in the Dickinson canon which are still to be cleared up. "I heard a fly buzz" has again and again been reprinted in the altered version of the early Todd-Higginson editions. This version substitutes "round my form" for "in the room" (second line), preferring an insipidity to an imperfect rhyme. It reads "The eyes beside" instead of "The eyes around," substitutes "sure" for "firm," and says in place of "witnessed in the room," "witnessed in his power." Both "sure" and "power" have generalized moralistic and honorific connotations which Higginson and Mrs. Todd thought (perhaps rightly) would be more pleasing to late Victorian readers than the poet's more precise, concrete words. These editors left the fourth stanza intact but wrote the third stanza thus:

I willed my keepsakes, signed away
What portion of me I
Could make assignable—and then
There interposed a fly.

To gain a rhyme, that is, they did not scruple to add the gratuitous and poetically neutral "Could make" and to sacrifice the voiced "s" sound which the poet had provided in "It was." Higginson and Mrs. Todd did not publish this poem at all until *Poems*, Third Series, in 1896. This leads one to conjecture that they thought it unusually awkward in its versification and that, consequently, when they did get around to publishing it, they edited it with unusually free hands. These are questions which can be an-

swered only by the much desired definitive edition of
Emily Dickinson's work.

Of the several poems which describe death as a gentleman visitor or lover the most familiar is also incomparably
the best:

> Because I could not stop for Death,
> He kindly stopped for me;
> The carriage held but just ourselves
> And Immortality.
>
> We slowly drove, he knew no haste,
> And I had put away
> My labor, and my leisure too,
> For his civility.
>
> We passed the school where children played
> At wrestling in a ring;
> We passed the fields of gazing grain,
> We passed the setting sun.
>
> We paused before a house that seemed
> A swelling of the ground;
> The roof was scarcely visible,
> The cornice but a mound.
>
> Since then 'tis centuries; but each
> Feels shorter than the day
> I first surmised the horses' heads
> Were toward eternity.

The only pressing technical objection to this poem is the
remark that "Immortality" in the first stanza is a meretricious and unnecessary personification and that the common sense of the situation demands that Immortality
ought to be the destination of the coach and not one of the

passengers. The personification of death, however, is unassailable. In the literal meaning of the poem, he is apparently a successful citizen who has amorous but genteel intentions. He is also God. And though as a genteel citizen, his "civility" may be a little hollow—or even a confidence trick—as God his "civility" is that hierarchic status which he confers upon the poet and for whch she gladly exchanges the labor and leisure of the less brilliant life she has been leading.

The word "labor" recalls Emily Dickinson's idea that life is to be understood as the slow labor of dying; now this labor is properly put away. So is the leisure, since a far more desirable leisure will be hers in "eternity." The third stanza is a symbolic recapitulation of life: the children playing, wrestling (more "labor") through the cycle of their existence, "in a ring"; the gazing grain signifies ripeness and the entranced and visionary gaze that first beholds the approach of death of which the setting sun is the felicitous symbol.

The last two stanzas are hardly surpassed in the whole range of lyric poetry. The visual images here are handled with perfect economy. All the poem needs is one or two concrete images—roof, cornice—to awake in our minds the appalling identification of house with grave. Even more compelling is the sense of pausing, and the sense of overpowering action and weight in "swelling" and "mound." This kinaesthetic imagery prepares us for the feeling of suddenly discerned motion in the last stanza, which with fine dramatic tact presents us with but one visual image the horses' heads. There are progressively fewer visible objects in the last three stanzas, since the seen world must be made gradually to sink into the nervously sensed world—a device the poet uses to extraordinary effect in the last stanza of "I heard a fly buzz."

Not more than two poems on the same subject come within hailing distance of "Because I could not stop for Death": "Death is a supple suitor" and "All that I do is in review."

The number of poems in which Emily Dickinson uses nature as a symbol of death or in which she contrasts the process of nature with eternal rest is very large. Of those poems whose main purpose is to bring nature and death into conjunction the most successful are "There's a certain slant of light," "Safe in their alabaster chambers," "I died for beauty," "The only ghost I ever saw," and "Death is like the insect."

Of those poems which describe life and death as a journey the best is "Our journey had advanced." One might add, however, "Through lane it lay, through bramble," a poem which speaks of the "children" who followed a perilous and lonely path through woods and clearings, encountering the wolf, the owl, the serpent, the tempest, and the lightning, and which concludes,

> The satyr's fingers beckoned,
> The valley murmured "Come"—
> These were the mates—and this the road
> Those children fluttered home.

Overtones of Genesis and folktale beautifully adapted to the poet's particular view of things make this a richly and at the same time a delicately rendered poem.

Miscellaneous poems on the theme of death which strike one as well above the average achievement are: "Her final

summer was it," "Today or this noon," "It knew no medi-
cine," "He scanned it—staggered, dropped the loop," "A
dying tiger moaned for drink."

I shall not detain the reader by detailing what seem to
me the many brilliant strokes occurring in poems which
fail as wholes. Such lines as

> Lay this laurel on the one
> Too intrinsic for renown. . . .

or

> Yet never met this fellow,
> Attended or alone,
> Without a tighter breathing,
> And zero at the bone. . . .

or

> And we, we placed the hair,
> And drew the head erect;
> And then an awful leisure was . . .

such lines would be recognized as expressing the accent of
a major poet even if she had written nothing else.

Many readers of this long chapter will find my mode of
criticism insensitive. The objections will arise among that
considerable body of Dickinson admirers who maintain
that the poet is capable of great successes in a wide variety
of styles and genres, and that her accommodation of experience and her range of vision give her the power, as it
were, to move forward simultaneously and with equal success on several fronts. I do not believe that this is true. And
it seems to me, also, that the more we abstract her from
her background and her temperament, the more we lose

sight of her particular qualities, the more we give her a seat in the general assembly of literature where every poet is facelessly identical simply by virtue of being a poet, the less able we are to perceive her enduring qualities.

Emily Dickinson's vision of things, when it is clear, is more than likely to be sternly limited. Great lyric poetry is not to be achieved without precision and discipline. As a reader of lyric poetry, one must do one's best to honor and to emulate this discipline.

I have consistently praised Emily Dickinson's "narrowness"—her strong preoccupation with death and her residual Calvinism. I have not meant, however, to imply that these or analogous preoccupations are necessarily beneficial to poetry. They were beneficial to *Emily Dickinson's* poetry. It has been said that many great American writers display in their works an obvious attempt to deal with the all but overwhelming abundance, the burgeoning vitality, the random superfetation of the American experience. Like Emily Dickinson, Whitman found that in the midst of a culture which seemed to demand literature in celebration of life, a preoccupation with death was in fact much closer to the source of genuine poetry than anything else. Considered as a poetic device, the theme of death was the necessary stratagem of both Whitman and Emily Dickinson in their attempts to make order out of disorder. Melville found the same stratagem only somewhat less necessary. Yet a poetry whose single theme is death is hardly a goal to be sought by all poets.

Nor does great verse have to issue from a system of religious dogma. It is surely not true, as the epigoni of some modern critics have supposed, that a great poet must either work unquestioningly within a system of dogma or, appearing when the system has collapsed, repossess it imaginatively. It has become fashionable to praise those writers of our past, like Melville, Hawthorne, and Emily Dickinson, *merely* because, cogently or not, they can be said to have affinities with religious belief, to entertain ideas of grace or evil. And it has become correspondingly fashionable to depreciate Emerson and Whitman because they lack these affinities or do not possess them readily or dogmatically enough. If I have had occasion to point out from time to time in the course of this book instances wherein the mind of Emily Dickinson seems more precise and profound than that of Emerson or Whitman, it is because I have been trying to describe the mind of Emily Dickinson, and not to condescend to Emerson and Whitman. The looseness, the vagueness, the over-optimism of these two writers must by now be sufficiently plain. We need not excuse or forget their failings in the necessary act of renewing our sense of their residual greatness.

Accordingly I should be most disappointed if anyone took my account of Emily Dickinson as a contribution to that current view of our literary history which prizes only those writers whose works resound with the overtones of religious dogma or plunge into the metaphysical darkness. I have already expressed my opinion that Walt Whitman makes a formidable claim to be our first poet. I shall venture to add the opinion that only after this fact has been accepted can we speak of the comparative merits of Emily Dickinson, and of such lesser poets of her century as Bryant, Poe, Melville, Emerson, and Lanier. To which one may add that, on any scale of poets who have written in English, Shakespeare, Milton, Donne, Keats, and Yeats, at least, must precede our American poets.

The Recluse

ONE of Emily Dickinson's obiter dicta is that "biography first convinces us of the fleeing of the biographied." However true this may be as a general proposition, it has its melancholy relevance to the later, even more than to the earlier years of her own life. We know the general tendency of her life between 1862 and 1874, the year her father died. We know that in these years the tendency towards seclusion, settling in her mind and temperament ever since her early twenties, was finally established as the only possible mode of existence open to her. The statement of 1870 to Higginson that "I do not cross my father's ground to any house or town" may be taken as announcing the final commitment to what was not only a surrender and a withdrawal but the final achievement of a way of life. After 1870 she left the house only to visit Austin and "Sister Sue" next door, or possibly, on rare evenings, other close neighbors, and to work at her garden. There were rumors in Amherst that she was accustomed to roll out a scarlet rug from the house to her flower plot, but we also have the somewhat more credible testimony that she merely used an old red army

blanket to kneel on as, dressed always in white, she trans-
planted or cut her flowers.

Other particulars remain. She was in Boston during the
summer of 1864 and for a longer period in 1865 in order
to have her eyes treated by an Arlington Street doctor. Her
long correspondence with the Norcross sisters, ceasing only
with her death, begins after these years, for she lived with
them in their boardinghouse during her eye treatments.
She always had a tendency toward myopia, but we may
suppose that her severe case of eyestrain was a product of
the general emotional turmoil she had known in the years
between 1859 and 1863 as well as of the intense poetry
writing she had quite possibly been doing in the last two
years of this period. She was forbidden to read, and—even
worse—to write. Reclusive by temperament and by choice,
she was perforce learning the peculiar isolation of the
semi-blind. Her eyes seem to have improved under treatment, for after these years we do not hear much about
them, beyond one gesture which she made in 1868 toward
returning to Boston for further treatment. She decided
against this move partly and perhaps entirely because, as
she said, her father preferred her to stay at home.

Besides her garden, she had, in these years, her usual
household duties, though these seem to have been somewhat specialized and delicate as compared with the more
vigorous managerial activities of her sister Vinnie. She carried on a thriving correspondence with her friends. There
were occasional visits from Mr. and Mrs. Bowles as well as
from less eminent acquaintances. In 1870 and again in
1873, there were visits from Higginson, whom she continued to regard as her tutor. In 1873 there was a visit from
Helen Hunt Jackson. Above all there was her poetry,

which she scribbled on odd scraps of paper at the small desk by the window of her comfortable bedroom, with its Franklin stove and pots of hyacinth.

The winter of 1870-71 was time of anguish: "The terror of the winter has made a little creature of me, who thought myself so bold." Edward Dickinson had fallen sick and his daughter's whole life had for the time been taken up with the ordeal. "Father was very sick," she writes to her cousins. "I presumed he would die, and the sight of his lonesome face all day was harder than personal trouble. . . . I think his physical life don't want to live any longer. You know he never played, and the straightest engine has its leaning hour." Nothing so engrossed the mind and being of Emily Dickinson as the idea that her father would die, that that straight engine, that "Cromwell" who stepped out to get the kindlings, would "cease."

It is apparent from her letters of these years, as it is also apparent from her poetry, that Emily Dickinson's mind continued to operate in oddly disparate ways, and that the disparities continued to have their indubitable relationship to her central vision of things. She continued to play at "little women" with her cousins. Her cousins, she likes to point out, are innocent, they play, and so they shall go to heaven: "Comfort, little creatures—whatever befall us, this world is but this world. Think of that great courageous place we have never seen!" She continues with her game of hierarchies, announcing that with the coming of spring "even the hens are touched with the things of Bourbon, and make republicans like me feel strangely out of place."

The life of the imagination, such as she could muster, she also carried on in her letters to Mr. and Mrs. Bowles and to Higginson. To these correspondents she repeatedly affirms a strong and enduring love of illusion, memory, and imagination as against the meager mentality of shallow realism. Mr. and Mrs. Bowles, she believes, must share with her the opinion that if one is to arraign the *Arabian Nights*, it is for "their understatement," for their underestimation of the wonder and the magical quality of life. That is indeed a "stale sagacity" which sees nothing in the *Arabian Nights* but a sham. To Higginson she writes that "it is difficult not to be fictitious in so fair a place." Illusions, so she thinks, should never be surrendered to merely prudential cunning or vulgar realism. They have no formidable enemies except experience and reality itself: "test's severe repairs are permitted all."

Reading the letters we gain a new sense of the purport of that curious and much remarked unevenness of the poet's mind, the marked disparities we see in her bad taste, her coyness, her playfulness good and bad, her elaborate artifice, her plain-spoken profundity, her marvelous clarity of vision, her sheer mastery of language.

The most general truth that may be stated about Emily Dickinson's letters is that they deal with death and the imagination. Her letters alternately plead and demand that her correspondents shall accept the pre-eminence of poetic thought and that they shall share with her a life of the imagination such as, given their character and ability, they may be capable of. It is clear that her belief in the magic power of words extended also to a belief in the magic power of letters. Letters, she suggests, partake directly of eternity—her highest possible praise. Emily Dickinson's description of her poems as "my letter to the world" has been construed in so many questionable ways, both sentimental and esoteric, that we are inclined to forget that it does carry meaning. She treated her poems as letters, refusing to have them published yet with some freedom sending them to her friends. Some are actually written in epistolary form. Her letters, too, were often written upon the sheet of paper in such a way that they give the visual impression of being poems.

A life of letter-writing suited Emily Dickinson's deepest proclivities. It was her chosen mode of association with others, entailing not only harmonious communication with her friends but offering also forms of subservience to them and domination over them. Her correspondence allowed her to associate with her friends without having to endure the amenities of genteel New England manners or the physical presence and the curiously inquiring eyes of friends in the flesh. Letters also provided modes of intimacy and seriousness which were difficult to establish in personal intercourse. Letters were, indeed, a form of magic by which Emily Dickinson could control her friends, could keep them at a suitable distance and in a certain relationship to her. They were the power by which she gained emotional and intellectual support in return for the devotion she offered, along with her aphorisms, her jokes, her news, and her profound thoughts. She demanded of all her correspondents that they share her cult of friendship and immortality. Sometimes she seems to be offering Mr. Bowles an eternal life or even to be forcing it upon him.

There can be no doubt that Emily Dickinson needed very desperately the support which her correspondence gave her—the sympathy, the confirmation of her views, the evidence that the rich inner workings of her mind could in some degree be shared by others, that they had some objective reference outside herself. The business of being a poet, and an unorthodox one at that, in nineteenth-century Amherst was not impossible but it was difficult and it required certain stratagems. The indispensable necessity was to create and sustain a structure of imagination, to reassure oneself over and over again that the visionary life was possible, to cloak the ordinary existence of a central Massachusetts town with the verdure of fancy and illusion, and to envelop existence with an aura of eternity, an intimate and blissful experience of which was something shared in friendship. Above all; the impression that in death one beheld the center of meaning must be repeatedly stated, explored, and affirmed. The most practical function of Emily Dickinson's letters is to propitiate, to praise, to sympathize with, to entertain, and if necessary to cajole her correspondents in such a manner that they will aid and abet her life of the imagination. The poet that signed herself "your gnome" was not thereby rendered incapable of making very imperious demands.

So great a commitment to letter-writing could not help being also a commitment to her correspondents, to their manners, their moral attitudes, their conventions of mind and spirit. For, though we cannot understand Emily Dickinson without considering her letters as acts of power, of self-assertion, and of self-confirmation, we cannot ignore either the fact that she had only a few correspondents, and that these were almost without exception of somewhat mediocre intelligence. It is true that she tended to write over the heads of Mr. Bowles and the Misses Norcross and that they were often baffled by her sibylline utterances. Yet her correspondence must surely have had the effect of confirming those elements of our poet's character and mind which she most readily found in her correspondents. The game of little women which she played with the Norcross sisters was warrant for her elaborate native playfulness and childishness. The rather vague spiritualism and the bad literary taste of correspondents like the Hollands helped to confirm similar tendencies in herself. Instinctively she did not finally regard Higginson very highly as a critic of poetry, or at least of *her* poetry, but she seems hardly to have questioned his general intellectual prowess. She believed, so she said, that everything he uttered in his writings was true. Higginson was certainly not a stupid man but neither was he a man to whom it ever occurred that to have a profound thought was *difficult*. He made thought seem remarkably easy—a warrant for those reflective or "thoughtful" poems which constitute a large part of Emily Dickinson's secondary verse. She shared her ideas about death and immortality with all her correspondents, but one may suppose that she found her strongest confirmation of these ideas in her correspondence with Wadsworth.

In one sense it is difficult to say whether Emily Dickinson retired from the world in order to write letters or wrote letters in order to retire from the world. In any case both her correspondence and the larger fact of her seclusion may be regarded as stratagems which she found it necessary to adopt in order to live as she felt she must. Not, of course, that her gradual seclusion was *nothing but* a consciously or prudentially chosen way of life. It involved flight and surrender; it entailed very painful and damaging renunciations. But it was also a consolidation of forces, an act of power.

In her use of aphoristic language and visionary perception Emily Dickinson is the spiritual descendant of another

New England spinster, Mary Moody Emerson. In the language of an earlier generation, Emerson's aunt called herself "a goody" and made just such imperious demands on society and the mysterious cosmos as did the poet who called herself a "gnome." Strongly Dickinsonian in tone and language are such of Miss Emerson's observations as "I like that kind of apathy that is a triumph to overset" or such descriptions of herself as "the puny pilgrim, whose sole talent is sympathy." Many of the aphorisms in the letters and diaries of Mary Moody Emerson are strikingly reminiscent of Emily Dickinson's manner:

Society is shrewd to detect those who do not belong to her train, and seldom wastes her attentions.

How insipid is fiction to a mind touched with immortal views!

Alive with God is enough—'tis rapture.

O the power of vision, then the delicate power of the nerve which receives impressions from sounds!

. . . the prospect of a dying bed reflects lustre on all the rest.

. . . 'tis benevolence enjoins self-denial.

Hard to contend for a health which is daily used in petition for a final close.

I learned the order of human events from the pressure of wants.

Emerson writes that the muses of his aunt's genius were Destitution and Death. She spoke of having lived in "dreary deserts"; she spoke of her solitude, of her power-lessness, of her intimacy with immortality. Her manner-isms were astonishing; they included sleeping in a bed made to resemble a coffin and wearing a shroud as a shawl. Like Emily Dickinson she took up her mannerisms gradu-ally and by an economy of means and ends prescribed by destiny: "My oddities were never designed—effect of an uncalculating constitution, at first, then through isolation; and as to dress, from duty." The oddities were both a prod-uct of genius and a tactic of self-defense. "She had the mis-fortune of spinning with a greater velocity than any of the other tops," says Emerson. And her relationships with her fellow man were consequently oblique, skirmishing, and paradoxical. She ardently loved all evidence of spiritual superiority in her acquaintances; she could cut her friends off with queenly disdain; she loved especially the company of the very young. Like our poet she regarded life as bleak and lonely unless in relation to death and eternity it could be flashingly illuminated by ecstatic insight.

Still orthodox in her Calvinism (though she had read and admired such different authors as Plato, Herder, and Byron), Mary Moody Emerson's thought was nevertheless more an affair of imagination and piety than of systematic theology. Of Byron she thought that "the fiery depths of Calvinism, its high and mysterious elections to eternal bliss, beyond angels, and all its attendant wonders would have alone been fitted to fix his imagination." Like Emily Dickinson, she had a special feeling for autumn, for the dying of the year. She wrote, "Never do the feelings of the infinite, and the consciousness of finite frailty and igno-rance, harmonize so well as at this mystic season in the deserts of life." And just as did our poet, she automatically turned from thoughts of nature to thoughts of death: "Oh, if there be a power superior to me—and that there is, my own dread fetters proclaim—when will He let my lights go out, my tides cease to an eternal ebb? Oh for transformation!" When we perceive that we exist in eternity, she wrote, we first perceive the joy of existence in this world. When we see that life is but the passage to the "cool, sweet grave," we are able to feel that "existence itself in any form is sweet." Emily Dickinson had herself come to this conclusion when, in 1870, she said to Higginson: "I find ecstasy in living; the mere sense of living is joy enough." Emily Dickinson might well have written: "Am I, poor victim, swept on through the sternest ordinations of nature's laws which slay? yet I'll trust." Both women regarded beauty as a "chastisement," as the intuitive perception of divine grace whereby we understand and acquiesce in the fact that nature is the condition of death and the assault of nature upon man the origin of beauty, truth, and joy. Both women made of their solitude a way of living imaginatively, of walking close to the "fathoms" (as Emily Dickinson said) and the abysses of experience, of suspending ordinary experience in favor of the dramatic and the ecstatic, of annotating the daily vicissitudes of a life lived close to the mystery of death. Both women used their nonconformity, as they used language—as forms of power over society and history.

The question of Emily Dickinson's withdrawal from the world cannot be considered apart from her extraordinary insistence upon ideas of status. In her remarkably suggestive chapter on the poet's seclusion Miss Taggard writes that Emily Dickinson "voices, for America, an art of choice which it has not yet learned or begun to practice. She pictures life in scale and in value, in choice and rejection, in form and design—not in mere quantity, mere bulk, mere amorphous welter." One must lower Miss Taggard's claims, remembering how little inclusive, how narrowly principled, and how meagerly political was our poet's mind. But then it is still possible to admit that her poetry was an attempt to picture life in scale and in value and that her seclusion was an attempt to *live* life in scale and in value. She could not, like Whitman, embrace America, man *en masse*. She could not tolerate, either, the formless ambiguities of Thoreau's withdrawal from society. She might proclaim in one of her poems that it was "dreary to be somebody" and that she was content to be "nobody," yet she receded only so far, and no farther, from the cognizance of others. She receded exactly far enough to define her position as a recluse, to adopt a set of mannerisms which would both adorn and demarcate her chosen status. She at least would not succumb to the powerful social pressure which urged everyone regardless of temperament and taste into the same amorphous welter. Again and again she had watched what seemed to her the painful indignities which society imposed upon Edward Dickinson, indignities which were the inevitable product of a society which called him "Squire" but lacked the systematic set of values this honorific title implied. Society perpetually transgressed the boundaries of Edward Dickinson's aristocracy. Society exalted him, it would seem, only to pull him down again to the common level—cheered him with heart-felt admiration and gratitude only, in the next breath, to cheer the insurance company with identical emotions. The merging, the blurring of distinctions, the settling down into the level and amorphous mass—this is the poet's idea of catastrophe, just as her idea of sin is the conventional obtuseness to experience which makes social, intellectual, and spiritual distinctions impossible.

Emily Dickinson's poetry strongly insists upon both the fact and virtue of separation, the disjunctions of the cosmos as well as the distinctions which ought to characterize social and intellectual life. Her seclusion is the practice of her preachment. If one is going to live according to an idea of status, one must adopt the manners that go with it, even though one's peculiar circumstances often force upon one's manners the appearance of mannerisms. The rococo convention of Emily Dickinson's poetry finds its counterpart in the carefully cultivated and inviolable mannerisms of her life. The purpose of the mannerisms, like that of the poetic convention, is to adorn and enrich the meagerness of ordinary existence and to delimit areas of thought and behavior. Thus if an elderly lady comes unannounced to call one afternoon, she will be ushered into the garden by Maggie the maid and asked to wait. After a considerable time Maggie will return to say somewhat embarrassedly that Miss Emily cannot see anyone today and to extend to the visitor a silver tray with a delicate doily on which there reposes a single clover blossom. The rules of this game of hierarchies are obdurate; they will not succumb to the easy assumptions of democratic social intercourse. And if, in one of her letters, she calls herself Xerxes, it is because she shares with the oriental monarch the knowledge that a hierarchy and one's place in it can be vivified and reaffirmed by keeping one's person invisible, unapproachable, and mysterious.

Emily Dickinson had discovered that in the America of the nineteenth century one of the few ways to have a set of manners which was not open to anomaly and subversion was to become a recluse. The idea that one might become an expatriate would hardly have occurred to her. The paradox is that in our country manners have been associated with nonconformity. Our public opinion associates manners with the odd, the irregular, the secretive, the snobbish, and even the demonic and the insane. So Hawthorne masterfully suggests in his story called "Feathertop." The protagonist of this story is a scarecrow into whom his mother, a witch, has temporarily breathed the spirit of life. Feathertop is the only character in the entire range of Hawthorne's works whom one can unqualifiedly call the creation of a novelist of manners. Feathertop, a figure stuffed with straw, is nothing but a collection of manners; he is an elaborately artificial contrivance for whom life in society quickly turns out to be impossible. This story has always seemed to me to be Hawthorne's apologia for not being more the novelist of manners than he was; for the story says in effect: in our American life only scarecrows —to which we may add, recluses and other odd characters —have a set of manners.

Miss Taggard charges to the poet's account a good deal of pride and even of vanity—vanity, that is, of that deeply rooted sort which in some part both issues from and takes the form of humility, shame, and fear. She speaks of the vanity which urged Emily Dickinson to conserve "all fragments of herself," her poems, her handwriting (which she did not like to expose to the public and so asked others to address her letters), her presence in company, her likeness (which she steadfastly denied to would-be photographers). Above all there was the increasing desire to conserve what Miss Taggard calls "the myth of her mannerisms." Emily

Dickinson refused both instinctively and on intellectual grounds the powerful demand of society that she give of herself what society thought proper. In her entirely personal way, she joined those pre-eminent Americans of her century like Hawthorne, Melville, and Henry Adams of whom it has often been observed that they said "No" to the general tendency of the culture they lived in. For if feminine vanity, fear, and Puritan fastidiousness were indeed strong elements of her character and strong forces in confirming her reclusive ways, her life had nevertheless the effect of a strong rhetorical statement of dissent.

In the only photograph of the poet as an adult, one senses the paradox of her character and her life. She is self-effacing, anonymous, and shy. The eyes, which do not easily focus, appear to indicate that she is on the point of seeking a refuge. The figure is slight, winsome, and appealing. At the same time the eyes express a will to power, an imperious demand upon the beholder. There were many elements of passivity and retreat in her reclusive life, responses to panic, insecurity, bereavement, sickness, and the morbidities of shame and shyness. Her seclusion was a way of maintaining in her inner life that precarious hold on sanity and vitality of which her poems often speak. It was a way of existence, an economy of life, within the Dickinson family circle, a way of controlling her relationships with her father, her mother, her sister, her brother, and her sister-in-law. Yet she gave to her seclusion a range of significance beyond herself and beyond her family circle. Her antagonist was nothing less than society itself, and the public opinion through which the values of society were forced upon the individual. She was entirely content to be what the world called a "nobody" so long as her position as "nobody" could be used as a vantage point of attack. And in her way she defeated the world, finally overwhelming its most stubbornly held redoubts. Her strategy was elaborate and extreme; it involved her own death. Emily Dickinson's seclusion—sad as it was and unpropitious for our culture—was yet one of the notable public acts of our history.

Friends and Relatives

OF THE few friends with whom Emily Dickinson had some personal and much epistolary intercourse during the last twenty years of her life, Samuel Bowles was in many ways the most typically an American of his time. His biographers testify to the nervous impetuosity of his temperament, to the vigorous and combative spirit which enabled him to rise from poor beginnings to the editorship of the Springfield *Republican*. The provincial newspaper in the nineteenth century was a thriving, independent, and influential force in the life of the nation, and under Bowles the *Republican* achieved a pre-eminence of which, even today, there remains some general impression. Bowles was the typical, almost the legendary, energetic newspaper man. He was not a profound or reflective man. But he was possessed of great energy, which he prodigally expended until his death in 1878, at the age of fifty-two. He became an influential force in Whig and Republican politics, and his editorials, which he wrote in a brisk and brief manner that set a new style, commanded respect in both Boston and Washington.

Emily established a kind of playful intimacy with

Bowles, who had long been a friend of Edward Dickinson. We hear, for example, of his habit of bounding up the stairs of the Dickinson house in pursuit of the elusive Emily, whom on these occasions he addressed as his "rascal." She acquiesced in his whim of calling her his "rascal" and signed at least one of her letters to him with this appellation. Mr. Bowles hardly had time to cultivate a taste in poetry though he is said to have often demonstrated a liking for it. The evidence is that he was no great critic. Emily Dickinson's poem on the snake ("A narrow fellow in the grass") was printed in the *Republican* through a process of connivance in which the poet herself had no part. So far as the evidence goes Bowles found the poem impressive because one could see from reading it that the poet was aware that corn would not grow in boggy soil.

Emily Dickinson exchanged letters with Mr. and Mrs. Bowles for over twenty years. As has been suggested in an earlier chapter, it is a little difficult to imagine what they made out of some of her communications, such as "Teach us to miss you less because the fear to miss you more haunts us all the time. We didn't care so much, once. I wish it were then, now, but you keep tightening, so it can't be stirred today. You didn't need to be worse, did you? Wasn't it a mistake?" Did the busy editor have time to reflect fully upon the statement that "you have the most triumphant face outside of Paradise" or to wonder what, exactly, his correspondent might mean by saying "The last day that I saw you was the newest and oldest of my life"? From a woman not yet forty, these strong asseverations must have sounded uncomfortably like a declaration of love. It was at any rate an act of assertion, a claim of possession. Mr. Bowles had been given a part in the poet's life, and he must accept the rules of the game. He must not be offended, for example, if instead of seeing her when he visited the house, he was expected to content himself with a letter the next day. In the friendship with Bowles she found a warrant of eternity, a partial answer to the question she asked him as early as 1858 or 1859: "Do you think we shall 'see God'?" On the occasion of Bowles's death, she writes to Mrs. Bowles, "He is without doubt with my father." As late as 1881 she writes to the widow, in the private language our poet had taught her to understand, of "the look of Arabia in his eyes." Mr. and Mrs. Bowles, surely, were somewhat baffled partners in a relationship of whose distant ranges and hidden profundities they cannot have been more than partly aware.

Dr. Josiah G. Holland was a friend more directly interested in literature than Bowles. Beginning in 1850 he worked with Bowles on the *Republican* and became coeditor. After 1870 he was editor of *Scribner's Monthly Magazine*, later called the *Century Magazine*. Holland's intelligence was not great and his taste was sentimental and stodgily conventional. There seems no reason to reassess the judgment of one of this author's contemporaries, an unnamed reviewer who wrote that "Dr. Holland . . . does not affect the play of the darker and fiercer passions, but delights in the sweet images that cluster round the domestic hearth. He cherishes a strong fellow-feeling with the pure and tranquil life in the modest social circles of the American people, and thus has won his way to the companionship of many friendly hearts." Possessor of the extraordinary pseudonym of "Timothy Titcomb," Dr. Holland was the author of such works as *Titcomb's Letters to Young People, Single and Married; Lessons in Life, Plain*

Talk on Familiar Subjects; and *Bitter Sweet, a Poem in Dramatic Form.* A biographer's description of him as "hopeful and somewhat sentimental" errs only in understatement. Very much interested in the problems of women, he was nevertheless ardently opposed to feminism. He remarks in one of his books that the "truly lovable, humble, pure-hearted, God-fearing, and humanity-loving women" of his acquaintance did not want the ballot box. One of the chapters in his *Letters to Young People* takes as its subject "The Beauty and Blessedness of Female Piety" and begins "Young women, this is my last letter addressed specially to you; and as I take your hand and give you my adieu, I wish to say a few words. . . ." After stressing the dependence of women because, for one thing, "your bodies are smaller than those of men," the inspirational sage goes on to advise women to live in an aura of sunniness, duty, and eternity. To the writer of these shallow and lugubrious works (or to his wife), Emily Dickinson sent such fine passages of prose as (what I have already quoted) "A woman died last week, young and in hope but a little while—at the end of our garden" and "To all except anguish, the mind soon adjusts."

She also sent some of her poems to Holland. His biographer points out that Holland's favorite authors were Longfellow, Whittier, Harriet Beecher Stowe, and Mrs. A. D. T. Whitney, that he commended Bryant, Emerson, Hawthorne, Lowell, and Holmes, that he was uneasy with Howells and James, and that he entirely disliked Poe, Whitman, and Thoreau. Though he had seen the poems of Emily Dickinson, he wrote in 1876 that Mrs. Stowe and Mrs. Whitney "are our best living female writers in America." It is therefore not surprising that as editor and critic he judged Emily Dickinson's poems as "really not suitable" because "too ethereal." If T. S. Eliot had by some quirk of history been isolated all his life on a farm in Missouri and had sent his poems to, let us say, the late Professor William Lyon Phelps, we should have a somewhat analogous situation.

Colonel T. W. Higginson is now remembered by many people only as the "tutor" of a poet whom he did not take, when he came right down to it, very seriously. Alice James voiced what early became the general opinion of the eminent critic when she expressed her fear lest the poems of Emily Dickinson had "been sicklied o'er with T. W. Higginson." In short she took him to be the essence of late nineteenth-century Boston gentility. There is no doubt that this description fits him very well, if we add the qualification that he belonged to the liberal, reforming wing of gentility. For though he shared most of the literary opinions of such "defenders of ideality" as Stoddard, Taylor, Aldrich, Stedman, Woodberry, and Wendell, he retained from his Transcendental beginnings a spirit of reform. He was a combination of all that was bland and easily accomplished in Emerson and Matthew Arnold. After a Harvard education, he was a Unitarian minister, until his principles led him to feel that he must resign entirely from the pulpit. He later became the symbol of cultivated taste to whom an unknown Massachusetts poet in need of guidance might naturally turn. A strong abolitionist, Higginson had principles to fight for in his years as a captain in the 51st Massachusetts Volunteers. Six months after he received the first of Emily Dickinson's curious letters he had become (in November 1862) colonel of the 1st South Carolina Volunteers, a regiment of former slaves. Always a literary man he wrote down the songs of his soldiers and in emulation of Sir Walter Scott presented to the attention of educated readers (by way of the *Atlantic*) the spirituals of the Negroes, as Scott had presented his native folklore.

Higginson made a public career out of reform. There is no doubt about his wit, his learning, his good intentions, and, on nearly every subject but the position of women, the lightness of his touch. He opposed much that Edward Dickinson stood for, such as tradition and privilege. He was in favor of, as in his earlier years he was one of, those "modern literati" whom Edward Dickinson warned his daughter against. As little like her father as possible, the poet's "tutor" was the gay reformer incarnate.

Higginson was an ardent and sometimes a fatuous feminist. The battle for the liberation of the Negro slave having been won, he turned to the liberation of women—and he collected the songs of domestic slaves as he had once collected those of the Negroes. In a quasi-Arnoldian essay of 1867 called "Literature as an Art" he wrote, by way of excursus: "We seem nearly at the end of those great public wrongs which require a special moral earthquake to end them. Except to secure the ballot for woman—a contest which is thus far advancing very peaceably—there seems nothing left which need absolutely be fought for." In his *Common Sense about Women* he expressed his fear that across the face of America there might pass, had indeed already passed, the "shadow of the harem." A chapter dealing with the plight of creative or literary women deplores the fact that they are the "intellectual Cinderellas" of our society and that they are likely to be ransomed from obscurity late in their careers, if ever. In an essay devoted to the "most eminent poetess of the world," he made Sappho herself one of his "intellectual Cinderellas." He insisted that the aura of scandal traditionally associated with the name of Sappho must be attributed to the disrepute into which women as a class always fall in the "coarse periods of the world's career." For though, as he wrote in "The Greek Goddesses," the Greeks had created the highest and most perfect idealization of women, their actual practice fell far short of their ideals. The Athenians might idealize the virginal Artemis, the lovely Aphrodite, and the motherly Demeter, yet the Athenian women were cruelly subordinated. And was it not the "reckless comic authors of that luxurious city, those Pre-Bohemians of literature," who stained the reputation of Sappho with their licentious and profligate jibes—as, one day, Voltaire was "to pollute . . . the stainless fame of his own virgin country-woman, Joan of Arc"?

In his *Women and Men* (a title which shows that the chivalrous critic was ever mindful of the maxim, "ladies first") he praised woman's influence on literary style, pointing out that the feminine touch consists of elegance, piquant simplicity, delicate propriety, wit, and social insight. Women, he tells the reader, are particularly adept at letter-writing, their letters being noteworthy for "the wit, the grace, the daring, the incisiveness, the 'lyric glimpses'" by which they are distinguished from the letters of men—one wonders if he was thinking of the letters of Emily Dickinson. Yet the feminine qualities of style must find their expression within the framework of certain more general artistic canons. His larger criteria were the image of conventional gentility: "these are the qualities of style that seem most obviously important—simplicity, freshness, structure, choice of words, and thoroughness both of preparation and finish." It is to be feared that in looking at the poems of Emily Dickinson, the critic must have found only one indubitable virtue, "freshness." As examples of "structural completeness" Higginson plausibly called to the reader's attention the *Oedipus Tyrannus* and *The Scarlet Letter*. As an example of failure in form, he cited *Leaves of Grass*: "It is no discredit to Walt Whitman that he wrote *Leaves of Grass*, only that he did not burn it afterwards and reserve himself for something better." Eccentricity, he thought, might be taken as a sign of vitality in a young writer, but it could only be a disfigurement in a mature work of art. In his essay on Whitman, Higginson described him as "of all our poets . . . really the least simple, the most meretricious" and maintained that Whitman was not equal to Lanier, a "man of more heroic nature and higher genius." Whitman, he concluded, "has phrase, but not form—and without form there is no immortality." His view of Emily Dickinson's poetry was in general his view of Whitman's.

Though he favored equality, Higginson's intentions towards his "intellectual Cinderellas" were distinctly princely. But if he looked forward to his first meeting with Emily Dickinson as a prince might look forward to a call graciously made upon a humble and obscure subject, he was somewhat taken aback to discover that the tables were turned, that he was paying court. The entry in his diary for August 16, 1870, records the fact that he had that day seen Miss Dickinson and that it had been a "remarkable experience." In a letter he described the occasion more fully:

A large country lawyer's house, brown brick, with great trees and a garden. I sent up my card. A parlor dark and cool and stiffish. . . .

A step like a pattering child's in entry, and in glided a little plain woman with two smooth bands of reddish hair and a face with no good feature—in a very plain and exquisitely clean white piqué and a blue net worsted shawl. She came to me with two day-lilies, which she put in a sort of childlike way into my hand and said, "These are my introduction," in a soft, frighted, breathless, childlike voice—and added under her breath, "Forgive me if I am frightened; I never see strangers and hardly know what I say"—but she talked soon and thenceforward continuously—and deferentially—sometimes stopping to ask me to talk instead of her—but readily recommencing.

Higginson recorded some of the poet's utterances which he remembered from the memorable interview. She had said that her father read only on Sunday and that he read nothing but lonely and rigorous books, that she knew a book was real poetry if it made her whole body so cold no fire could warm it or if she felt that the top of her head had been taken off, that women talk whereas men are silent and that that was why she dreaded women. He recalled her saying, "I never knew how to tell time by the clock till I was fifteen. My father thought he had taught me, but I did not understand and I was afraid to say I did not and afraid to ask anyone else lest he should know." He remembered too that she had suddenly asked, "Could you tell me what home is?"—a question, it must be admitted, rather hard to answer, especially while holding two day-lilies on one's lap.

At the end of this report on what Miss Dickinson had said, Higginson wrote: "I never was with anyone who drained my nerve power so much. Without touching her she drew from me. I am glad not to live near her." Emily Dickinson was not in the least like the members of the Women's Clubs before which Higginson was accustomed to expound culture. As for the poet, she somewhat mysteriously wrote to Higginson after his visit to compare his coming to Amherst with the coming of Birnam Wood to Dunsinane. It had been, for her, a great, if indescribable, occasion. She could even think that it had put her newly in touch with eternity.

A second visit, on December 3, 1873, appears to have been very much like the first. Miss Dickinson, so Higginson wrote to his sisters, "glided in, in white, bearing a *Daphne odora* for me, and said, under her breath, 'How long are you going to stay?'"

Higginson was entirely capable of patronizing Emily Dickinson, though he seems not to have done so outside of private letters. After the 1870 visit, which he described as a visit to "my partially cracked poetess at Amherst," he wrote (in a letter to his sister): "I saw my eccentric poetess Miss Emily Dickinson who *never* goes outside her father's grounds and sees only me and a few others. She says, 'There is always one thing to be grateful for,—that one is oneself and not somebody else,' . . . I am afraid Mary's [Mrs. Higginson's] remark, 'Oh, why do the insane so cling to you?' still holds."

Yet according to his lights Higginson was faithful to the trust Emily Dickinson had placed in him. Her poetry, no less than her personality, baffled him from the start. His essay on her in the *Atlantic* in 1891 candidly admits that he is still puzzled by this curious poetry. "What place ought to be assigned in literature to what is so remarkable, yet

so elusive to criticism?"—no one would call it an easy question, and he did not know the answer. "The bee himself
did not evade the schoolboy more than she evaded me;
and to this day I still stand somewhat bewildered, like the
boy."

Higginson was always dubious about publishing the
poems. He knew as a general proposition that great genius
was often neglected and misunderstood in its own time. He
wrote in "Literature as an Art," "Probably the truth is,
that art precedes criticism, and that every great writer creates or revives the taste by which he is appreciated." He
knew also that "the writer, when he adopts a high aim,
must be a law to himself, bide his time, and take the risk
of discovering, at last, that his life has been a failure."
Hawthorne, he saw, had taken this risk and had won out
in his own lifetime. It is a little too easy from our vantage
point to chide Higginson for not seeing in Emily Dickinson's poetry what we see: the art that precedes criticism
and creates taste. Before 1890 he had always thought, perhaps rightly, that if they were published Emily Dickinson's
poems would be received with indifference or ridicule.
But his caution surely verged upon timidity. He would not
have collaborated in publishing the 1890 volume except
for the pressure of Lavinia Dickinson, Mrs. Todd, and
others. The preface which he wrote for this edition is a
curious mixture of diffidence and positiveness. He begins
by informing the reader that the contents of the book are
emphatically what Emerson had long since called "the Poetry of the Portfolio," that the poems were written without thought of publication, and that they therefore lack
"whatever advantage lies in the discipline of public criticism and the enforced conformity to accepted ways." The

reader is told that the poet is a recluse, the daughter of an eminent citizen of Amherst, Mr. Edward Dickinson, and that to meet her face to face is to have the "impression of something as unique and remote as Undine or Mignon or Thekla." Seeking a straw for the reader to cling to, Higginson suggests a parallel between Emily Dickinson and Blake. In both poets will be found "flashes of wholly original and profound insight into nature and life; words and phrases exhibiting an extraordinary vividness of description and imaginative power, yet often set in a seemingly whimsical or even rugged frame." He concludes with the cheerful observation that "After all, when a thought takes one's breath away, a lesson in grammar seems an impertinence."

Though not brilliantly perspicacious or assertive, Higginson's preface, in comparison with his usual conventionalism, is by no means contemptible. But it surely reaffirms the fact that he shared the inability of our poet's other literary friends fully to accept her as a poet. The literary culture in which she existed had very limited notions of what poetry could be and do. It had a few convenient categories, into none of which Emily Dickinson's verse could be placed. A poet was someone whose verse did not depart too far from the manner of Longfellow or of Tennyson and could be praised by the rather finicking Stedman or Aldrich—the latter of whom unhesitatingly pronounced Emily Dickinson's verse a "poetical chaos" when he read it in 1891. A poet wrote about such matters as Life, Love, Nature, Time and Eternity. It is not surprising, then, that Higginson's relationship with Emily Dickinson consisted of his attempts to mold her into this or that image of the Poet and of her witty and profound evasions, her interplay towards him of subservience and domination, and her final refusal to conform to any of his images of what she ought to become.

Miss Taggard has observed that Higginson offered Emily Dickinson a literary personality, which she declined. Actually he offered her several literary personalities out of his somewhat limited stock. When she first sent her poems to him he praised them but suggested that she might sing more metrically and with more exact rhyme, perhaps like Mrs. Spofford, another of his "intellectual Cinderellas." Sensing a relationship between Emily Dickinson's verse and Whitman's (not a very flattering comparison, given his opinion of Whitman) he appears to have suggested that free verse might be her proper style, that she might give up rhyme altogether. To the suggestion that she might become a kind of female Whitman, she replied coyly that she had heard Whitman was "disgraceful"; at any rate, she could not do without rhyme, could not "drop," as she chooses to say, "the bells whose jingling cools my tramp." Higginson offered to model Miss Dickinson into a devotee and perhaps an idol of intellectual meetings. He urged her to come to Boston. Was Emily Dickinson—like Verena Tarrant in James's *Bostonians*—to be pressed, cajoled, and coddled into expressing herself, into pouring out the inspired song of her soul as a contribution to culture and women's rights? Higginson suggested, at least, that she attend meetings on the thirtieth of every month at Mrs. Sargent's, where papers were read and discussions carried on. Or, if this seemed impossible, would she not consent to attend a meeting of the Woman's Club at Tremont Place to hear him read his paper on Greek goddesses? She, of course, resisted all these appeals. But Higginson brought her to the attention of at least one woman's club, when, in 1875, he delivered a lecture to the ladies of Newport on "Two Unknown Poetesses," one of whom was Emily Dickinson and the other of whom was Higginson's sister.

Clearly, Emily Dickinson did not want any of the literary personalities Higginson had to offer. One may ask why, in this case, she kept up her relationship with him, why she should have insisted through the twenty-four years of her life after 1862 that they should exchange letters? She gave their friendship considerable complexity and meaning. She was his "gnome" and his "pupil." She was ill-educated, feminine, and awkward—"a kangaroo among the beauty." Could he help her? Then again she was a sibyl, or a queen, who could not be seen in the flesh without protocol. In another mood she was the unquestioned equal of Higginson who could write him with deep fellow feeling when his small daughter died. This much intimacy she achieved with him despite the fact that unlike nearly all of her other correspondents, Higginson was not a friend of the Dickinson family.

There were numerous reasons why Emily Dickinson should want to keep up this somewhat uneasy correspondence. If she was lonely, a letter from Higginson was a blessing, confirming as it did her personal relation to the man whose voluminous writings she faithfully read in the magazines. Higginson praised her work, and this too was a comfort even though she sensed his bafflement. She might have corresponded with greater men. Why, for example, had she not sent her poems to Emerson? A response such as he gave to Whitman after reading *Leaves of Grass* would have been unparalleled in her experience, far outweighing the approval of Higginson. The fact is that she found something specially and uniquely valuable in her correspondence with Higginson which went beyond her loneliness or her desire to be praised. What she found in him was, in a word, culture, the official Boston culture of her time. In her mind, Higginson was the flawless symbol of the literary and intellectual part of that society, that public opinion, with which she skirmished from the vantage point of her seclusion. Her idea was to keep this culture in a steady relationship to herself, never allowing it to come too close nor to go too far away, steadily resisting all of its demands which threatened to obscure or destroy the true qualities of her genius, giving just enough of herself and her poetry to keep the relationship alive, gracefully baffling her culture by alternately showing herself to be more humble and greater than it was. One gathers that Higginson was aware of a certain calculatedness, a certain purposeful seduction, in her treatment of him, that he sensed in his unprofound way the real felicity of calling Emily Dickinson, as he did in his preface to her poems, an "Undine or Mignon or Thekla."

Our poet numbered among her friends one of the most productive woman writers of the time, Helen Hunt Jackson. The famous author of *Ramona* and *A Century of Dishonor* (an indictment of our Indian policy), as well as voluminous magazine fiction and poetry, had herself been born in Amherst. The daughter of a rigidly orthodox Calvinist, a professor at the college, she was almost exactly Emily Dickinson's contemporary, having been born in 1831. One hardly knows how to understand Emily Dickinson's remark to Higginson that "Mrs. Jackson soars to your estimate lawfully as a bird" in view of the fact that Higginson's estimate was in truth preposterous. "The poetry of

Mrs. Jackson unquestionably takes rank above that of any American woman," wrote Higginson, though he had the grace to add (but too late for our poet to read his words): "its only rival would be found, curiously enough, in that of her early schoolmate, Emily Dickinson." Higginson found in Mrs. Jackson's prose writings "an even excellence of execution . . . which is surpassed by hardly any American writer." It is impossible to reconcile such an estimate with the crude bathos, sentimentality, and general disorganization of Mrs. Jackson's writing. One can only suppose that Higginson was gallantly complimenting one of the writing ladies whom he regarded as his protégées and that Emily Dickinson was both chaffing her tutor and joining in his praise of a friend.

If Emily Dickinson wished to observe what sort of life might be open to a woman writer with a background similar to her own who did not become a recluse, Helen Hunt Jackson was an admirable example. Although she obviously had a gift for literature and could sometimes write eloquently, she nevertheless strikes one as an almost classic example of the neurotic writer. "It is undoubtedly true," said Higginson, "that she wrote her first poetry as a bereaved mother and her last prose as a zealous philanthropist." Her life was pathetic enough. Her first husband, Major Hunt (with whom Miss Pollitt mistakenly supposed Emily Dickinson to be in love), was killed in 1863 while experimenting with a device for firing torpedoes. Their two sons died in childhood, the younger after promising, at the age of eleven, to speak to his mother from the spirit world in case this should prove possible and after obtaining from his mother the promise that she would not kill herself after his death. Only after these tragedies did she take to literature. She turned out a very large number of stories and poems during the next ten years, until her marriage to a Mr. Jackson of Colorado and her conversion (for it had that force) to Indian philanthropy. If our poet was extremely jealous of her anonymity, Mrs. Jackson was equally jealous of her pseudonymity; she usually signed herself "H. H." though she used several other literary names. She strongly resented any public knowledge of even the most unimportant facts about her life. Yet she cherished the possibility of exercising a public power. The hard bargains she drove for her writing were famous among editors. Her investigations into the injustices of Indian policy were strenuously public acts, and one of her last acts before her death in 1885 was to write a letter to President Cleveland about the Indians. As a writer and reformer she drove herself from one illness to another, and her later years consisted of incessant restless changes of residence in search of health. It is impossible not to see in Mrs. Jackson, besides the "brilliant, impetuous, and thoroughly individual woman" Higginson describes, an unhappy, compulsive, and disoriented woman.

Mrs. Jackson (then Helen Hunt) visited Amherst in the late summer of 1873. Her biographer tells us that she was in one of her periods of ill health, and the move to Amherst, she hoped, was a move toward recovery. She wrote to ask about living quarters, and Emily Dickinson suggested a house which was well protected against dampness and in which her two cousins—who "were timid themselves"—had comfortably stayed. Whatever Mrs. Jackson's living quarters turned out to be, we know from the report of Lavinia Dickinson that she stayed at the Dickinson house for two weeks and from her biographer that she soon left Amherst, again in pursuit of health. We hear from Lavinia of much private literary conversation between her sister and Mrs. Jackson during these two weeks. Like Higginson, Mrs. Jackson came to Amherst in an aura of literary fame and with hopes of introducing the unknown poet to the literary world. She was much more sanguine than Higginson about publishing Emily Dickinson's poetry, an eventuality to which she apparently saw no obstacle but the poet's unaccountable diffidence. She made at least two attempts in later years to induce her friend to publish, once in 1876, when she stopped at Amherst and endeavored to secure some poems for a projected anthology to be called *A Masque of Poets*, and once in 1884, when in a letter she reminded Emily Dickinson of the "portfolios full of verses" which by this time she must have. She spoke of the "cruel wrong to your 'day and generation' " which was being done so long as the verses remain unpublished, and she urged her to consider whether "we have a right to withhold from the world a word or thought any more than a *deed* which might help a single soul." It is sometimes suggested that Emily Dickinson was about to yield to the pressure of Mrs. Jackson and others and consent to publication. A letter of 1883 to Thomas Niles, the publisher, expresses her wish to deserve "the kind but incredible opinion of H. H. and yourself." If there was a genuine possibility of publication at this time it was defeated by the death of Mrs. Jackson and a marked decline of health in Emily Dickinson. The assault upon the portfolios liberated but one poem: "Success is counted sweetest." In some manner, without Emily Dickinson's consent but without arousing in her any ostensible resentment, this poem was published anonymously in *A Masque of Poets* in 1878.

It may be said that if Higginson came to Amherst as a

representative of official genteel culture, Mrs. Jackson came as the representative of public opinion itself. She does not appear to have been interested, as was Higginson, in the quality of Emily Dickinson's poetry and the question of how it would be received if published. She expressed instead her sorrow and, almost, her sense of outrage that anyone should write portfolios of poems and then perversely desire to keep them to herself. Despite her reluctance to expose the details of her own career, Mrs. Jackson was in favor of publication as a way of life. Having herself given up, or been deprived of, nearly all forms of private life, she found in Emily Dickinson first an object of entranced fascination and then a gifted citizen remiss in her duty. It is rather more difficult to imagine precisely what our poet saw in Mrs. Jackson, since, of course, she speaks of her in her letters with vaguely extravagant praise ("Helen of Troy will die, but Helen of Colorado, never"). It is certain that she did not share Mrs. Jackson's notion of the poet's duty to mankind. She had written to one of the Norcross sisters in 1872 to tell them about another attempt to induce her to publish, and the opinions she expressed were certainly not equivocal: "Of Miss P— I know but this, dear. She wrote me in October, requesting me to aid the world by my chirrup more. Perhaps she stated it as my duty, I don't distinctly remember, and always burn such letters . . . I replied declining. She did not write again—she might have been offended, or perhaps is extricating humanity from some hopeless ditch. . . ." Emily Dickinson can hardly have helped entertaining similar thoughts about Helen Hunt Jackson.

But if she could not give her friend what she asked, she could yet give her something. Like Emily Dickinson's other friends, Mrs. Jackson must not be allowed to come too close, but neither must she be allowed to disappear entirely. During the two weeks' stay at the Dickinson home, the poet took her friend somewhat into her confidence, allowed her to read her poems and told her, it seems likely, about her relationship with Newton and Wadsworth. She could hardly have been innocent enough not to know that to tell such things to Mrs. Jackson was to offer oneself as material for fiction. *Mercy Philbrick's Choice* and *Esther Wynn's Love-Letters*, published in the years immediately following the Amherst visit, present heroines who are composites of three ideal images: the sunny and soulful women admired by Dr. Holland (often Mrs. Jackson's editor), Emily Dickinson, and Mrs. Jackson herself. Mercy Philbrick is a suffering and intellectual young lady who finally becomes an eminent poet. She is helped along the spiritual path by a Mr. Allen, who somewhat resembles Newton, and by a Parson Dorrance, who resembles Wadsworth, and, to some extent, Higginson. Like Mrs. Jackson, Mercy becomes a widow early in life. *Esther Wynn's Love-Letters*—a story which would have strongly appealed to "Ik Marvel"—concerns the discovery, fifty years after they were written, of a remarkable collection of the letters and poems of an obscure woman who was in love with a man she could not marry. The documents are found under a staircase by an extraordinarily spiritual old man and his young niece, the relationship between whom apparently struck Mrs. Jackson's readers as the essence of spotless sentiment but which strikes the modern reader as verging upon impropriety. The poems discovered among Esther Wynn's papers are indeed reminiscent of Emily Dickinson's verse; they are very mediocre imitations by Mrs. Jackson. Taken together with the letters attributed to Esther Wynn, they are revealing evidence of the author's idea of Emily Dickinson, of the personality she wished to bestow upon her. Esther Wynn is a fancied version of Emily Dickinson who can write to her beloved: "But all that you have so much loved and cared for, dear, calling it intellectual growth and expansion in me, has been only the clearing, refining, and stimulating of every faculty, every sense, by my love for you. . . . But, precious one, it is ended. The whole solemn, steadfast womanhood within me recognizes it." Whereupon Esther Wynn travels in search of health to Jerusalem, where she dies—as had Mrs. Jackson's father.

These stories were not intended to be actual or detailed fictional studies of Emily Dickinson. Mrs. Jackson was indulging in fantasies according to which the poet ceased to be herself and emerged in an image more acceptable to the general opinion of the time. Above all, the point of the fantasy is that Emily Dickinson surrenders her private self and her private life, and also, of course, her genius. Mercy Philbrick becomes famous during her lifetime; the letters and poems of Esther Wynn cease to be a private possession.

Yet Mrs. Jackson's atttitude toward the woman recluse remains somewhat ambivalent. Esther Wynn is not openly condemned for keeping to herself and for not publishing her poems, even though one is distinctly invited to breathe a sigh of relief once the manuscripts are rescued from their secret crypt. We may suppose that in her reaction to Emily Dickinson, Mrs. Jackson was as ambivalent as public opinion itself; she disapproved but she was entranced. Behind the poet's extravagant praise of her friend, behind her beautiful devotion, there was certainly a similar ambivalence. Contemplating the two women together one senses anew the rightness, for her, of Emily Dickinson's life, the rightness of her jealously guarded privacy and of her strategy of keeping society at arm's length. The feminism of the time, a most striking phenomenon in our history, was surely admirable in many of its ideals. Yet the pitfalls which it offered to creative woman were numerous and dangerous. While it liberated the minds and lives of some women, it urged others into all sorts of unnatural situations, inventing for them new forms of suffering and breakdown while it imposed upon them the norms of an inferior intellectual culture. These hazards to the talented woman could be clearly seen in the broken and unhappy life of Helen Hunt Jackson. In her decades of skirmishing with Mrs. Jackson and Higginson, we see that Emily Dickinson perceived the dangers offered to her by the feminism as well as by the general culture of the time and that—though she fell far short of perfectly succeeding—she was determined to protect herself and her art.

Amy Lowell proposed to write a book about Emily Dickinson in relation to the members of her family. And were sufficient evidence available, such a study might indeed be fascinating. Of Austin and Emily we may say, at least, that they do not seem to have continued into later years the close intellectual kinship to which the letters of the early twenties testify. Occasionally they exchanged ideas; a letter to Mrs. Holland, written as late as 1880, mentions a discussion with Austin about whether consciousness extends beyond death, a discussion which their mother thought "improper." Emily suggests that her mother would have thought even more improper, had she heard it, Austin's statement that no such man as Elijah ever lived. Yet the relationship with Austin in these late years is perhaps accurately described in the great letter of January, 1875, to Mrs. Holland, wherein we read that Austin had spent four weeks in his father's house while his family was away but that to Emily he remained inaccessible, his stay reminding her only the more poignantly that their early attachment was "Antediluvian." Their devotion to each other and to their early comradeship seems never to have flagged. But Austin Dickinson was not disposed to consider very closely the meaning of his sister's secluded life. He regarded it as "natural" in the light of her plain appearance, her shyness, and her love of literature.

Austin himself differed from the traditional Dickinson character. We may suppose that we behold in him—besides the Squire, the respected citizen, and the successful lawyer —those uneasy stirrings towards adventure, life, and culture which the novelists have noted in the late nineteenth-century well-to-do American. Here in the eighth generation of a New England family the inherited temperament began to feel a pervasive dissatisfaction, an uneasiness with the long routine; and it began to make tentative motions toward the intellectual and the aesthetic life.

Outwardly Austin Dickinson easily fulfilled the requirements of his prominent position in Amherst. One hears of his tall, erect bearing and the familiar Dickinson air of importance, respectability, and, on occasion, haughtiness. In public he was likely to be reserved and even, as one writer testifies, slightly defiant. His head was more massive than that of his father and though his features might at times be as hard and strong, the whole appearance took on a larger expressiveness from the copious shock of reddish-brown hair and the spacious side whiskers. As town moderator, as treasurer of the college, as a pillar of the Congregational Church no one could have been more proper or more efficient. But occasionally some outer sign of imaginative verve would be visible, perhaps in the wide-brimmed planter's hat or in the flying figures of his horses, to which he sometimes gave full rein in the streets of Amherst. He was not, indeed, the severely aloof man his father was. He is said to have bent over his father's coffin, to have kissed his forehead, and to have remarked, "There, father, I never dared to do that while you were living."

Beneath the exterior there stirred a certain wayward and fitful passion, a flamboyance of imagination, and a thirst for modes of experience which he failed to find in his public career. He was entirely capable of deploring "materialism" and of commenting on the anomaly of his being treasurer of the college when, as he wished it to be known, he did not really approve of "handling dirty money" and could find no pleasure in doing so. Such remarks as this, or the remark that he would never believe anything that stultified his reason or that he was going to vote for Cleveland, were likely to be made when he temporarily abandoned his public personality and called, for example, upon Professor and Mrs. Todd, in whose music case he kept a velvet cap which he wore during his visits. His daughter remembered being often taken to Boston and New York (where they visited the literary Hollands) and of having trouble to keep up with her father's enraptured pursuit of color and drama, of beholding with him the paintings in the museums and the acting of Bernhardt in *Camille* or of Austin's "Idol," Tommaso Salvini, in *Othello*. His pleasure in collecting art-works was sometimes indulged to the point of straining the family budget. President of the Village Improvement Society, he far exceeded the zeal of the other members in the matter of tree-planting, a pursuit to which he was much devoted. A large share of the arboreal charm of present-day Amherst may be attributed to the imaginative and enthusiastic tree-planting of Austin Dickinson. He was entirely capable of digging up and replanting several trees which the Improvement Society had lately planted in order to produce an aesthetic effect by irregularity of arrangement as opposed to the perfectly straight line in which the trees had been set. In this act we have a fitting symbol of the life and character of Austin Dickinson. He did not seek to revolt from the ways of Amherst and his father; he sought rather to relax the ancient strictures, to provide room within the pattern for an imaginative waywardness and for aesthetic strivings. It was a decision he had made in the 1850s when he had risen to the call of adventure in the West but allowed his father to persuade him to remain in Amherst.

It is hard to imagine how Emily Dickinson would have got on without her devoted sister. Lavinia was vigorous, quick, and active about her household duties and became more and more the overseer of the domestic economy as their mother gradually declined towards her death in 1882. The poet's letters show a humorous indulgence of Lavinia's odd characteristics, an indulgence which is saved from condescension by the genuine sisterly devotion which she also felt. She is capable of referring to a letter written by Lavinia as "one of her mental products" and of commenting to a friend that Vinnie is "spectacular as Disraeli and sincere as Gladstone." Lavinia's vehement treatment of an unruly tradesman or a would-be invader of the household is reported thus: "Vinnie is full of wrath, and vicious as Saul towards the Holy Ghost, in whatever form. I heard her declaiming the other night, to a foe that called—and sent Maggie to part them." However well intended, Lavinia's cantankerousness must have become something of a burden in her later years. Yet there is no reason to suppose that Emily ever questioned her firm conviction that her bond to Lavinia was "early, earnest, and indissoluble."

That Lavinia would marry was always assumed in her youth, since she had a kind of dark and sparkling beauty never possessed by her sister. The fact that she remained a spinster may be provisionally attributed to a certain harshness in her character, a certain Dickinsonian pride and aloofness. She appears to have fallen into the routine of her predestined life without emotional hardship, and the poet benefited by the domestic services which might otherwise have been rendered to a husband. Lavinia's devotion to all the Dickinsons, and especially to Emily, verged upon fanaticism.

Lavinia Dickinson was noted not only for her quick, nervous, vehement temperament but for the grim and salty witticisms, which in later life constituted her observations on the world, and for the virulence and shrillness of her anger. Her humor—harsh, paradoxical, concerned with death and near-obscenities—was and still remains the common property of numberless aging New England widows and spinsters. It is inevitable, of course, that the sharp and mobile features, the shrill voice, the oddity of dress, even the air of being unkempt should have invited the thought of witches. One of Lavinia's jokes, recorded by Mme. Bianchi, is standard American humor. A salesman called at the Dickinson house and inquired of Lavinia if she had any rats, mice, or beetles, to which she answered that she had not but that she believed she would not take any this morning. Another joke recorded by Mme. Bianchi is perhaps more native to New England. Lavinia, it seems, was accustomed to say that she had had a dream that she was dead but could not make up her mind which of two coffins she should choose, whereupon she sent for Sue, her sister-in-law, who resolved the dilemma by saying that Lavinia must choose the handsomer one and "go in style." In a similar vein she was in the habit of making rather grisly witticisms out of the circumstance that she had been born on the twenty-ninth of February. Mrs. Todd jotted down some of Lavinia's aphorisms, and these too will be recognized as standard taste among certain classes of New England spinster: "He is a runaway corpse"; "Her voice was sharp—it needed oiling"; "He preached one of his cancerous sermons. It would be well to have a little chlorate of lime sprinkled down the aisles, there is so much 'sewer' in his sermons."

In 1896 Lavinia Dickinson brought a lawsuit to recover a strip of land which she had previously deeded to Professor and Mrs. Todd. Her brother Austin had urged her to deed the land by way of recompense for Mrs. Todd's editorial labors in preparing the first volume of Emily's verse. The result of the lawsuit was the estrangement of Mrs. Todd from the Dickinsons and, apparently, a general sense of revulsion and disillusion which made it impossible for her to continue editing and publishing the poems. She put aside copies of several hundred unpublished poems, and these were not destined to be published until 1945, when *Bolts of Melody* was brought out by herself and her daughter Mrs. Bingham.

Mrs. Todd came to Amherst in 1881 with her husband, who was to take up a professorship in astronomy. She was twenty-four and her previous life, in Washington, had accustomed her to somewhat more freedom and excitement than she found in Amherst. She believed, and probably with justification, that some of the ladies of Amherst (those whom one would as soon assault as one would a plush) thought of her as an immodest woman. Her photographs show a certain piquant assertiveness, a womanly defiance which is both humorous and provocative. This is the notable expression of the face that looks out at us from the photograph of Mrs. Todd as an actress in the cast of a college play and in the kimono which, with parasol, she affected for the camera during a trip to Japan with her husband.

In the last years of Emily Dickinson's life, Mrs. Todd formed the habit of visiting the Dickinson house to play the piano. The poet, who had perhaps almost literally never heard Scarlatti, Bach, Beethoven, and Chopin, displayed a touching gratitude to the talented young woman who came to play the works of these composers. She hovered, of course, in the hall while the pianist played in the parlor. Mrs. Todd remembered the vibrant voice of her unseen listener. After one of these informal concerts, the performer was presented with a cream whip and a card which bore the words "Whom He loveth He chasteneth."

In the years after Emily Dickinson's death, Mrs. Todd was intermittently engaged in sorting out, arranging, and copying poems from the manuscripts made available to her by Austin and Lavinia. It was she who performed most of the labor in publishing the early volumes, for though she was ostensibly collaborating with Higginson in the editorial task, his largest contribution was to be his prestige.

Before Austin Dickinson died in 1895, it was generally supposed in Amherst that he had formed an attachment to Mrs. Todd which overreached the bounds of mere friendship, that in fact a village romance had developed. Lavinia Dickinson became querulous and impatient as she grew older, and she found many reasons to rationalize her growing enmity towards Mrs. Todd, as well as her ingratitude. Yet there seems to be no question that one reason for bringing the lawsuit in 1896 was to punish a woman whom she suspected of being a licentious schemer. She wished, at least, to reclaim everything which she regarded as inviolably Dickinsonian. She wished to protect the family name and to annihilate every trespasser on the family domain. The lawsuit was the last of her many protective actions.

She had no case. Her only plea was that she had signed the deed without knowing that it was a conveyance of property. In her testimony before the court she played her best part. Wearing yellow shoes, a blue flannel dress, and a voluminous mourning veil, she was elusive and grossly humorous. She maintained that she knew nothing of business, that she could not distinguish between a deed and any other piece of paper, that her father had always handled the family business. Asked if the signature on the deed was truly hers, she answered that it was her autograph, that she had written her name on the paper under the impression that she was giving her autograph to someone in Boston who had requested it. She played a part she had long been rehearsing —the harsh, profane, mock-foolish New England spinster.

If the case had been decided on its merits, Lavinia Dickinson would obviously have lost the suit. The fact that she won is clear evidence that the real question before the court was the inviolable reputation of the Dickinson family. This was reaffirmed by the decision. A legal injustice had surely been done, and much righteous wrath had been directed, by strong implication, against Mrs. Todd.

The direct descent of the poet's branch of the Dickinson family came to its conclusion in the generation to which she belonged. A provincial Electra, Lavinia Dickinson devoted herself to the justification of her family and to the protection of a timid sister and a wayward brother. In retrospect she must have thought that her mission had been given to her early in life. She survived her father, her mother, her sister, and her brother. And when she died in 1899 she might well have felt that it had been her destiny to watch over the dissolution of her family, to tend the brief, fitful, and sometimes brilliant flame in which the energy of her family's generations expired.

The Last Years

THE last twelve years of Emily Dickinson's life—from 1874, when her father died, to 1886—were the final fruition of a mode of existence which, though she had chosen it, had nevertheless the inflexibility of fate. These years were, as she said, the autumn of her life. The rapt attention to eternity was no longer occasioned by the wakening lights of the spring nor by the rich and enigmatic mood of summer. The colors now darkened; existence surprisingly yawned before her in its infinite depths; the golden bowl was breaking. Even less than the earlier periods of her life were these last years a time of serenity. The fruits of the imaginative life, the rewards of a dedicated career, were being secretly born. Yet the death of friends and of relatives constantly reminded her that what she had learned as a child remained true: that to live was to renounce, to be robbed, to be left desolately alone. Her imagination matured and deepened as life itself became more and more impossible. If her last years display some of the qualities of a ripe fruition, they display as many of an exacerbated and terrifying anxiety. "The 'golden bowl' breaks soundlessly," she writes. But the calmness and the acceptance of her tone are dispelled by such an anguished cry as this:

> Good-night! I can't stay any longer in a world of death. Austin is ill of fever. I buried our garden last week—our man, Dick, lost a little girl through the scarlet fever. I thought perhaps that *you* were dead, and not knowing the sexton's address, interrogate the daisies. Ah!—dainty Death! Ah! democratic Death! Grasping the proudest zinnia from my purple garden, —then deep to his bosom calling the serf's child!
>
> Say, is he everywhere? Where shall I hide my things? Who is alive? The woods are dead. . . .

These great lines are surpassed only in the letter of January, 1875, where she writes: "Mother is asleep in the Library—Vinnie—in the Dining Room—Father—in the Masked Bed—in the Marl House."

The signal event of Emily Dickinson's last years was, of course, the death of her father, which occurred in June, 1874. Having lost "that pause of space which I call 'father,' " existence must of necessity be more empty, more formless, less abrupt, less meaningful, and less principled.

There had been, at least, a moment of unwonted intimacy between father and daughter on the day before the tragic event.

> The last afternoon that my father lived [she wrote to Higginson], though with no premonition, I preferred to be with him, and invented an absence for mother, Vinnie being asleep. He seemed peculiarly pleased, as I oftenest stayed with myself, and remarked, as the afternoon withdrew, he "would not like it to end."
>
> His pleasure almost embarrassed me, and my brother coming, I suggested they walk. Next morning I woke him for the train, and saw him no more.

His heart was pure and terrible, and I think no other like it exists.

On the evening following that "next morning," "we were eating our supper . . . and Austin came in. He had a despatch in his hand, and I saw by his face we were all lost, though I didn't know how. . . . Father does not live with us now." Edward Dickinson had collapsed in the State House at Boston while making a speech on Massachusetts railroad policy and the Hoosac tunnel. Recovering somewhat he returned to his hotel room at the Tremont House, sent for a doctor, and began packing his bag. The doctor pronounced it a case of "apoplexy" and administered morphine. Edward Dickinson died in the hotel room. It was Austin's curious idea that morphine was a poison to his father and that the drug had been responsible for his father's death.

The town of Amherst had lost one of its first citizens, and the funeral of Edward Dickinson was an unusually striking one. Mme. Bianchi, the poet's niece, remembered the odor of June flowers, the assemblage on the Dickinson lawn of numerous settees brought from College Hall, the heavy grief of her father, Austin Dickinson. During the service the members of the family sat in the library. Emily, however, remained in her room upstairs, her door far enough ajar so that she might hear the prayers and the eulogies.

Doubtless it is not for us to chide Emily Dickinson for refusing to attend her father's funeral—for that is what her conduct amounted to. But sentimentality must not keep us from sensing in its full extent the uningratiating coldness, even the cruelty, in which her mode of life involved her. There can be no doubt that the fine objectivity of the poet was accompanied by a certain callousness of spirit in the woman, which, though by itself it hardly determines our final judgment of Emily Dickinson, must be nevertheless apparent to any candid observer. Consider the question she poses to the Norcross sisters in 1886: "Don't you think fumigation ceased when father died?" Though we may be inclined to recall that these words were written by a dying woman, a woman suffering, furthermore, from Bright's disease, we may also think that we sense in them, more sharply than in anything else she wrote, a strong residue of the Puritan coldness, remoteness, and rigidity. The chilling question she asks of her cousins sums up in its starkest form her relation to her father. Though much more besides, he was the grand principle of sanitation in her life. He was the living emblem of that *cordon sanitaire* which she so elaborately threw around herself by means of her poetry and her letters—and her white dress—against the day, as we may think, when her father should live no more.

Emily Dickinson knew that the death of her father had made very great changes in the inner personal life of herself and her family. But aside from a growing antipathy between her household and Austin's wife Sue, the Dickinsons endeavored to live as they had before. In 1878 she could write to Higginson that "We dwell as when you saw us, the mighty dying of my father made no external change. Mother and sister are with me, and my brother and pseudo-sister, in the nearest house." If any outward change could be discerned it was the gradual decline of her mother: "When father lived I remained with him because he would miss me. Now, mother is helpless—a holier demand." She believed that her mother's will had "followed" her father, that her mother's heart would never be anything but idle and listless for his sake.

Emily Norcross Dickinson suffered a paralytic stroke a year after the death of her husband, and she gradually declined into invalidism during the eight years after 1874. In 1882 Emily Dickinson wrote: "Our mother ceased." The invalidism had been a long and wearing strain. Yet in the long months and years of anxious watching and waiting, of endless domestic and sickroom duties, Emily first became acquainted, it may be, with her mother. She found that her mother's dying "almost stunned" her "spirit." And she wrote to her cousins that Emily Norcross Dickinson "was scarcely the aunt you knew. The great mission of pain had been ratified—cultivated to tenderness by persistent sorrow, so that a larger mother died than had she died before." As Emily watched "the illumination that comes but once" as it "paused" on her mother's features, could she not feel the poignancy of having discovered a mother only at the moment of losing her?

Emily Dickinson had good reason to feel that death had become an "intimate friend." She was saddened and sickened in the autumn of 1883 by the death of Austin's eight-year-old son Gilbert, who had been a great favorite of his aunt and who had played a prominent part in the curious games she continued to share with the neighborhood children as long as she had strength. Samuel Bowles died in 1878, Dr. Holland in 1881, and Helen Hunt Jackson in 1885.

It is impossible to calculate the effect on our poet, in 1882, of the death of Wadsworth. That the effect was considerable we must conclude from her letters, after 1882, to J. D. and C. H. Clark, in which she movingly speaks of the "beloved clergyman" and declares her undying devotion to him. These passionately written reminiscent letters furnish strong evidence both that Emily Dickinson had been in love with Wadsworth and that he remained for her a somewhat mythical and remote figure. One may conjecture (though it is dangerous to do so without the letters that passed between Wadsworth and herself) that this was exactly the ambiguous manner in which she wished to possess "her dearest earthly friend." Given the circumstances, it was of course the only way she *could* possess him. Yet in her descriptions of him as a "dusk gem" and a "Man of Sorrow," do we not sense once again her instinctive strategy of friendship, suffused and magnified, however, with the large feelings only one human being had aroused in her? In the act of her possession of Wadsworth resides also the act of translating him out of the human condition and into the realm of myth. The more passionately and powerfully present he is the more remote and ideal he becomes. Like the relationship between Henry James and Minny Temple, the Wadsworth-Dickinson connection was one of those which can only be sustained by a love which involves the renunciation of the beloved. The relationship with Wadsworth was a grand replica of our poet's relationship with the world in general; it was second in its power and influence upon her life only to the relationship with her father.

Emily Dickinson's last interview with Wadsworth took place in the summer of 1880, nearly twenty years after their previous meeting. She writes in a letter that the last time "he" came "in life," he found her among her lilies and heliotropes. Lavinia heralded his approach by saying that the gentleman with the deep voice wished to see her. The interview seems to have been brief and the conversation somewhat random, having to do at one point with frogs. The poet records her strong sense that she was speaking to an apparition, in whose substantiality she could hardly bring herself to believe. Where had he come from? she asked. And why had he not let her know that he was coming? He answered that he did not know himself that he was coming, that he had stepped immediately from his pulpit to the train. And how long had the journey been? she inquired—to which Wadsworth answered with intentions hard to fathom: "Twenty years." His manner of saying this struck Emily Dickinson as "inscrutable roguery." Apparently nothing happened during this meeting to modify the deep ambiguity of their relationship, the sustained tension of intimacy and remoteness. The meeting merely served to confirm the essential qualities of the relationship obliquely described in the letters to the Clarks after Wadsworth's death two years later.

A few glimpses of Emily Dickinson's ordinary life remain from the last years. Cooking activities of a limited sort engaged her energies. Mme. Bianchi remembered that her aunt was rather "précieuse" in the kitchen, that she chose to stir with a silver spoon and to measure with a glass. A kind of "imaginary line" or taboo separated her cooking utensils from those used by Maggie and Lavinia. Her niece's memory is that Aunt Emily's craftsmanship was delicate and precise in such feats as sliding the wine-jelly uninjured from the mould. In making even such delicacies as the one she called Homestead Charlotte Russe, she rigorously curbed the temptation to imaginative improvisation and stuck closely to the rules, lest, as her niece remembers her to have said on one occasion, a "quarter of a teaspoon of Eternity" should get in by mistake.

The poet's love of childhood and of children strengthened as she grew old. In 1874 she wrote "Affection is like bread, unnoticed till we starve, and then we dream of it, and sing of it, and paint it, when every urchin in the street has more than he can eat. We turn not older with the years, but newer every day." It was one of her ideas, as we see, that in growing old one was in some sense growing a child again, since only thus could one be finally taken into the kingdom of heaven. She believed, of course, that the strongest of childhood emotions was the sense of deprivation, of hunger. She formed a kind of league with the neighborhood children, among them those of her brother, in opposition to the rest of the world. Mr. MacGregor Jenkins, who was one of these children (though not after 1878, when his parents moved from Amherst), recalled that he and his playmates were accustomed to play a variety of games on the Dickinson grounds but that the general theme of these games was "starvation." When the starvation became acute there would be a knock at the window on the second-floor or a dimly flourished handkerchief. The window would open and amid a conspiratorial state of expectancy the children would gather around to await the basket of gingerbread shortly to be lowered to them from above. While the children ate their gingerbread, the gamesome poet, we may be sure, supposed herself to be tasting eternity.

The imaginative life of Emily Dickinson remained active to her dying day. In her last years she repeatedly asserts her idea that for her no disillusion is possible. To Mrs. Todd she wrote, in 1882, that "maturity only enhances mystery, never decreases it." In the next year she wrote that "Fathoms are sudden neighbors," a trope which, though she had always used it in one way or another to express the depths and the mysteries of experience, becomes almost the key metaphor in the letters of her last years. The death of Higginson's daughter, aged seven weeks, elicited a letter in which she spoke of the sudden intimacy of eternity, the sudden sense of the universe opening deeply out before us like a foreign landscape. In a note to Mrs. Todd she wrote, "I trust that you are well, and the quaint little girl with the deep eyes, every day more fathomless."

As she grew older her own past opened out to her imagination in new depth and she was led to praise memory as the highest function of the imagination, as "the most consecrated ecstasy of the will." Memory led one to a sense of the eternal, and in these last years the poet was intoxicated with eternity, if not with God. She looked into the "fathoms" which imagination delved through the surface of ordinary life, and she found that the mere fact of existence was to her an appalling mystery, quite overpowering the less vivid and engrossing emotions offered by books, as she intimated to Higginson. To tend one's flowers, whether in the garden or the small conservatory where fern and heliotrope might be kept alive all winter, was to sense a pathos more moving than literature. "The career of flowers differs from ours only in inaudibleness. I feel . . . reverence . . . for these mute creatures whose suspense or transport may surpass my own." More and more she came to modify the intransigence with which she had sometimes separated nature and man. The letters of her late years imply a kind of Gnostic vitalism, a personal version of Transcendentalism, which pictures "life" as a magic power or spell and

s of it as the principle of eternity in this world.
course not a new idea to Emily Dickinson; it is a predictable emphasis of her later thought. As life grew more and more precarious, it came to seem more and more like a spell, "a spell so exquisite that everything conspires to break it."

Emily Dickinson was increasingly ill and weak after 1884. The years of 1882 and 1883 had been especially hard to bear, for those years had brought the death of her mother, of Wadsworth, and of her nephew Gilbert. In the autumn of 1884 she fell ill: " . . . I was making a loaf of cake with Maggie, when I saw a great darkness coming and knew no more until late at night. . . . Then I grew very sick and gave the others much alarm, but am now staying. The doctor calls it 'revenge of the nerves'; but who but Death had wronged them?" The attack which brought the great darkness exhibits all the symptoms of nervous breakdown. She enjoyed periods of partial recovery from this attack, resuming some of her usual duties, continuing to write letters and verses to her friends, taking enough interest in books to watch "like a vulture" (in 1885) for the expected biography of George Eliot and to enjoy with her Norcross cousins a "haunting" and "greatly impressive" novel entitled *Called Back*, by "Hugh Conway." Yet she gradually receded and by 1886 became dangerously ill: "I have been very ill, and begin to roam in my room a little." Just before her death, she sent the following note to the Norcross sisters:

> Little Cousins,—
> Called back.
> EMILY

Mrs. Todd noted in her diary that by May 15 all hope had been given up and that Emily Dickinson died quietly at about six o'clock in the evening of that day.

T. W. Higginson attended the funeral and read "No coward soul is mine" by Emily Brontë. He recorded his impressions in his diary on May 19: "The country exquisite, day perfect, and an atmosphere of its own, fine and strange, about the whole house and grounds—a more saintly and elevated 'House of Usher.' The grass of the lawn full of buttercups, violet, and wild geranium; in house a handful of pansies and another of lilies of valley on piano. E. D.'s face a wondrous restoration of youth—she . . . looked 30, not a grey hair or wrinkle, the perfect peace of the beautiful. There was a little bunch of violets at the neck and one pink *Cypripedium*: the sister Vinnie put in two heliotropes by her hand to 'take to Judge Lord.' "

The King had at last been witnessed in the room. Yet Emily Dickinson belonged not to him but to her privileged posterity.

Bibliographical Note

THE large collection of Dickinson manuscripts released in 1950 from the possession of the Bianchi family and its heirs and acquired by Harvard University is now in the process of being edited by Mr. Thomas H. Johnson, who has assumed the important task of bringing out new and definitive editions. Meanwhile a number of variously imperfect editions are available. In 1937 Martha Dickinson Bianchi, the poet's niece, published in collaboration with Alfred Leete Hampson *The Poems of Emily Dickinson*. This volume includes all the poems published in the 1890s by Mabel Loomis Todd and T. W. Higginson, to which was added a variety of further poems, such as those published by Mme. Bianchi in *The Single Hound: Poems of a Lifetime* (1914). *Bolts of Melody* (1945) added well over six hundred poems and poetic fragments to the Dickinson canon. This volume, edited by Millicent Todd Bingham and her mother, finally placed before the public the poems which remained untouched in Mrs. Todd's possession for nearly fifty years after the lawsuit which Lavinia Dickinson brought against her. *Bolts of Melody* profited by the editors' candidness; the text is very little, if at all, bowdlerized and the transcription is more accurate than that of earlier editions. The publication of this volume made available nearly all the poems Emily Dickinson is known to have written.

The most important collection of the poet's letters is *Letters of Emily Dickinson* (1931), edited by Mrs. Todd. Further letters appear in Mme. Bianchi's *The Life and Letters of Emily Dickinson* (1924) and in the same author's *Emily Dickinson Face to Face* (1932). Another important collection is Theodora Van Wagenen Ward's *Emily Dickinson's Letters to Dr. and Mrs. Josiah Gilbert Holland* (1951). Further letters of minor interest are to be discovered in Helen H. Arnold's article called " 'From the Garden We Have Not Seen': New Letters of Emily Dickinson," *New England Quarterly*, XVI (1943), 363-75.

BIOGRAPHY

A generally dependable account of Emily Dickinson's life was first made available by George Frisbie Whicher in his *This Was a Poet: A Critical Biography of Emily Dickinson* (1938). Genevieve Taggard's *The Life and Mind of Emily Dickinson* (1930) and Josephine Pollitt's *Emily Dickinson: The Human Background of Her Poetry* (1930) examine certain phases of the poet's life not touched upon elsewhere, but both these books make erroneous assertions about Emily Dickinson's alleged love affairs. The biographies of Miss Taggard and Miss Pollitt suffer somewhat by a lack of "aesthetic distance," a lack of objectivity, a tendency to make a cult of Emily. Further biographical sources are MacGregor Jenkins, *Emily Dickinson: Friend and Neighbor* (1930), a slight volume of reminiscences of the Dickinson family by the son of an Amherst clergyman; Martha Dickinson Bianchi's *The Life and Letters of Emily Dickinson* (1924, but see later editions) and the same writer's *Emily Dickinson Face to Face* (1932). Observations on the poet will be found in T. W. Higginson's *Carlyle's Laugh and Other Surprises* (1909). Mrs. Todd's *Ancestor's Brocades: The Literary Debut of Emily Dickinson* (1945) provides an exhaustive account of how the poet's verse was edited and published, as well as many biographical details concerning the Dickinson family.

CRITICISM

Useful insights into the poetry are to be discovered in Henry W. Wells's discursive and many-sided *Introduction to Emily Dickinson* (1947). An interesting assessment is Stanley T. Williams, "Experiments in Poetry: Sidney Lanier and Emily Dickinson," *Literary History of the United States* by Spiller *et al.* (1948), II, 899-916. A brilliant essay in history is Allen Tate's "Emily Dickinson," *Reactionary Essays on Poetry and Ideas* (1936), 3-26; reprinted in *On the Limits of Poetry* (1948), 197-213. The best account of the poet's use of language is Richard P. Blackmur's "Emily Dickinson: Notes on Prejudice and Fact," *The Expense of Greatness* (1940), 106-38. A severe but on the whole just view of Emily Dickinson as "of all great poets . . . the most lacking in taste" is Yvor Winter's "Emily Dickinson and the Limits of Judgment," *Maule's Curse* (1938), 149-68. F. O. Matthiessen's "The Problem of the Private Poet," *Kenyon Review*, VII (1945), 584-97, is ostensibly a review of *Bolts of Melody* but is also a sane general assessment of Emily Dickinson as poet. The chapter called "How to be Lonely—With Examples" which appears in Miss Taggard's biography, 224-50, is a discerning account of the meaning of Emily Dickinson's seclusion.

Among several other useful critical comments one may mention Conrad Aiken's introduction to his *Selected Poems of Emily Dickinson* (1924); Mark Van Doren's introduction to *Letters of Emily Dickinson* (1951)—a reprint of Mrs. Todd's edition of 1894; Eunice Glenn, "Emily Dickinson's Poetry: A Revaluation," *Sewanee Review*, LI (1943), 574-88; Morton Dauwen Zabel, "Christina Rossetti and Emily Dickinson," *Poetry*, 37 (January, 1931), 213-16; Marianne Moore, "Review of *The Letters of Emily Dickinson*," *Poetry*, 41 (January, 1933), 219-26; Babette Deutsch, "Miracle and Mystery," *Poetry*, 66 (August, 1945), 274-80; Edwin Moseley, "The Gambit of Emily Dickinson," *The University of Kansas City Review* (Autumn, 1949), 11-19; Mary Elizabeth Barbot, "Emily Dickinson Parallels," *New England Quarterly* XIV (1941), 689-96; Millicent Todd Bingham, "Emily Dickinson's Handwriting—A Master Key," *New England Quarterly* XXII (1949), 229-34; Ruth Flanders McNaughton, "The Imagery of Emily Dickinson," *University of Nebraska Studies, New Series No. 4* (January, 1949).

A useful account of the poet's reception is Anna M. Wells, "Early Criticism of Emily Dickinson," *American*

Literature, I (1929), 243-59. Two of the most memorable early reactions to Emily Dickinson's verse are Thomas Bailey Aldrich, *"In Re* Emily Dickinson," *Atlantic Monthly* (January, 1892)—the doctrinaire response of gentility—and William Dean Howells, "Editor's Study," *Harper's Magazine* (January, 1891)—a much more perceptive and, according to our modern notion, a much more correct judgment of the poems. Other brief but intelligent early comments are a letter of 1891 written by Samuel G. Ward to T. W. Higginson (see *Ancestor's Brocades*, 169) and Alice James, *Alice James, Her Brothers—Her Journal*, ed. by Anna Robeson Burr (1934), 248.

Further critical pieces are Gamaliel Bradford, "Emily Dickinson," *Portraits of American Women* (1919), 229-57; Alfred Kreymborg, "Emily Dickinson," *Our Singing Strength* (1929), 193-205; and Granville Hicks, "Emily Dickinson," *The Great Tradition* (1935), 124-30. To these may be added Hart Crane's poem called "To Emily Dickinson," *The Collected Poems of Hart Crane*, ed. by Waldo Frank (1933).

BIBLIOGRAPHY

Emily Dickinson: . . . *A Bibliography*, published in 1930 by the Jones Library at Amherst, preface by Professor Whicher; Thomas H. Johnson, "Emily Dickinson," *Literary History of the United States*, III, 467-70.

Of Potosi and the mine,
Reverently to the hungry
Of your viands and your wines!

Cautious, hint to any captive
You have passed enfranchised feet!
Anecdotes of air in dungeons
Have sometimes proved deadly sweet!

The poem states that it is imprudent or irreverent to speak too lavishly of riches to beggars, of food to the hungry, or of freedom to prisoners, since death may ensue. Obviously the words *beggars*, *hungry*, and *captive* are being used with general reference. The beggar begs not for money but for love, wealth of experience, esteem, marriage, regality, and immortality—in short, for spiritual fulfillment or redemption. And so with the hungry. The captive is imprisoned in a number of unspecified ways: by circumstance, by renunciation, by the flesh. Being set free involves "air" and sweetness—that is, spirituality or immortality (air as opposed to earth) and bliss or (again) immortality. Having discovered that the poet is as usual speaking of this life in relation to the next, we perceive the one element of the poem which is of any real interest as poetry: the implication that wealth, food, and freedom are so consuming that not only may the deprived die according to physical law, by partaking too suddenly, but that having discerned the complete fulfillment of desire to be unattainable short of eternity, they will die in order to find fulfillment.

Index